PROFILES IN ENTERPRISE

Peter Church OAM, B.Com (UNSW), LLB (Sydney), LLM (London) is a lawyer and corporate adviser by profession and has spent more than 30 years living and working in the South East Asian and Indian regions. He was awarded the Medal of the Order of Australia (OAM) in 1994 for his services to the promotion of business relations between Australia and the South East Asian region. He has written a number of other books on the Asian region, including *Added Value – The Life Stories of Leading South East Asian Business People* (Murmeli, 1999), *A Short History of South East Asia* (John Wiley, 2009) and *Added Value – The Life Stories of Indian Business Leaders* (Roli, 2010).

ALSO BY PETER CHURCH
Added Value: The Life Stories of Indian Business Leaders

OTHER LOTUS TITLES

Ajit Bhattacharjea	*Sheikh Mohammad Abdullah: Tragic Hero of Kashmir*
Amarinder Singh	*The Last Sunset: The Rise and Fall of the Lahore Durbar*
Anil Dharker	*Icons: Men & Women Who Shaped Today's India*
Aitzaz Ahsan	*The Indus Saga: The Making of Pakistan*
Alam Srinivas & TR Vivek	*IPL: The Inside Story*
Amir Mir	*The True Face of Jehadis: Inside Pakistan's Terror Networks*
Ashok Mitra	*The Starkness of It*
Dr Humanyun Khan & G. Parthasarthy	*Diplomatic Divide*
Gyanendra Pandey & Yunus Samad	*Faultlines of Nationhood*
H.L.O. Garrett	*The Trial of Bahadur Shah Zafar*
Hindustan Times Leadership Summit	*Vision 2020: Challenges for the Next Decade*
M.J. Akbar	*India: The Siege Within*
M.J. Akbar	*The Shade of Swords*
M.J. Akbar	*Byline*
M.J. Akbar	*Blood Brothers: A Family Saga*
Maj. Gen. Ian Cardozo	*Param Vir: Our Heroes in Battle*
Maj. Gen. Ian Cardozo	*The Sinking of INS Khukri: What Happened in 1971*
Madhu Trehan	*Tehelka as Metaphor*
Mushirul Hasan	*India Partitioned. 2 Vols*
Mushirul Hasan	*John Company to the Republic*
Mushirul Hasan	*Knowledge, Power and Politics*
Nayantara Sahgal (ed.)	*Before Freedom: Nehru's Letters to His Sister*
Nilima Lambah	*A Life Across Three Continents*
Robert Hutchison	*The Raja of Harsil: The Legend of Frederick 'Pahari' Wilson*
Sharmishta Gooptu and Boria Majumdar (eds)	*Revisiting 1857: Myth, Memory, History*
Shrabani Basu	*Spy Princess: The Life of Noor Inayat Khan*
Shashi Joshi	*The Last Durbar*
Shashi Tharoor & Shaharyar M. Khan	*Shadows across the Playing Field*
Shyam Bhatia	*Goodbye Shahzadi: A Political Biography*
Thomas Weber	*Gandhi, Gandhism and the Gandhians*
Thomas Weber	*Going Native: Gandhi's Relationship with Western Women*
Thomas Weber	*Gandhi at First Sight*
Ullekh NP	*War Room: The People, Tactics and Technology behind Narendra Modi's 2014 Win*
Vir Sanghvi	*Men of Steel: Indian business leaders in conversation*

FORTHCOMING TITLE
Kunal Purandare	*Ramakant Achrekar: A Biography*

PROFILES IN ENTERPRISE
INSPIRING STORIES OF INDIAN BUSINESS LEADERS

Peter Church

Lotus Collection

© Peter Church, 2015
Second impression, 2015

All rights reserved. No part of this publication may be reproduced or transmitted, in any form or by any means, without the prior permission of the publisher.

The Lotus Collection
An imprint of Roli Books Pvt. Ltd.
M-75, G.K. II Market, New Delhi 110 048
Phone: ++91 (011) 4068 2000. Fax: ++91 (011) 2921 7185
E-mail: info@rolibooks.com; Website: www.rolibooks.com
Also at Bangalore, Chennai and Mumbai

Cover Design: Rohina Thapar

ISBN: 978-81-7436-989-5

Typeset in Warnock Pro by Roli Books Pvt Ltd
Printed in India at Rajkamal Electric Press, Haryana

For Ginny and for my evergrowing brood of grandchildren –
Daisy, Polly, Harry, Fox, Lily, Charlie Rose, Chance and Harvey

CONTENTS

ix   Acknowledgements

1   Introduction

8   Radhe Shyam Agarwal – *Emami*

20   Subroto Bagchi – *Mindtree*

38   Professor Bala V. Balachandran – *Great Lakes Institute of Management*

52   Shobhana Bhartia – *HT Media*

66   Ela Bhatt – *Sewa*

84   Ajay Bijli – *PVR*

102   Anand Burman – *Dabur*

114   Ramesh Chauhan – *Bisleri*

128   Adi Godrej – *Godrej Group*

144   Sanjiv Goenka – *RP-Sanjiv Goenka Group*

158   Bhavarlal H. Jain – *Jain Irrigation Systems*

176   B.K. Jhawar – *Usha Martin*

190   Naveen Jindal – *Jindal Steel & Power*

204   B.M. Khaitan – *Williamson Magor*

216 Sanjay Lalbhai – *Arvind*

232 Keshub Mahindra – *Mahindra & Mahindra*

242 Sunita Narain – *Centre for Science & the Environment*

258 Sanjay Nayak – *Tejas Networks*

274 Harshavardhan Neotia – *Ambuja Neotia Group*

290 Ajay Piramal – *Piramal Group*

304 Ronnie Screwvala – *UTV / Disney India/Unilazer*

318 Venu Srinivasan – *TVS Motor Company*

334 Arunachalam Vellayan – *Murugappa Group*

Endnotes to each chapter provides a brief description of the subject's business or organization.

ACKNOWLEDGEMENTS

In any project such as this, the first and most important contribution is obviously made by the interviewees themselves and, as we all know, their extremely important secretaries and assistants, without whom there would be no book. I found all the subjects to be easy to interview and generous with their time.

It would also be remiss of me not to acknowledge and thank for the assistance given to me by many other people who helped me shortlist those to be interviewed. Amongst these were my colleagues Shiban Bakshi, John Bond and Suresh Iyer.

As you would no doubt understand interviewing the fascinating people covered in this book is the easy part. The more arduous task is converting what they told me into the chapters of this book. In this regard I would like to particularly thank my brother-in-law, Antony Nash who helped me with the initial drafts.

I would also like to thank Lena Law, my assistant at Stephenson Harwood who had no idea when we started working together that this project was underway, and no doubt might have thought twice about agreeing to work with me had she known!

Finally, I would like to thank Pramod, Kapil and Priya Kapoor and Neelam Narula of Roli Books for taking on the challenge and publishing, not just this book but also my previous book on life stories of Indian business leaders. I am thankful for their expert advice and assistance along the way.

The life stories in this book are the result of my interviews with the subjects over a three-year period, so they might not be completely up to date as at the date of publication in December 2014. These are their stories and each of them approved the text for his or her chapter. If any mistakes remain, then the responsibility rests with me.

INTRODUCTION

This is my second book featuring the life stories of Indian business leaders.[1] I knew that in a country of over one billion citizens, I had barely scratched the surface with my first book and, as I found each of the subjects' stories fascinating, I was interested and encouraged by others to write a follow up.

As with the first volume, this is not a book about wealth but certainly many of those interviewed are wealthy. It is more about the lives of leading Indian businessmen and women who have added value to their businesses or professions and, in many cases, to India as a nation. The book also focuses on their thoughts on success and its ingredients.

Through my involvement with the countries of Asia over the last 40 years, first as a student, then as a lawyer and corporate adviser, I have met and observed a number of the 'movers and shakers' in the region. Usually, when I read about them in the press or hear others talk of them, what is reported is how much money they have, what huge deals they have cracked, or the wonderful lives they lead. There seems little interest in their life stories which, for me, are far more interesting than speculating about how many dollars they have in their bank accounts. How did they do it? Was it luck? Was it just hard work? Or are there a number of factors or threads which could guide others to success?

In 1999 I wrote a book[2] on the life stories of some 65 leading South-East Asian businessmen and women from the ten countries making up the Association of South East Asian Nations (ASEAN). The book answered many of these questions, and, the most important ingredient to success so far as I could ascertain was *timing*. There seems to be a time to get into businesses, a time to grow businesses, and a time to get out of businesses. For a number of older people interviewed, the right time came in the years following the Second World War and as their nations gained independence.

Not surprisingly there are many similarities but, as you will read, the history and culture of India is different in many respects from the countries of South-East Asia. Certainly India, like all the countries of South-East Asia, with the exception of Thailand, was colonized by a Western power but India created some amazing twists and turns for many of those interviewed for this book.

What looms largest in the stories of many of these men and women is the long dark shadow cast by the 'licence raj' when one almost needed a licence to breathe. Even large industrialists suffered. How individual men and women prospered in that period is almost beyond belief. For those who did, I think the personal characteristic that shines through most is their grit and determination to never give in.

And again, as in South-East Asia, timing shines through as a key ingredient in the success of many of those covered in this book. They were in the right place at the right time when the 'licence raj' drew its last breath. But, of course, their success is far more complicated than this.

Apart from external factors like timing, what then are the characteristics one expects to find in successful entrepreneurs? Many psychologists have spent their careers trying to identify these. The precise definition of exactly what the word 'entrepreneur' means seems to be the subject of some debate and the definition I most enjoy is the one of Peter Kilby in his classic essay 'Hunting the Heffalump'.[3] He likened the search for an entrepreneur to be like hunting the Heffalump, a character from A.A. Milne's 'Winnie the Pooh' that, in Kilby's words '...is a rather large and very important animal. He has been hunted by many individuals using various ingenious trapping devices, but no one so far has succeeded in capturing him. All who claim to have caught sight of him report that he is enormous, but they disagree on his particulars.'[4]

Fortunately, many psychologists such as Reg Jennings, Charles Cox, and Cary L. Cooper[5] do agree on several key 'particulars'. As you read the life stories in this book, I suggest you bear in mind the characteristics they identified from their research. Although their study was of Western entrepreneurs, I think you will be surprised to see how many of the following apply to the Indian subjects in this book:

- **Assertiveness** – the grit and determination I mentioned above, not surprisingly, tops the list and I think is exhibited by every person in this book;
- **The Learning Curve** – the ability to learn from setbacks or failures;
- **Ambition** – being highly proactive and responsive to challenge;
- **Achievement Orientation** – the need and belief to succeed;
- **'The Internal Gyroscope'** – a clear and positive view of where they are going;
- **An Integrated Value System** – clear values with one of the most important being *dependability*. *Wealth* and *power* rank lower in importance for most entrepreneurs than *people* and *relationships*;
- **Effective management of risk** – most take much bigger, and sometimes all or nothing, risks earlier in their careers which become more calculated later in their careers;
- **Goals: 'Do-able' lists versus 'wish-lists'** – most entrepreneurs seem to focus on realistic goals rather than absolute fantasy;
- **High dedication** – in terms of effort and time put in – every person in this book exhibits this characteristic;
- **Intrinsic Motivation** – most love what they do and have high energy levels in pursuing their chosen field;
- **Well-organized Lifestyle** – most have the unshakeable support of a spouse and apparently 'entrepreneurial duos' are not that unusual;
- **Pragmatic Approach** – most entrepreneurs have a pragmatic approach to life rather than an intellectual approach;
- **Sound Analytic and Problem-Solving Skills** – and don't these have to be applied to succeed in India!
- **High Level of 'People Skills'** – to achieve their objectives entrepreneurs usually need the assistance of others. Most seem to operate an 'open and consultative' style but with strong authoritarian back-up;
- **High Level of Innovation** – entrepreneurs are more at ease creating new ways of doing things rather than just adapting existing models;
- **Parental Influence** – interestingly most independent entrepreneurs have mothers who played a dominant role in

their early childhood and career path. Few apparently reported poor relationships with their fathers;
- **Social Origins** – socio-economic background affects development and behaviour. In India it is well known that certain ethnic groups such as the Marwari produce a high percentage of entrepreneurs. It is also interesting to note that in the research done by Jennings, Cox and Cooper, they found elite independent entrepreneurs mostly had working-class origins and did not have entrepreneurial parents. Given India's caste system I am not sure if India would bear this out;
- **Education** – regardless of the education received the research indicates that successful entrepreneurs usually see any misfortune they may have had in not receiving a good education as just another hurdle to overcome in achieving their goals;
- **Career Development Patterns** – nearly all entrepreneurs have had to cope with failure of some sort and most see it as a positive to learn from one's mistakes and failures. Most exhibit extreme resilience and the ability to bounce back;
- **Work History** – most entrepreneurs did not spend very long as employees before taking the plunge in creating their own businesses;
- **Philanthropy and Pro-social Behaviour** – the research suggests altruism stems from parents and religious teachings of moral obligations and a strong work ethic, combined with internalized norms of behaviour and the concern for others' needs;
- **Marginalization** – Many entrepreneurs come from socially marginalized groups.

There are also some unique aspects of Indian life which have touched many of the lives in this book. The most prevalent of these is the concept of a 'joint family'. Whilst Indian readers of this book will all too well understand exactly what this concept means, it may be helpful for others to have some explanation. Essentially a joint family is an extended family arrangement; particularly prevalent amongst Hindus and under which several generations will live under the same roof. All the male members are blood relatives and all the women are either mothers, wives, unmarried daughters, or widowed relatives, all bound by the common sapinda[6] relationship.

The family is headed by a patriarch, usually the oldest male, who makes decisions on economic and social matters on behalf of the entire family. The patriarch's wife generally exerts control over the kitchen, child rearing and minor religious practices. A daughter cannot remain the member of her father's family after her marriage and the sisters, though they were once entitled to a share in the property, would lose their right and would be entitled to only maintenance until their marriage and their marriage expenses.

Six key aspects of joint family are:
- all members live under one roof;
- share the same kitchen;
- three generations living together (though often two or more brothers live together, or father and son live together or all the descendants of male live together);
- income and expenditure in a common pool – property held together;
- a common place of worship; and
- all decisions are made by the male head of the family.

The most critical element of the joint family from the point of view of an entrepreneur is that all money goes to the common pool and all property is held jointly. As you will see in many of the life stories in this book, it is this element that often leads to the break-up of the joint family. The common pool concept probably worked well in more traditional times and may still work well where the members of the family have few opportunities and little wealth. But in the India of today, and particularly urban society, one can see the enormous pressures this must bring. What if one member is lazy or incompetent? What if one member wishes to take risks and others don't? What if the patriarch lacks the skill and experience to manage the businesses? As you will see, different entrepreneurs have handled it differently but there is no doubt that the entrepreneur only starts to 'fly' once he is on his own. What some families have done is to learn from successful European and US families that have not only survived, but prospered, over many generations through means of structures such as family constitutions. What is particularly interesting is that a number of these new Indian family constitutions treat men and women equally; something one would not typically have seen only ten years ago.

Inextricably tied up with joint families and the lives of many of the subjects of this book is how they 'handle' the next generation coming into the business they have built or inherited. Most of the entrepreneurs seem to be following the European and US concept of 'family offices' where the businesses are run by professionals and the family office acts more like a holding company.

There is one element not mentioned above which the psychologists I have read do not seem to touch on with respect to whether an entrepreneur succeeds or not. This is the concept of 'luck'. Perhaps there is no such thing as 'luck' or, as one hears from time to time, that people make their own destiny. But most of the entrepreneurs covered in this and my earlier book on Southeast Asia admit there is an ethereal element that defies description and could be called 'luck' for want of a better word. Timing could well be a part of luck but the entrepreneur still needs to seize the opportunity which he has identified.

I should mention how the businessmen and women were chosen. First, I sought guidance from my Indian friends and from Australia's and India's diplomatic and trade missions in asking them to provide me with a list of 20 names of Indian entrepreneurs who succeeded in the chosen profession or business and who have the respect of their peers and the wider community. In reviewing these lists it was surprising how many names appeared multiple times. I then set about approaching my short list and this book is the result. Some I approached declined to be interviewed, but they were very few.

I conducted all the interviews face-to-face. Many of my friends and colleagues who knew I was writing this book asked whether I had 'grilled' a particular person on some event or rumour about their lives. I always replied that this book was not meant to be investigative journalism. Indeed, I sent a draft of my interview to each person for approval and, in most cases, only minor changes were made to correct mistakes in names or dates.

Some readers familiar with the lives of particular individuals may observe what they believe to be inaccuracies in the stories. Any such inaccuracies would be irrelevant to my overall objective of seeking common threads in the stories of their successful business and professional careers.

The relevance or importance of chasing wealth was something else which interested me and I was pleased to find that, for most, the key was doing something they liked and doing it well. The wealth followed. Most seemed to think that if one just chased money, then other important elements of success, such as ethics, tend to go out of the window. If one loses one's way ethically, then the general opinion is that, while a short term gain may be enjoyed, one could easily lose one's name and reputation and that would impact the rest of one's life.

For me one of the most interesting things to come out of the various meetings and which should spur many young people from around the world is that not all of the people were brilliant academically. Certainly many are, but quite a number were not and were quite relaxed to say so. And by no means were all the subjects compliant and well behaved in their childhood.

All in all, I hope this book enables Indian and foreign readers, both young and old, to understand what makes these successful entrepreneurs 'tick' and to understand a little better the challenges they have had to overcome to achieve that success. In doing so, I hope in particular younger readers who are budding entrepreneurs will realize that all is not lost if they do not stand first in school and university, but also clearly understand that the path of an entrepreneur is difficult, full of risk and rarely one of never-ending success.

---

1 Peter Church, *Added Value – The Life Stories of Indian Business Leaders*, Roli Books, 2010.
2 Peter Church, *Added Value – The Life Stories of Leading South East Asian Business People*, Sydney, Murmeli, 1999.
3 P.M. Kilby, *Entrepreneurship and Economic Development*, New York: Macmillan (1971).
4 I wonder if this revelation could lead to some new nicknames of the entrepreneurs covered in this book by their children and grandchildren?
5 R. Jennings, C. Cox and C.L. Cooper, *Business Elites: The Psychology of Entrepreneurs and Intrapraneurs*, London: Routledge (1994).
6 Sapinda relationship with reference to any person exists as far as the third generation (inclusive) in the line of ascent through mother, and the fifth (inclusive) in the line of ascent through father, the line being traced upwards in each case from the person concerned, who is to be counted as the first generation.

> The West does not know the meaning of friendship. Friendship is a matter of what we call *sambandh* in Hindi, which means equal relations – equal bondage to each other. There is usually no equal bondage in the West.

RADHE SHYAM AGARWAL

Founder and Chairman, Emami[1]

Radhe Shyam Agarwal (almost always known as RS) had broken a bone in his foot which meant he had to work from his home in Kolkata. I arrived for the meeting to find that on that very day, he was having a family get-together to review all Emami's businesses. Senior executives and family members were milling about waiting to do their presentations and I wondered how on earth I would be able to get his attention on such an important and busy day. And so it was when RS arrived, I learnt that he could only afford a short time that morning but suggested we meet instead for a relaxed lunch the following day. This was clearly going to be a better outcome and so I readily agreed.

The following day produced one of those beautiful November Kolkata mornings. RS welcomed me to his apartment wearing a white cotton kurta pyjama. His foot was clearly troubling him as he was using a walking frame to get about and when we settled down for the interview, he elevated his injured foot up onto a coffee table beside us. He was clearly in some discomfort during the meeting, but he never complained and was in full-flight espousing many of his philosophical views on life. I must say he reminded me somewhat of a younger version of AVS Raju of Nagarjuna Constructions. Behind RS was a picture window giving an excellent view of the surrounding suburbs.

As we started the interview, I was quickly to learn that the lives of RS and his partner and namesake, Radhe Shyam Goenka, are inextricably intertwined and that in many ways they are alter egos. They reminded me of the extraordinarily successful Australian business partnership between Franco Belgiorno-Nettis and Carlo Salteri, the founders of Transfield. In that case, however, whilst they brilliantly complemented each other in business, I do not believe they were particularly close in their private lives. RS and Goenka are on a completely different level where the closeness permeates every crevice of their lives. In fact, just shortly before completion of the book for publication, RS told me that Goenka and he had decided to both change their family names to 'Emamiwala'!

RS was born on 18 February 1945 and RS Goenka one year and one day after him. And not only that, their wives too were born on the same day in the same year. And this doesn't end here, as RS added, 'Our first child is a girl and we each have two sons. While I was born in Bikaner [like BK Jhawar's forebears] he was born in Churu in Rajasthan, but both of our parents moved to Kolkata from Rajasthan. We ended up in the same Hindi language medium school in the sixth grade and soon became friends. Following primary school, I went on to St. Xavier's College [to which most of the Kolkata subjects of this book went] whereas RS Goenka went to another college. Our parents never became friends but for some reason we just "clicked" and we have met each other almost everyday since primary school.

'My family was very wealthy by the time I was born as it had a successful business in Bikaner making dyes that was run by my four uncles.' The way RS speaks at times might be seen by some as over-confidence, but I think he is just one of those rare individuals for whom everything is crystal clear and coming to a decision is a simple matter for him. He listens to the facts and 'bang' he has an answer or a view. At St. Xavier's College, he was a good student always among the top three in his class. He was excellent at sport, captaining the school teams in cricket, football, and hockey. But he says he was no 'goody goody' and was quite rebellious.

But RS' life was to dramatically change while he was still at school. 'My father and one of my uncles speculated in silver bullion and lost a lot of money, and then they speculated on the Indian currency and had large holdings of one thousand rupee notes which were suddenly cancelled by the government. It was not an overnight collapse as my father tried to save the situation by selling everything off, including his properties and my mother's jewellery. First went the building our family owned and lived in, and then we started a process over several years of moving to smaller and smaller rental properties.

'Luckily for me, this happened towards the end of my school days so I did not notice it and, in any event, I had no understanding of the meaning of money at that point. The upshot was that my father never recovered the lost family fortune, and I was never able to forgive him for the sufferings he brought on my mother who constantly reminded us of our previous life with maidservants and lots of works of art. I was extremely close to my mother who always had great faith in me. She told me "never borrow money from anyone, and never bow your head in front of anyone or else bad times will come".

'The decline also hurt the family socially. My father's explanation of what had happened to his wealth was to blame it on others who owed him money and never paid him back. Whilst this may have been true to some extent, the real reasons were the ones I mentioned earlier. So embittered did he become that he felt that the world seemed to reward dishonest people and that he, who in good times had helped many people, suddenly found they were not there to help him when he needed it. Our Marwari community indeed is very helpful in assisting budding young entrepreneurs get started, but it was not in a position to help someone like my father who had lost a large fortune. Above all, my father was ashamed and became a recluse and split from his brothers.

'Actually, not every business of my father was lost. The one business he managed to salvage was Lalji, a general goods store that had belonged to my father's family for 70 years. It still exists, and today it is one of the biggest shops in the wholesale market. But in those days, it was just a small shop and it was where I spent time working after I left school and while I was studying to become a chartered accountant. My father wondered why I did not immediately look for employment, but I felt my destiny was to be an entrepreneur if I was to restore the family name and fortune and, which I dearly wanted to do for my mother. I subsequently did my articles with S.R. Batliboi & Company, which at that time was the biggest firm in Calcutta and was associated with Ernst & Young.'

In 1971, not long after RS became a chartered accountant, he joined Birla Brothers where RS Goenka was already working. Goenka did not become a chartered accountant but along with RS studied for a bachelor's degree in law and a master's degree in commerce. When I asked what had made the two of them such good friends, RS replied, 'God and destiny are the essence of such a good friendship, and the key is to treat the other as you would like to be treated. It is important in such a relationship to give and not seek. These principles have stood us in good stead over many years.

'I got on extremely well with Goenka's father, and he implored me to treat his son as a younger brother. Goenka had only had one younger brother so it was a very small family for that time and I think his father saw me as somewhat of a mentor to his elder son. His family was reasonably well off, and certainly in comparison to how my family ended up. His father had great personality and we all thought he was extremely good looking as, being quite fair, he looked like an Englishman. In fact, his father spent most of his time in the British business community as he worked as a broker for British businesses.

'I got married in 1971 at the age of twenty-six, and in the same year, I joined Birla Brothers. Actually Goenka married seven years before me but, as I mentioned, we both had our first child in the same year. Mine was an arranged marriage. That did not mean that I had no choice at all, but I met one girl and that was final.

'I joined Birla as the company secretary, responsible for all the company law issues. Subsequently, I became a vice president and started to look at financial issues and the strategy for growth. But my real chance came when Aditya Birla, who was running Birla Brothers at that time and who knew me from college, took over four companies and asked me to streamline the systems which I did quickly and successfully. This gave me an opportunity to work with him very closely and I became his "blue eyed" boy, analyzing potential takeover targets and how the existing businesses were performing. He was a brilliant entrepreneur. He not only had a chemical engineering degree from MIT, but he had fire and ambition oozing from within. Even though he was only one year older than I was, I learnt a lot from him and think he also learnt a little from me in the areas of my expertise.' RS Goenka was meanwhile working for the K.K. Birla Group, streamlining their taxation systems.

'In 1976, after five years of working for Birla Brothers, I submitted my resignation to Aditya Birla. He was shocked as he was about to appoint me as President of Industrial Plants Limited. I told him that I did not want to betray his confidence but service was not my objective and I wanted to start and grow my own business. By that time I had a car, a flat, and other facilities from the company and he asked me whether I was prepared to give all that up. I told him that this did not bother me and that I just wanted his blessing.'

I asked RS whether his wife had been worried that he was giving up such a good job. 'Frankly, I did not ask her or any of my peers or seniors, other than, of course, RS Goenka with whom I had discussed everything as we were going to strike out together. That is why I told you that I am a rebellious and aggressive man and if I decide that I want to do something, I will simply do it. Goenka has a far more calm personality than me, and that is one of the reasons why I suspect we get on so well. We are perfect foils for each other.'

RS then told me an interesting story about what happened on leaving Birla Brothers. 'Aditya Birla called me up and said, even if I was leaving them, he was so happy with my performance that he wanted me to come to the office once a week where I would find I still had an office and secretary and that he would keep paying me my weekly salary. I think he actually hoped that if my attempts to be an entrepreneur failed, I would come back to Birlas. And so I would go each week to the office and collect the cheques for my salary but would never encash them. About a year later, he called me up and said, "What are you doing? Have you become idle? You are not even depositing your cheques." I told him I could not accept his money to which he replied, "But I ordered you to. These are my instructions. Now please deposit the cheques and come and meet me tomorrow." When I went to his office the next day, he was with a few of his friends and told them what I had done and said, "Would you all behave like this? This boy will do very well because of his self respect." Even before RS and Goenka left Birlas, they had decided on getting into cosmetics. 'We chose cosmetics as a start-up because it is a business with minimum risk of losses. I was always toying with the idea of finding a business where the losses would be at a minimum, and the upfront requirements for sales would also be at a minimum. We both researched books on cosmetics and created some of our own formulations.

'We started Kemco Chemicals in 1974 with a capital of 20,000 rupees and opened a small office of some 100 square feet. The brand name for our products from the very beginning was Emami. I do not remember exactly where the name came from but I think there was an unrelated product we found with the brand name "Amami". Goenka and I were clear it was to be a 50-50 partnership.

'Those were difficult days in Calcutta due to the Communist government and unions. But we have always had very good relations with our workers. Today we have around 20,000 people working for Emami and have never lost a single day due to a strike or lockout.

'Our business expanded quickly. In four years, we were number two in creams, after Ponds' well-known "Vanishing Cream". And in cold creams we were number two or three. So we were almost immediately rubbing shoulders with all the big multinationals. They were definitely surprised by our success given that our prices were often higher that theirs. We then took over two companies – Himani and Boroplus – in 1978 and 1984 respectively. Boroplus Antiseptic Cream has over the years become a household name.'

I asked RS what the balance was between RS Goenka and himself, which made their relationship so successful. 'That is pretty simple,' he said 'I am primarily responsible for planning and the creation of ideas and Goenkaji is responsible for execution and implementation. There has never been any overlapping, there has never been any contradiction, and there has never been any confusion. I do sometimes get into too much detail; but not in matters of routine. However, whenever either of us finds a problem, we sit together to find a solution or make the final decision. You cannot completely compartmentalize our work and say that this is your part of the job and this is my part, and that is why I said "primarily responsible". I do not think any partnership or any relationship works that way.

'Too much structuring of any relationship can destroy the quality of that relationship. It is not good to be too logical or too rational, because the rationale and the logic may change with the passing of time – after maybe six or seven years, things may change. In my opinion that is also why many couples decide to separate or divorce. After twenty or thirty years, a wife may say "I never knew that you would be like this" or the husband may similarly say "I never knew that you were like that". They have not tried to understand each other properly over the years. But if you try and put yourself in the "shoes" of the other, then you will see the whole picture. But if there is no love for each other, then your mind has no peace and that brings discomfort. And with discomfort comes stress, which leads to dispersion of energy and in turn you lose wisdom. Totally perplexed, we try and find fault in each other. Instead of accepting things as they are, we expect the other party to accept our desires and failings, but we do not do the same for them. Once we do that, we lose happiness and if that happens, then you lose touch with divinity too.

'I have several ways to determine whether a person is or should be happy or unhappy. In my opinion, to live a happy life one needs to care and put time into one's family, health, business, and also one's spiritual needs. If any of these pillars is weak, then the building of happiness is at risk.'

Wanting to know more about the friendship between RS and Goenka, I started by suggesting that in the West, we say that you should not do business with friends, but I was interrupted, 'The West does not know the meaning of friendship. Friendship is a matter of what we call *sambandh* in Hindi, which means equal relations – equal bondage to each other. There is usually no equal bondage in the West. The beautiful English word of "intercourse" to me implies not only a physical relationship but an emotional one as well. I believe between a husband and wife one can talk about intercourse, whereas between a man and a prostitute it is only physical and the English word of "intercourse" should not be used. Please forgive me for using such an example, but my intention is to try and explain that *sambandh* means a very deep kind of friendship. If one can do business with a complete stranger, how can one not do business with a friend?'

I asked RS whether the friendship between him and Goenka has continued into the next generation. 'Yes. Our children are also very close which you would have seen yesterday when everyone was here for the family meeting. Even Goenka's grandson is a friend of my grandson. You know, all this depends on how you maintain good relations and how selfish or careful you are. We think it is also a matter of being just. With the next generation, if you start from the principle that I will look after my son and Goenkaji will look after his son, then you are going to have problems as far as the relationship is concerned. So it is important not to differentiate between his and my children.

'Emami is therefore run like a large joint family business. Maybe we both will change our family names to Emami. The only possible problem with that is somebody said that the name Emami sounds like a Muslim name, which might cause offence.

'Nor do we have problems when our children marry. We have a forum consisting of members from both the families to discuss this. All the daughters-in-law, as well as our daughters, regularly meet to discuss problems and they also do this with their husbands. We also have a system where nobody can, for example, buy jewellery just for themselves. We give a limit to each and every member of the two families and everyone has to go by these rules. We have created a family constitution as well as a business constitution and it is the same constitution for both the families. Everyone is treated as part of one family. Also, if any member of the two families wants to do something independently, then we have allowed some freedom for that too.

RS's two sons, Aditya and Harsh, and his daughter, Priti Sureka, are on the board of Emami and RS Goenka's younger brother and his son Mohan are also on the Board. His other son Manish and his nephew Prashant are part of the key management team. All six of the next generation are aged between thirty-five and forty.

'Goenkaji and I are planning to retire within the next two years. We are forming a committee to manage the retirement, as nobody knows what the future holds, including of course for how long they will live. We are still making certain there are very strong guidelines for those who take over the company. Some of these guidelines are recommendatory and others obligatory. There are also sanctions if one strays, but one cannot be expelled from the family against their will. If anyone wants to leave, they have the option to sell all or a part of their shareholding, but only to other family members, not to outsiders. Up till now, nobody has left and I am not expecting anyone to leave any time soon.

'There have been some tough times in the past. And, as for debt, it is as I told you it was my mother's wish that I should never take on any debt. But we have started to learn how debt can be used in a wise and conservative way and we do need such debt if we wish to grow bigger.'

And then RS said something that proved, not long after we met, to be eerily prescient. He said, 'But we can never anticipate what is going to happen. This is a very unpredictable world and these are unpredictable times. I believe in three things – there are certain factors we know, certain factors that are unknown, and there are certain factors that are unknowable. Known factors affect whatever I am doing. Factors that may be unknown at this moment may actually be predictable, in which case it is good to develop strategies to handle them. As for the unknowable, we can do nothing but deal with them when they happen. The earthquake that caused the Japanese tsunami and the nuclear accident exemplify this. A sudden death or accident may happen at any time. Always remember that the unknowable is 80 per cent of life but it may affect 100 per cent of your life – you only know 20 per cent of your life.' Within a month of my meeting RS, a major fire was reported at a hospital in which RS and Goenka were shareholders and which sadly led to loss of life. This has led to court cases against multiple parties and which are wending their way through the labyrinthine processes of the Indian court system. It is an event that I suspect RS would definitely place in the unknowable category.

RS is one of the more philosophical of the entrepreneurs I have met and again, for me, this reminded me of AVS Raju. Towards the end of our meeting RS espoused more of his thoughts, 'God smiles at one person leading to him being successful and making the person feel it is all of his own doing. But it is not; it is God who has caused this to happen. Luck and destiny and God are all intertwined; it is God who creates or does not create luck for you. What is the reason that Rahul Gandhi is born in his family, and I am not, and you are not? Why did Prince Charles marry Princess Diana when there so many to choose from? All of these things are beyond our comprehension.'

Like many of the people I meet for my books, RS finds clarity where for many of us there would be confusion. And the main takeaway for me is his philosophy that no matter how successful one might be, we need to realize it is not all of that person's brilliance or doing, as there are other deeper spiritual elements at play. And, above all, we all need to be cognizant that around the corner there may be an unknowable event that changes everything.

---

[1] Emami Limited (www.emamiltd.in) is one of India's leading personal and healthcare businesses. The group was established in 1974 and makes over 300 products based on ayurvedic formulations; many of which are also sold outside India. Emami had a turnover of some USD 300 million in 2012.

> I think that the next seven years will be the defining years for Mindtree. We are making the transition from being a culture-led company to an expertise-led but culture-backed company, and that is an interesting and fascinating journey because it is not the journey of a company; it is the journey of people. In my view when people go to a destination, they take the company with them.

SUBROTO BAGCHI
Chairman, Mindtree[1]

India constantly surprises me, despite all the time I have spent there. And so it was on my way to meet Subroto Bagchi, the founder of Mindtree. For much of the journey from my hotel in Bangalore (now Bengaluru) to his office in Global Village, I was on a dusty road and then we turned off and suddenly 'Bam' I felt I was in another city as we drove down an 'LA-like' boulevard tastefully bordered with palm trees. In fact, the whole complex was extremely well-planned and landscaped creating a feeling of space; a rare commodity in urban India.

I was surprised again when I was ushered in to meet Subroto. Firstly, his office is not at the top of the building, as I have found is often the case with founders or CEOs, but was on the ground floor with a number of large windows looking out into the gardens. Not only that, the layout of the office was unique as it was more like a meeting room. Subroto sits on the inside of a large semi-circular desk with space for a dozen people to sit around the outside of the semi circle. Needless to say Subroto, has a magnificent view of the gardens outside his window and it dawned on me why his office was not at the top of the building.

We started our meeting with my observation that Subroto was a common name in Indonesia and wondering if there were any Indonesian links in his family. He laughed and said, 'I hope it means good stuff there. "Subroto" is actually a Sanskrit word. In Sanskrit, it is written as Subrat – "Su" means "good" and "Brat" means "resolutions"; so it means he who makes good resolutions. But the Bengalis are like the French and would pronounce it very differently. The Bengalis pronounce it "Subroto" and I have chosen to be pronounced the Bengali way.'

We then turned to the story of his family. 'My grandfather was a doctor in Bihar; he had migrated to Bihar from West Bengal sometime around the turn of the twentieth century. My father in turn travelled from Bihar to Odisha where he worked for a small-time king or maharajah in the days before Indian independence in 1947. Before independence, India was a land full of these tiny kingdoms. People working in these princely states were often given fancy grandiose titles and my father's was, believe it or not, "Assistant Secretary for War Affairs". Most of these kings did not speak English, but because they were subjects of His Majesty the King of England, he would send them war dispatches from time to time. So somebody had to read that stuff and make sense of it to the king and, in that process, those small kings felt both important and part of the larger agenda. So my father's official job was to read the war dispatches and brief the king. But as sometimes happens in India even today, his unofficial job was often far less glamorous. At one time he told me his role included escorting the king's daughter along with her two dogs to Calcutta to have her baby.

'My mother came from Bengal. Together, my parents had five children, all boys; I am the fifth and last one. Then came independence in 1947 and these maharajahs lost their kingdoms and so my father transitioned to becoming an employee in the state government. So, he lived, worked and died a state government employee in Odisha, which was, until recently one of the poorest states in India. It is a very interesting state – full of history, literature, and culture, but it is steeped in poverty. We grew up mostly in the mountainous part of the state. My earliest recollection of my childhood is of a place called Koraput where we did not have electricity or water. In fact, the first time I saw electricity in a dwelling was when I was eight years old. I did not go to school until I was eight because there were no schools nearby. And, until about the age of ten, we would bathe from a public tap that was somewhere down the road and fill up two buckets with water to bring home for mother's kitchen. So, that is how my life started.

'There was a big age difference among my brothers and me because the first three came in quick succession and the last two happened as afterthoughts. The gap between my eldest brother and me is fourteen years. It is interesting because he became my surrogate father. My father retired when I was in eighth grade. As a small-time government servant, he did not even have a house of his own and so, on his retirement, my parents with their two youngest children moved in lock, stock and barrel to be part of my eldest brother's household. And that arrangement continued until I branched out on my own. My eldest brother was and remains very inclusive: if he could have his way, the whole world would be part of his household; but his wife had to bear the brunt of the burden at that time. Economically, it was a huge burden on him. My father's pension was meagre. When he retired in 1969, his monthly salary was about 300 rupees (roughly $5 at today's exchange rate) so it was not a lot of money.'

I wondered if education was important to his parents. 'Yes, it was. My father came from a highly-educated family, because his father was a doctor and a landowner as well. My father had to drop out of engineering when my grandfather died and he came to Odisha. But when he was growing up, he and his elder brother had access to good education. In fact, an Englishman was hired to teach them English and he was paid in gold coins. My grandfather wanted to make sure that these two boys spoke English the way English should be spoken and wrote English the way that Englishmen did. And they were brought up to be equal to London matriculates. So, although my father was a man of very humble means he took it upon himself to make sure that his five sons also were equivalent to London matriculates. He taught us English and made sure that our academic ambition and performance were high. My mother was barely able to finish high school but was very erudite; she loved literature and she would recite Tagore's poems to us. I was home schooled between these two parents until I went to school.

'In addition to my parents, two out of my five brothers had a huge influence on me. The first was my eldest brother, Dadamoni, who took us under his wings. He joined the elite Indian Administrative Service and retired at the end of his career as Chief Secretary of Odisha. This would be a big deal for any family and we were enormously proud of him.

'My third brother, Amitav, took a completely different path. Amitav studied and practiced law. Then one day suddenly he gave everything up and became a monk. In substance, he abandoned his family for fifteen years. He eventually came back but continues to be more of a monk than a responsible family man. If he feels like pushing off somewhere for three weeks of pilgrimage, he will just push off. So, he is not accountable. He is only accountable to himself.' In his book Go Kiss the World,[2] Subroto summed up the different influences of these two brothers: 'I learnt the importance of ambition and achievement from Dadamoni whereas from Amitav I learnt that our achievements are only as good as the value they create for others.'[3] Of my other two brothers, the second brother was in the Air Force but passed away many years ago. And the fourth was in the Army, and then became a banker.'

I asked Subroto to share a little more about his grandfather. 'His family owned land in Bengal. While he was alive he had sixty to seventy acres of fertile land on the Ganges, but that did not become part of the family inheritance. He left all that behind when he came to Bihar. Both my grandparents died quite young leaving behind some of their children who were still infants. No one really knows what happened to the land. I think there may have been some changes in the land laws that caused some of the land to be forfeited but certainly most of it was just squandered away by family members. For my family, we did not know what we might have missed, so it had no relevance.'

I asked Subroto whether his father ever felt that he had not really achieved his potential due to the changed family circumstances. 'Well, my dad was a very different kind of a man. Although we might have lived in places where there was no electricity and no water, there were four things he did and over which there could never be any compromises. Firstly, he always drank good tea; he drank tea the way the British would drink it. Number two, whether the world was going to the dogs or not, it was absolutely essential that he had a packet of cigarettes. He smoked one packet of cigarettes a day and that had to come out of the grocery money. Thirdly, he had to have his daily newspaper, the Statesman. Quite often it came one day late because it had to come by bus, train, truck, mule, or whatever, but it was very central to him. The family did not have a transistor radio, so in the evenings he would go to the so-called "Officer's club". There, while others played bridge, he indulged in his fourth passion of listening to the BBC's news bulletin and then the English news from Delhi. Once that was over, he would come home.

'As a result, whilst he may have had a very low paying and fairly meaningless job, he was up to date on world news, whether it was concerning the President of the US or the Prime Minister of the UK. In later years my father would be tracking where Kissinger was going today and tomorrow, much to the chagrin of my mother whose main concern was the more practical issue of making ends meet. He was definitely a man who defied his surroundings. He was the quintessential Indian-Englishman. When the Union Jack came down at the time of Independence, he thought that the country was going to "go to the dogs". But my mother was the opposite. She was patriotic and garlanded Subhas Chandra Bose when he arrived in Dhaka after the Indian National Congress broke up. Subhas became the symbol of the armed struggle against the British so you can see there was an enormous difference in political outlook between my parents.'

When I asked whether there were not arguments over that, Subroto burst out laughing. 'Oh, argument was fundamental to the Bagchi household. There used to be a lot of discussion and debate and we were all very passionate in our views. If you had any two of us converse on any subject for more than five minutes, there would be a fair degree of passion. But most of these debates were issue based: whether, for example, the US or Indian governments were doing the right thing or not. It was a funny household, which was less concerned about the next meal and more concerned about world affairs. So, it was never boring and all in all was good fun and educational at the same time.'

I asked Subroto to expand on the educational aspect of his upbringing. 'I always went to government schools. Certainly we did not have enough money for us to go to English schools.' Subroto reflects on some of his early memories of his schooling: 'When I went to a school in a backward district called Keonjhar, I used to sit with forty odd children on a dhurrie on the floor. Only from the seventh class on, you could sit on a bench. The school had a science lab but no apparatus. We never did any experiments and the roof made of earthen tiles leaked in monsoon and often during the rest of the year sparrow eggs fell on our heads, eliminating the need to look for protein-rich shampoo! It was perhaps not surprising that one of the first visions of the putative Mindtree[4] was to commit a significant portion of the profits every year to support enhancement of primary education in the societies that Mindtree was to work in.

'My father was a very private individual but, as the spoilt youngest child, I could break this down a little by jumping into his arms when he came home from work. He would just take me from one room to another and put me down. This often lead to father-son conversations during which I would complain to him about my mother or one of my brothers and ask him to throw out the one who was annoying most at the time. He would calmly tell me, "Okay, you have to write it down as we have to do this in a systematic way as there will be a court hearing with me as the magistrate presiding to deal with your complaints." I would ask him what a magistrate did and what a policeman did and he would explain all the procedures to me, hoping that I would forget all about it. But little did he know in the beginning that I would produce the petition for him the next day. This was all part of my education.

'My eldest brother taught economics in the university before he joined the IAS. He would explain to me the law of supply and demand and I knew about concepts like the law of marginal returns when I was eight years old. He would occasionally show me off to his students by asking me in his class to tell them about some or other economic principle. And he would teach me stuff like Schumacher's theory and tell me about ideas that the poor are poor because they are poor – about the vicious cycle of poverty. I knew about all that by the time I was a teenager.'

I suggested that it did not sound as if he had been much involved in playing games or just mucking around. 'That's true. Early in life, I got interested in debates and again this was something that my eldest brother also initiated me into. I became a voracious debater at school, going here and there and taking part in competitions and this lessened any time for games. Also when my third brother did well at the National Cadet Corps (NCC) he became a role model for me. NCC is a very serious organisation and you have to put in a lot of time and effort to do well. This certainly took my time away from playing games. But NCC was a lot of fun and eventually I was a part of the first batch of civilian para-jumpers, which took me to take part in the Republic Day celebrations in Delhi. I was recognized as the best cadet in the country which led me to have breakfast with Prime Minister Indira Gandhi and to be introduced to the President of the country.'

I suggested that all of the foregoing implied that he was a very serious child. 'I would say I was not only serious, but very focused and achievement-oriented.' When I asked why he thought he was like that, he replied: 'It is very difficult to answer because this is an area that has been my study for much of my life and particularly in the last ten years after founding Mindtree. I have been working very closely with leaders and studying leadership. My current role at Mindtree requires me to spend one-on-one time with the top hundred people in the company. So I work with them closely and I ask myself this question, from where do people get the determination to achieve? I have spent time with doctors and psychologists and we really do not know. The interesting thing is that when you are conceived, your DNA is created. It is just a set of protein molecules coming together to form your DNA and they are not necessarily solely from your parents. In fact, out of so many molecules only one or two may be from your immediate parents and some may come from thousands of years back. So, at that moment, that is your combination locked in. Now, today, thanks to the way the study of DNA has developed, we know that your DNA in turn is going to decide what kind of chemical factory your body will become. The chemical combination of your body determines the synaptic actions in your brain. So it is a very complex thing. There is also, on the other hand, a theory about nurture versus nature and the human brain as a plastic space waiting for the impress of nurture. There is an interesting overlap taking place between biosciences, diagnostic imaging, and psychology. When you combine these three things, you realize how little we really know about the human brain and human thinking and why a person does what he does. The reason I am telling you all this is that, let us say there is a crisis, two different individuals may react in two very different ways to the crisis, so that their reactions may seem random at first glance. Sometimes you do not know why you do or why you not do whatever it is. Now how much in any moment is training development and adaptive behaviour, on the one hand and how much, on the other hand, is your DNA springing up, we really do not know.'

We returned to our discussion as to how Subroto became the top cadet in the country. 'It's quite an amazing story. There were eighteen states in India at that time and each state nominated its best cadet. So ultimately it's a competition between eighteen cadets. Among those eighteen, no one could really be eliminated on the basis of his turnout, on the way that he marched, on his basic level of firearm competency, none of that stuff. There was a group of selectors from the army to interview the eighteen candidates. And then the selection committee would select four for an interview with the Director General of the NCC. At the initial selection meeting, an Australian Major – can you believe it, he was the last Australian in the Indian Army, asked me: "Mr. Bagchi, have you heard of Diego Garcia?" Now, you will remember my father's four passions included the Statesman and BBC. We used to read out the Statesman's editorial at tea. So at the age of eight I had been reading this editorial without understanding anything. But Diego Garcia had been a topic that I vividly remembered. For the next ten minutes the selection committee did not know what had hit them. I told them about Diego Garcia during the 1971 Indo-Pakistan conflict and about Diego Garcia as an island in the Indian Ocean. I told them the length of the runway, how many B52 bombers were based there; how long it would take for a B52 bomber to take off from there, come to India, and go back without refueling. Now, what I am trying to convey in this story is that there is a randomness that is not totally random. This Major asked me about Diego Garcia. What if he had asked me about something else that I could not answer? And what were the chances that I might not have paid attention to all the facts about Diego Garcia? So there were ten minutes of my answer; it was like a machine gun. I gave them the whole nine yards on Diego Garcia and they did not ask me another question after that.'

I asked Subroto how he could remember all this. 'This was probably not that old news. Diego Garcia had been in the news in

1971 and this was only four years later, in 1975. The issue was not about knowing something about it – many people would have heard about Diego Garcia – but it was the level of depth that was the issue. There were two things: one is the capacity to be present, the capacity to seize that moment and perform. The other is the capacity to see more than the question – the capacity actually to raise it to a different level. I think, looking back, I did have the capacity to build memorability – the ability to make even a small transaction memorable. The whole world is looking for memorability. And memorability is not understood by CEOs because we do not understand the nature of what makes something memorable. Why is it that an Apple iPad is not an MP3 player? What makes Apple do something that makes their products memorable? I think memorability is the key to differentiation in the world of today where there is both information overload and attention deficiency. When people have attention deficiency, when even adults and organizations have attention deficiency, how do you stand out in a crowd? I guess I wanted to stand out to demonstrate that I was very ambitious and clever.' In his book Go Kiss the World, Subroto shares that his purpose in writing about the best cadet story is not to emphasize his achievement but instead to show the importance of creating memorability in a first meeting with anyone. 'Most people we meet do not have a special reason to remember us nor are they interested in what we have to say or what we actually do. Given that, it is important that in every situation one has to be not only well prepared but razor sharp to create instant engagement... the question on Diego Garcia had given me that short window to make my mark. It is what I call the Diego Garcia moment of my life.'

I asked Subroto whether he had known what he wanted to be. 'Oh, I wanted to be many things. And eventually it did not work out like I had wanted because as someone has said man has two futures: the future of desire and the future of fate – and seldom the two shall meet. My desires for the future were different at different times. There was a time when I fancied joining the army. There was a time when I fancied becoming a diplomat because that was something discussed in the family – we have a son who is an IAS officer, a son in the air force, another in the army, and another who is a lawyer – and I should therefore join the foreign service. Also, there was a time when I wanted to teach. I knew I was academically bright and was usually in the top two at school. And I was ambitious and focused. I wanted to stand out. I think I had this desire to make my family proud of me. Looking back I was always performing for my eldest brother. I was like his "dog" – but in a very loving way and not in a pavlovian way. He would take me on the tours of the district in his official jeep and he would explain to me the intricacies of development economics. No doubt this would have been very boring stuff for most kids; but for me it was interesting.'

When I asked Subroto whether his family had high expectations of him, he replied: 'No. In fact it is fascinating that you should ask that question. I tell my leaders all the time that we are so obsessed with measuring output, we should spend more time measuring input. And what I got as a child was inputs without questions, inputs without people trying to measure outputs and while my eldest brother showed me off and stuff like that, I was never put under pressure to perform. I was pulled to excel – I was not pushed. And I liked being shown off. I think it is interesting to compare humans to dogs. I love dogs and I think dogs are quite like smart people. When you show off a prized dog in a dog show, the dog is fully aware of what the hell is going on – dogs and horses are different that way – dogs and horses know that they are being shown off. I was like that – but there was no pressure.

'My life took a very funny turn after all the success of being the top cadet and being a national celebrity at eighteen. It seemed like everything I touched turned into "gold". I joined BJB College in Bhubaneswar in Odisha where I studied political science. I wanted to study economics, but my eldest brother said, "It is better to be a first-rate political scientist than a second-rate economist". Next I wanted to study international relations at post-graduate level. That was not only because of the influence of my upbringing, but also because I loved political theories. I hoped that the study of international relations would mean either a diplomatic or academic career. But this would have required me to go to the Jawaharlal Nehru University in Delhi that was the only university teaching international relations. Although I was a national scholar, I acknowledged I was increasingly a burden on the family and particularly on my eldest brother – for that matter I had been a burden for seven years already and it was becoming difficult. The bottom line was that we could not afford Delhi.

'As a result I took admission for post-graduate study in the local university, Utkal University in Bhubaneswar. I studied there for two months until I realized I was wasting my time as I was not learning anything new and it was all very uninspiring. So, I told myself, let me go and take up a job. We are talking about pre-industrialized India, so jobs were not easy to come by, other than joining the government. If I were to write the Civil Services examination, it would have taken another two years, because you had to be twenty-one. So, at the age of nineteen I joined a nearby Odisha State Government office as a clerk. Because to be a clerk, there was no age restriction – it was as if I had started as a bricklayer's assistant. I informed my parents who were quite shocked. I remember my father calling me and saying, "what do you think the interviewers at the Union Public Service Commission will ask you when you go there finally? Obviously, this is a stopgap job and eventually you will write the Civil Services examination, and what do you think they will think about this and what will they ask you?" I remember telling him that "I think they will be proud of me and, if they are not, then I don't care". So I started my working life in a government office, and I worked there for one whole, very difficult, year. It may sound romantic to do what I did, but it was quite tough. Everyone knew that I was only a passing passenger, who was going to drop off at any moment, but I loved the people around me and I think they too loved me. I found a new universe there with people twice my age. They were not mothering or fathering me; they were treating me as an equal. In the beginning they looked at me oddly and no doubt were saying to themselves what the hell is this guy doing here?

'After a year there, in 1977, I wrote an examination to become a management trainee for the DCM Group which was at that time the seventh largest industrial house in the country. DCM was run by the father and uncle of Arun Bharat Ram [see my previous *Added Value* book[5]]. Their management trainee scheme was a big deal. The conventional wisdom was you joined the Civil Services if you were bright and wanted a career in government but, if you decided to work for the private sector, the top management traineeships were ether with Tata or DCM. I had no idea that I would join the private sector. I was considered the outlier in my family because nobody worked in the private sector.

'When I got the DCM job in 1977, I said to myself it is time to get married. I had met Susmita when she was only fifteen and I was eighteen. The upshot was that we had known each other for a number of years and were in love, so we ran away from home and got married. I became a father at twenty-five and then again at twenty-eight. My parents were okay – I have told you the kind of people they were. But my wife's parents were scandalized because she did not come from Bengal – I was a Bengali but she was an Odia and interstate marriages were frowned upon. The only one of my brothers who had an arranged marriage was the one who left his family to become a monk – maybe there is a connection. My mother also lived with us until she died. So I have always been a minority male in my house with my mother, Susmita and our two daughters.' Laughing Subroto says, 'One day out of disgust and anger and retaliation, I brought in a Golden Retriever and I made sure that the fellow was a male. But he very quickly understood where the power in the household lay.'

I suggested that Subroto Bagchi and his wife might be alter egos. 'Yes, I am a Gemini and Susmita is a Libra. She is a true Libran. I always want to go to a new place to eat; I want to find a hole in the wall – I want to eat in a place where nobody speaks English and the menu is not in English. She wants to eat in the same restaurant and order the same dish. I drive her up the wall all the time. But the nice thing is that she is a writer so she understands me as a writer. She gave up working full time and chose to be writer instead to be able to accommodate my moving from here to there. We have moved home seventeen times in thirty-three years of marriage, so that requires Susmita to be a combination of a CEO and an Army General so that I am able to do my thing. That is a huge thing. I know it is very fashionable to make such statements, but when I tell people that we have moved homes seventeen times in thirty-three years, I want to emphasize that that is not possible without that alter ego with a good solid understanding and the sort of entrenchment which will push back. She cuts me down to size let me tell you. I get zero respect at home.'

I asked about his daughters, 'The younger one, Niti, is a student of Greek and Latin. She went to Columbia and is doing her PhD in Classics at the University of Pennsylvania. The older one, Neha, graduated from the Tepper School of Business of Carnegie Mellon

University. She taught for two years in the Bronx before she went to Carnegie Mellon after she had been an undergraduate at Rutgers University. But both the girls have so far rejected the corporate world. I do not think it will be for them. The older one put me in my place when I tried to do career counseling to her after high school. I said to her "let us have a father-daughter talk. Given the chance, what would you like to be?" So she looked at me as if I was from another planet and replied "I would like to be a poor musician". So they are not corporate material like me, and that is fine.

'I worked at DCM for five years in plant administration and learnt a lot but eventually fell out with Brihaspati Dev Pathak, who had been brought in by DCM management to run the Delhi cloth mills. In his book Go Kiss the World,[6] he tells a story of an important lesson he learnt from Dev Pathak. When Subroto became frustrated with the way his immediate superior was running their part of the business he broached this subject with Dev Pathak. Dev Pathak's response was 'Have you ever seen a seed sprouting from under a big boulder?' Subroto replied that he had. Dev Pathak continued, 'When the seed is under the huge rock, which has the upper hand, the greater power?' To this, Subroto replied, 'The rock, so?'

'Precisely', said Dev Pathak 'the relative balance of power is in favour of the rock. The rock can crush the sapling. The sapling, however, does not assert itself, does not fight the rock as it gently circumvents the rock and keeps growing along its side. And one day the sapling becomes a huge tree. At that time, where do you think the rock sits?' Subroto was silent. So, Dev Pathak answered the question for him, 'it remains at the foot of the tree forever.'

Eventually Subroto realized that he had to leave. He heard of an opportunity for entry-level sales people at an IT start-up called HCL. There the guaranteed monthly salary would be 40 per cent less than what he had been receiving at DCM, although there was the possibility of earning commission income also. Without the commissions Susmita and he would have serious cash flow problems as she was still at college and they also needed to send money home every month. Subroto said, 'Sometimes in our moments of conflict we come across the sign that in a flash helps us reach a decision which hours or days of frustrating reasoning cannot achieve. Almost magically the options or answer becomes clear. One evening, whilst walking in Connaught Circus, I saw a book with the rather unusual cover. It showed a bird in flight, wings outstretched. It was Jonathan Livingston Seagull by Richard Bach. I bought the book on an impulse and began reading it as soon as I reached home. I could not put it down once I started. The protagonist of the book, Jonathan Livingston Seagull, taught me that life's true purpose is not to live to earn; it is about having the courage to take flight. Susmita also read the book and, suddenly, the decision we had to take was clear – we would take the risk, a leap into the future. Cash flow became unimportant. If I did well, we would be able to make up the lost income through sales commission, if I did not, it did not matter.

'At that point the IT industry was just beginning to happen. I joined HCL in 1981 and worked for a number of people in a number of different roles in both HCL and MMC Digital Systems, which was a Mahindra outfit. I learnt about sales and marketing in these jobs. Then I tried my hand at entrepreneurship and ran a start-up company called Project 21 for three years along with a couple of other people, but that folded because of cash flow issues. In 1988, I joined Wipro where I worked for ten years.

'When I left Wipro I thought that it would be a good idea to try my hand at a multinational, so I joined Lucent. Lucent was setting up what they called their Bell Labs Development Center at Bangalore, and it took me a year to realize that this was not my life script and that this was not what I wanted to do for the rest of my life. Then it occurred to me that if I was unhappy with the system, then I could either fix that system or I could build a better system. So I said in conversation with myself "Why are you complaining about this or that; if you really want to do something worth while, then go and do it." That is when I started talking with my ex-colleague, who was still at Wipro, Krishnakumar Natarajan; he was the chief executive of one of the business units. He and I got together and, as a result, Mindtree was conceived, thirteen or fourteen years ago.'

The beginnings of Mindtree in 1999 was the story of ten founders coming together out of their corporate successes to do their own thing in their own company. Six of them had worked together at Wipro, including Ashok Soota who became the Chairman. He had been the President of Wipro Infotech from 1984 until the foundation of Mindtree. Subroto says, 'Susmita taught me the importance of being a good human being, before trying to be a leader. From Ashok I learnt what it takes to be a good leader.'

The story of the development of the Mindtree logo as told by Subroto in each of *Go Kiss the World*[7] and *Making of the Mindtree*,[8] is illuminating. While he was at Wipro, Subroto was introduced to the Spastics Society of Karnataka. And during his first visit to the Spastics Society, he met Sheena Watson, a visiting art teacher from Ireland, who was painstakingly trying to teach the young children with cerebral palsy how to hold a paint brush. For her, it was not just an effort to make the children creative, it was therapy for the more fundamental problem of muscular control. Probably because many of these children cannot speak or express themselves without severe effort, Subroto found their paintings to have extraordinary vibrancy and creativity. So he suggested to his co-founders that it might be a good idea to see if the cerebral palsy children could design Mindtree's logo. After the enthusiastic approval of his co-founders and with the agreement of the Spastics Society, he and some of his colleagues spent time with the children to try and explain to them what Mindtree was about. From amongst the ten designs they received, Subroto said it was not difficult to pick the astounding work of seventeen-year-old K.S. Chetan who said in support of K.S.' work 'the upward blue stroke in his creation stood for boundless imagination, the red background denoted action, and the yellow dots were "bubbles of joy".[9] (The logo has since been gifted to Mindtree Foundation and Mindtree has got a new logo after a recent rebranding exercise.)

'Now I am no longer "hands on". Krishnakumar Natarajan is the CEO of the company and I am the Vice-Chairman on the Board and the understanding that we have is he will oversee operations and I am making sure that when he and I move out at sixty, which is the age that we have decided that all founders must step down, the next set of people are ready to take the company to the next level by 2020. So, as I mentioned earlier, I focus on the top hundred. I also focus on the communities of practice and am internally the drag-and-drop icon so that I can work with groups as compared to going and hustling for business or saying, 'let me do a deep dive here and fix something for you.'

In his *Go Kiss the World*,[10] Subroto described how this change in role occurred. 'On 31 May 2007, I turned fifty. I took the day off and spent time with Susmita in a quiet, reflective mood. A deep sense, fulfillment pervaded. In the silence I began to hear the "little drummer" in me. First the beats of a barely audible, like a faint whisper coming through the mist of a dark winter night. Then it began to get louder and nearer. I recognized the beat; I had heard it many times in my life. It signaled a crossover; every time it brought a new beginning. The next day, I spoke to Ashok and conveyed that I would like to step down from the position of authority in Mindtree to take on a position of service. "What will you call yourself?" he asked. I heard myself say "Gardener". "This is a good thought. Write down the role description," Ashok replied. Almost a year later, on 1 April 2008, Mindtree had its first "Gardener". It is in this role, my task is to focus on creating leadership capacity within the top 100 people of Mindtree and where it was necessary to break the traditional mould and work without a formal structure.'

I suggested that his role as 'Gardener' had been him creating his perfect job. 'I have always done that. In fact, that is one thing that I have reflected upon about my own life that, whatever job I have done, I have done it my own way. Most of the jobs that I have done did not exist before I came along; the role, the title, and the responsibilities did not exist except only once or twice in my life. This was true even in my first job as a clerk. This was especially true at Wipro. That was amazing because, during my ten years there, none of the jobs existed before I took them on. I did four jobs in Wipro, and none of them had existed beforehand.'

Not too long after I met Subroto, Ashok Soota decided to seek a new challenge himself by being involved in the founding of a new company at the age of almost seventy. This turn of events led to Subroto getting back into a more active role as Chairman of Mindtree with K.K. Krishnakumar Natarajan as the CEO.

I noted to Subroto that Mindtree is listed. 'Yes, we had venture capital investment initially but now we are listed. I own a little more than 5 per cent of the company now. Ours is a fascinating industry and I keep telling myself and my leaders all the time that we walk in the "shadow of giants". We have always walked in the "shadow of giants". I think that the next seven years will be the defining years for Mindtree. We are making the transition from being a culture-led company to an expertise-led but culture-backed company, and that is an interesting and fascinating journey because it is not the journey of a company; it is the journey of people. In my view when people go to a destination, they take the company with them.'

As I left Subroto and drove back down the beautiful palm bordered avenue to the dusty streets of Bangalore, I started thinking of some of the words from Frank Sinatra's classic song 'My Way'. There is one stanza I thought particularly appropriate to Subroto's life to date:

Regrets, I've had a few
But then again, too few to mention
I did what I had to do and saw it through without exemption
I planned each charted course, each careful step along the byway
And more, much more than this, I did it my way.[11]

---

[1] Mindtree (www.mindtree.com) is a global information technology solutions company with annual revenues of over USD 435 million involving 13,000+engineers.
[2] Subroto Bagchi, *Go Kiss the World*, Penguin, 2008.
[3] idem p.50.
[4] Subroto Bagchi, 'The Making of Mindtree', www.mindtree.com
[5] Peter Church, *Added Value*, Roli Books, New Delhi 2010, pp.196-207.
[6] Subroto Bagchi, *Go Kiss the World*, p.84.
[7] ibid., pp.180-82.
[8] Subroto Bagchi, 'The Making of Mindtree'.
[9] Subroto Bagchi, *Go Kiss the World*, p.182.
[10] Subroto Bagchi, *Go Kiss the World*, pp.216-17.
[11] *My Way* lyrics © Universal Music Publishing Group, Warner/Chappell Music, Inc.

"I would create a movement with youngsters of my own age and go on the social media and do what the two guys in Egypt did, create a wave and then eliminate the damn cancer of corruption which we have somehow got in this country. Youngsters between thirty and forty years would have to take charge of the administration and governance of the country. I agree that this is revolutionary because the evolutionary way in India is just not realistic."

PROFESSOR BALA V. BALACHANDRAN

Founder Great Lakes Institute of Management[1]

I met Professor Bala Balachandran for breakfast early one morning at the Sheraton hotel in Chennai together with his colleagues, Professor Sriram and G.R. Venkat from Great Lakes Institute of Management, and my own colleague, Suresh Iyer. Bala, as many know him, was back in Chennai from his base in the US at Kellogg School of Management at Northwestern University to spend time with the 'baby' he created, Great Lakes Institute of Management.

Professor Balachandran was born in 1937 in the village of Pudupatti, which is close to the city of Pudukkottai in Tamil Nadu. He was the first child of his mother, who was the second wife of his father. His father had one son from the first marriage who was ten years old at the time Bala was born. His mother went on to have four more sons and a daughter. His half-brother left home to continue his studies at Christian College in Chennai while Bala was still very young making him, in effect, the eldest child in the family and certainly of his mother.

'My father was an advocate. He started with a small practice but it flourished after he successfully represented one of the most famous Indians of that era, Raja Sir Satappa Ramanatha Muttaiya Annamalai Chettiar[2] in a case in Burma.' Raja Annamalai came from a family of famous bankers who were involved in the establishment of the Bank of India. Raja Annamalai was a board member of this bank for many years. He was highly respected by Indians as well as the British for his contribution to India's banking and education sector (he founded Annamalai University at Chidambaram). This led to him being knighted by the King of England in 1923, and later honoured again by the King in 1929 as the first Rajah of Chettinad (being a hereditary title).

The Chettiar caste (of which Sir Annamalai was a prominent leader) were traditionally involved in finance and had become enormously successful and influential in Burma as financiers. During the 1930s, Britain introduced legislation that discriminated against the rights of Indians living in Burma and particularly the finance business of Chettiars. This was largely brought on by the Great Depression of 1930, which led to Burmese farmers being unable to pay back their loans to the Chettiar financiers. This, in turn, led to the financiers being entitled to seize the land of the farmers under their security arrangements. There was resentment amongst the indigenous Burmese and the British responded by seeking to introduce legislation restricting the rights of Indian nationals living in Burma. Influential Indian Chettiar, such as Sir Annamalai, made several trips to Britain to lobby for changes in the law, but the Second World War[3] interrupted a final outcome. Immediately after the war, the pressure for independence grew enormously and the position of Indians in Burma continued to be threatened. It was during these circumstances that Bala's father had to spend a year in Rangoon arguing the Chettiar position. Bala commented, 'This created significant respect for him amongst the influential Chettiar community in Burma and back in Chennai. As a lawyer yourself, you can imagine the impact this had on his legal practice as Chettiar from far and wide then sought his legal advice.

'My uncle S. Satyamurti was one of the famous freedom fighters from the Madras state. A well-respected Member of Parliament (the

Imperial Legislative Council) before independence, he was the political mentor of K. Kamaraj, later chief minister of Tamil Nadu and president of the Indian National Congress. In 1942, when I was five years old I had the opportunity to meet Mahatma Gandhi when he came to our city of Pudukkottai at the invitation of my uncle. As it happens, Gandhi was denied permission to enter Pudukkottai by the last Rajah (King) of the city. Rajagopal Tondaiman as the Rajah was under the influence of the British; provided he "toed the line" with what the British wanted, he did not have to pay any taxes. As Gandhi was not allowed to enter the city, my uncle and I met him on the outskirts. I was running around while they talked. At some stage, he must have noticed me and asked my uncle who I was. Gandhiji asked me to sit on his lap. He then asked me what I would do for India. I do not know why I said it, but apparently I responded immediately that "I would die for the country". At this, he cried, and I can vividly remember this, as it was unusual to see adults crying. Of course, as a child I did not appreciate the full significance of who Gandhiji was, but there is no doubt that, for me, it is one of my most significant memories.'

I reminded Bala Balachandran that he had described himself as mischievous. 'At one time, yes. I must have been around twelve then, I spent a lot of time playing cricket and generally not applying myself to my school work, so much so I got some bad results including flunking an exam. The school regularly sent progress reports and I knew this would make my father very angry. As at the best of times he was short-tempered, I knew that he was going to give me hell. So what did I do? I forged my father's signature on the report acknowledgement and then gave it back to the school principal. Unfortunately, there was an idiot relative of mine in my class. He came to my home and asked my father what he thought about me flunking the exam. Of course my father had no idea and eventually my "crime" was uncovered. In his rage, he took out his belt and didn't know whether he was using the buckle or the leather end of it on me and ended up using it the wrong way. One of the strokes was too high and the buckle pin went straight into my head. Blood started pouring out and I fainted. He immediately realized he had overreacted and rushed me to a hospital. This was an important lesson for me – I had committed two crimes; one crime is all right – I flunked – that was enough, but why the heck had I forged my father's signature?

'But I also learnt something else from this experience and that is anger, if not controlled, is a dangerous emotion. Anger can cause one to lose one's mind, do stupid things and then regret them forever. Fortunately, I did not inherit his short temper, but from that time on, when somebody makes a mistake which affects me, I practice *chalta hai* which, in Hindi, means "let it go".'

I asked Bala whether he was brought up in a joint family. 'It was a joint family for most of my childhood. In the family home lived my parents and siblings, as well as my uncle and his children and an unmarried aunt. At some stage, the tension between my mother and my uncle's wife became unbearable so my uncle and aunt and their children moved to another house in a nearby street. Eventually my aunt who lived with us got married and then it was just my immediate family.'

Bala was educated at the Christian Swedish Mission High School or CSM High School. 'It was a little bizarre because by the time I finished school, I probably knew more about Christianity than my religion of Hinduism. The reason was because we had Christian religious studies at school whereas no one taught us Hinduism – we just absorbed it from our life outside the school. When I went to the temple I would not know why everyone went clockwise but just copied them.'

I asked Bala about his studies. 'Whilst I was an excellent student later in my career, when I was younger I just messed around and had fun. There was a particular Brahmin community near where we lived where the priests wore their hair in a tuft. For fun, I suggested to my friends that we should tie a coconut to the tufts on two priests and bang the priests together to see if we could crack the coconuts. My friends thought I was mad as I am a Brahmin myself and what was I doing was making fun of my own community. Thankfully, it was just a joke!

'My birth star is Rohini, and it so happened that this was also the birth star of the Rajah of Pudukkottai. In fact, we were born on the same day but different years. Every year on his birthday, the Rajah would ride into the city on an elephant with two other elephants in front of him. As he went down the main street, he would throw coins to the people. And the dogs would go berserk barking at the elephants. My mother would say to me, "Bala look at those dogs barking but the elephants don't react even though they could easily annihilate the dogs by stepping on them." She asked me why the elephants did not do this. Her explanation was that the elephants concentrate on carrying the Rajah and do not allow themselves to be distracted. The message she was conveying to me was that it is the company one keeps that is most important; the elephants knew the Rajah was most important for them and that they should ignore the dogs. She told me that I should remember this throughout my life and I have.'

Bala's mother is ninety-four years old and lives in Madurai. 'My mother was a very big influence on me as a child, in fact, much more than my father who was always away earning money for the family. Even though she only studied up to fourth grade at school, this never embarrassed her. She used to tell me that Kamaraj, the chief minister at that time was also only educated to the same level and that both of them were trained by my uncle Satyamurti. She believed she was not inferior to anybody.' He added that it was his mother who taught him and his siblings about life, including responsibility and affection. 'In short, she was my "university" when I was young.'

A number of Bala's siblings have also had successful careers. His younger brother is the head of marketing at Stanford Business School. Even though he was a topper at school, he was not given admission to engineering at either Annamalai or Madras University because the system at that time discriminated against Brahmins in favour of other castes. He spent a year at home preparing for the competitive examination to enter the prestigious Indian Institute of Technology in Chennai and was accepted. In due course he graduated at the top of his class with the gold medal. Another brother was also a gold medal winner in Geology and went on to become the Director of Exploration and Development at ONGC – the Oil & Natural Gas Corporation – at Dehradun.

But Bala was the only child who enjoyed and excelled at mathematics and also helped his brothers in the subject. 'My younger brother who went to IIT ranked 14th in all of India in one of their mathematics' exams, so he must have been okay too,' he says with a laugh.

I asked Bala what made him interested in maths when neither his mother nor father showed any interest. He told me: 'Around 1950, when I was about twelve or thirteen years old, my mathematics teacher gave the class three problems and said if any one of us could solve the problems and also top the class in the next exam he would give half a rupee, about two cents at that time. The money did not matter to me but I wanted to top the class. So I worked hard and solved all three problems. Apparently our teacher was shocked as he told me he himself could not solve two of them. He was so impressed he doubled the prize and gave me a rupee. I learnt that what really mattered to me was, not the money, but being at the top. I think I would have to say I am an intensely competitive person who wants to excel at whatever I do. For example, my Ph.D. thesis on my specialization of Operations Research was awarded the top global prize in 1973 by the Operations Research Society of the US. Nobody from my university, Carnegie Mellon had ever won that award. But my competitiveness extends to everything I do. Usually it takes four years to do a Ph.D. but I finished mine in two. This is the basis of another of my life mottos – "be distinct or extinct".

I asked Bala why he thought that Indians were so good at mathematics and mentioned that I understood it was an Indian who created the concept of zero. He burst out laughing and asked if I was aware that one of India's ex-presidents, Sarvepalli Radhakrishnan [1888-1975] is credited with having said "India has given nothing to science"! '"Nothing" of course is another word for "zero" and that is why many of us were amused by his comment.' Bala told me he believes food habits have a bearing on whether one is good at Maths. 'There is a vegetable which we call *okra* in the US but Indians call it *lady's finger*. I believe this food has a specific property – something to do with high viscosity – that improves brainpower and makes brain cells work faster and stronger. So diet is extremely important.

'Secondly, our education may not be the best but I believe it is a strength that we are taught in the beginning to learn things by rote. For example, I learnt as a young boy that the square root of 2 is 1.414 and the square root of 3 is 1.732 etc. I do not know why the heck I need to know this, but somehow I do and I can do virtually all multiplications in my head.

'There is also the example of a very well-known mathematician called Srinivasa Ramanujan [1887-1920]. He did work on number theory and infinite series but was by and large a self-taught genius. When he was taking admission in Cambridge, he was asked why he was so good at mathematics. He responded somewhat strangely by saying that his family goddess, Namagiri of Namakkal – the city where he was groomed – would come to him in his dreams and he would receive visions of scrolls of complex mathematical content unfolding before his eyes. I am not sure if I believe that is true but that is what he said. Srinivasa was also a Brahmin, a Vaishnavite Brahmin.'

I asked Bala to go back to his own education. 'Even though I got 100 per cent in a state-wide examination, due to quota reservations and system discrimination against Brahmins, I could not get into engineering at the College of Engineering, Guindy, which is now part of Anna University in Chennai. My father wanted me to join the Indian Administrative Services, which was considered extremely prestigious and ensured a stellar career in the government. I sat for the exam to join Presidency College where they only had fourteen seats but again, due to discrimination, I did not get in. Fortunately for me, Annamalai University, which was founded by Rajah Annamalai, who we talked about earlier, started a statistics honours degree course into which I was admitted – no doubt largely due to my father's relationship with the Rajah. In 1959, I got my B.Sc (Hons.) in Mathematics and Statistics, and an M.A. in Mathematics and Statistics in 1961, and an M.Sc. in Applied Statistics in 1963. To support myself, I became a lecturer in Statistics at Annamalai University from 1960.

'While I was teaching, there was an interruption in my academic career. In 1962, Pandit Jawaharlal Nehru was the prime minister and he greatly admired his counterpart in China, Zhou Enlai and his "Panchsheel" being "the Five Principles of Peaceful Coexistence". To Nehru's surprise, our soldiers in the Ladakh area of Kashmir were attacked by the Chinese. It was manslaughter as the Chinese had machine guns, whereas our soldiers only had single shot Lee-Enfield .303 rifles. As a result, many thousands of our Indian troops perished. This incensed me greatly and without telling my father, I joined the army. As I had been in the National Cadet Corps part time, I had the rank of lieutenant while I was a lecturer. Upon enlisting, I was immediately appointed a commissioned officer on an emergency commission.

'My father was furious, he said, "Are you nuts; the military is only for high school dropouts. You are a bloody educated guy, why the heck would you join the army?" I told him I was angry at what China had done to our people and that I wanted to kill at least five

Chinese myself before going back to teaching. As luck would have it, I had a stupid high school dropout as my Battalion Commander with the rank of a Lieutenant Colonel. I was a Captain, his administrative officer. I think he was jealous of my education and wanted me out of the way. He would keep teasing me by calling me an idiot and that he was the stronger man. I got my chance to really annoy him one day when he asked me what the muzzle velocity of my rifle was. I was mischievous again – and told him that he was an idiot. I said that in the first place he really meant "vector" not "velocity". He asked me what I meant by vector. I told him that it was not a linear scale and deliberately teased him by saying that he might not understand it because he did not have college degree in physics. "That is it, get out," he said. I told him that he could not throw me out as I was a commissioned officer like he was and that there was therefore no insubordination. In any event it was clear to me that the army was no place for me and I had to acknowledge to my father that he was correct. I left the army after one and a half years and returned to Annamalai University where my place had been kept for me during my leave of absence.

'I returned there just in time to meet the man who would change my life. Professor Landis Gephart was based at Wright-Patterson Air Force Base and worked for the US Strategic Air Command. He had a Ph.D. and was a full colonel in the US Army and also a professor at the University of Dayton in Ohio. He had come to Chennai on a USAID project with the objective of propagating an understanding of reliability engineering and Quality Control and also to find students who could be recruited to go to the US to do a Ph.D. in that field. The upshot was that I was selected from the Statistics Department of my university. I told him that there was a catch, as I knew my father would not let me go. My father had told me often that he felt he might die soon and that if that happened as the eldest son, I would have responsibilities to take care of the rest of the family after his death. Gephart said to me, "All right, let's go." I wondered what he meant. He told me that he wanted to meet my father to which I responded that he did not live in Chennai but in Pudukkottai some 200 miles away. He said, "I don't care, let's go and get the train." You can imagine how shocked I was. I was terrified to think of what my father would say and whether he would be polite in telling this American that it was not up to him to decide my future. So we took the train and met with my father. He told him that I was gifted at mathematics and that he would ensure I got a Ph.D. and that all costs including my travel and living expenses would be born by the US Government. Can you imagine that this father of mine, who was short-tempered and had shouted at me that I was stupid to want to go to the US, responded immediately that of course I should go? At that time, this was the power of the "white man", seriously! My father did not trust his own damn son. But he believed somebody whom he had never seen before and just said "yes". I was furious, but my dad said that this guy was right. I asked him in Tamil so as to not embarrass the professor how he knew and he just repeated that Professor Gephart was right and added that he was a "white man" and would know what was best for me. Okay, great! The job was done but I was really upset.

'I left for the US in 1967 and right from the beginning felt that America was the place where I wanted and needed to be. Professor Gephart took me to the Wright-Patterson Air Force Base and immediately put me on some classified projects to work on. We were working on a weapon system effectiveness program in 1972 and also published a report where there was a big seal on the file which stated "This file is highly classified and not to be seen by any foreign national etc." I said to Professor Gephart, "Bloody hell, I am a foreign national." Professor Gephart was shocked, as he had thought I had become a US citizen. You will never guess but, in less than one day, I had my fingerprints done and I was dragged all over the place in Cincinnati and by the end of the day was a US citizen. It shows the power of the US military and it also shows how relaxed they were then. If 9/11 had happened before this, it would never have happened.

'Before that, in 1968, I completed my Master's of Engineering at the University of Dayton in one year as promised by Professor Gephart. Whilst I could have gone on to do my Ph.D at Dayton, I knew the two top universities in my field at that time were Carnegie Mellon and MIT. Fortunately, I got admission to Carnegie Mellon and that is where I met the second great influence in my career, Gerald L. Thompson, who was Professor of Systems and Operations Research and supervised my thesis. With his guidance and assistance, in 1973, I received the Gold medal for my Ph.D thesis conducted by the Operations Research Society of America and went on to publish six papers with him.'

I imagined that with the gold medal from Carnegie Mellon, it would not have been difficult for Bala to find a role at a leading university. 'Indeed, I was offered roles at Stanford and Harvard, whereas University of Chicago and Northwestern both offered an Associate Professorship immediately. And so in 1973, I joined the Kellogg School of Management at Northwestern University and have been there ever since. And it was at Kellogg where I met the third major influence in my life, Donald Jacobs. He was Dean of Kellogg's Business School for more than 25 years, and prior to that had been chairman of Amtrak, the major US railroad. We somehow hit it off and he got me involved in all sorts of important initiatives for the university, such as chairing the Strategic Planning Committee. We set ourselves the objective of becoming the No. 1 business school and specifically beating Harvard and Stanford. At that time, we were ranked seventh. In order to get from seventh to first, everybody was saying that first you needed to go from seven to six, then from six to five and so on. But Don wanted to jump straight from seventh to first in one go, and he asked me what it would take. At that time, I was doing lot of work on business process re-engineering and had written a book on the subject. I told him that it would take twenty million dollars and that we would need to recruit three superstars to our school and to create new programs for them to teach. When the *Wall Street Journal* interviewed us and asked what our goal was, I said that we wanted to be number one and the journalist just laughed. I told him that it was our goal, and that it was possible we would not make it but that was what we wanted. Believe it or not, we did indeed make it in our first year. From 1988 until 1994, Wharton, Harvard, Stanford, and everybody else were chasing us. We then dropped back for a couple of years before regaining the top spot for another long run. We are still in the top three.

'This experience led me to want to do similar things for India. I went to Don and asked him if I could have 3 months off each year to work in India. I started at the Management Development Institute [MDI] in 1991 and then worked with the Indian School of Business [ISB] and finally founded Great Lakes Institute of Management.

'I have now retired from Kellogg, though I still teach one course each year and they have honoured me by appointing me Professor Emeritus. I am still extremely busy in the education sector as, in addition to my role at Kellogg and Great Lakes where I am Dean as well as founder, I am a Strategic Advisor to the Dean at Bauer College at the University of Houston. I am also still active with my consultancy in the area of re-engineering or cost management for Tata Group and a number of banks, including the State Bank of India and ICICI.' In fact, post my interview with Bala, I was not surprised to find he was on the Board of Directors of some of the companies covered in this book.

Finally, I asked Bala what he would be doing if he were a young Indian today. 'I would create a movement with youngsters of my own age and go on the social media and do what the two guys in Egypt did, create a wave and then eliminate the damn cancer of corruption which we have somehow got in this country. Youngsters between thirty and forty years would have to take charge of the administration and governance of the country. I agree that this is revolutionary because the evolutionary way in India is just not realistic. So there has to be some other means – just like when I went to attack China – that was a rash and stupid decision but I was emotionally charged up. I do not know why people of amazing talent and knowledge in this country remain silent. But I am positive that the conventional methods of strikes and hunger strikes and Gandhism will not work. Of course, I do not want and nor do I support terrorism. In three years' time, I think there will be a major change in India because people are not going to take it any more.' With these comments, we brought our meeting to a close and I headed out to Great Lakes to see the impressive campus and to give an impromptu lecture on doing business in South-East Asia to a class of MBA students.

As I write this chapter several months after meeting with Bala, the horrifying rape and death of the young female student in Delhi has led to massive demonstrations and social media outpourings – and many of the comments from youth echo Bala's above comments that Indian youth have had enough. Bala's vision of the future may indeed be prophetic.

[1] Great Lakes Institute of Management (www.greatlakes.edu.in) is a business school with campuses in two metros Chennai and Gurgaon near New Delhi. The institution aims to fill the vacuum for a top-flight business school in Tamil Nadu and put it on par with the three other southern states that boast of top-rung management institutions: the Indian Institutes of Management in Bangalore and Kozhikode and the Indian School of Business in Hyderabad.

[2] The Chettiars or, to give them their traditional name, the Nagarathars came from a sun-baked homeland in basins of the Sittang and the Salween. The original Chettiars in Burma set sail from some Coromandel port and, hugging the coast, reached Rangoon after many weeks of sailing. It seems the Chettiar used to spend three years in Rangoon and then three years back in India before repeating the cycle again. Strangely, it was the opening of the Suez Canal in 1869 that was the genesis of the finance business for the Chettiar in Burma. Europe was clamouring for rice and the Chettiar identified that lower Burma with its plentiful rainfall was an ideal place to grow rice, albeit to that point the Burmese only grew enough for domestic consumption. For whatever reason the British Government were unwilling to finance the development of the area. And it was into that void stepped the Chettiars. Rice production increased one hundred fold as seven million tonnes of rice were produced. The Chettiar earned enormous profits with interest rates said to be above 30 per cent. Whilst without the Chettiar taking the financing risk the Burmese economy would never have developed like this, there is little doubt that many Burmese resented the influence and high profits of the Chettiar. See http://www.archive.org/stream/rajahsirannamala030779mbp/ rajahsirannamala030779mbp_djvu.txt for a description of the situation by the Rajah Sir Annamal Commemoration Volume.

[3] Almost half of the population of Rangoon (now Yangon) at the start of the Second World War was Indian and perhaps 20 per cent of the total population. Most of them fled back to India before the Japanese took the country. Most had to walk by foot and many thousands perished. At the end of the War few Indians returned to Rangoon as it was clear that Burma was heading for independence and that the rights of Indians would not be protected. After Independence, Burmese law treated a large percentage of the Indian community as 'resident aliens'. Though many had long ties to Burma or were born there, they were not considered citizens under the 1982 Burma citizenship law that restricted citizenship for groups immigrating before 1823.

❝ To my father, the thought that the paper should be benchmarked against others is something that he would never have considered. For him, the Hindustan Times was still the media vehicle that was used for the Independence struggle. ❞

SHOBHANA BHARTIA

Chairperson and Editorial Director, HT Media[1]

I met Shobhana Bhartia, the Chairperson and Editorial Director of the *Hindustan Times*, for tea one afternoon in the group's headquarters on KG Marg in New Delhi. I had not met her before and, I don't know why, but I was quite unprepared to see before me a strikingly elegant middle-aged woman who gave the immediate impression of being someone who was relaxed and at ease with herself.

As you would have read in earlier stories in this book, I usually begin these interviews with a question about family background and childhood, but Shobhana deflected my first question into an account of her start at the *Hindustan Times*, 'I was very keen on public life and public affairs. So from a young age I would be tracking newspapers – I was quite a voracious reader. When I moved as a young woman to Delhi from Kolkata, my association with the *Hindustan Times* grew. This became the first paper that I would read each morning and I would benchmark it against other newspapers. I would give my father, who was at that time the chairman, suggestions on what I thought – where we scored better than others or where I felt that we had not done as well. One day he said, in exasperation, why don't you get formally involved with the newspaper since you are devoting so much time to it? It happened quite suddenly, and was not something that was premeditated and arranged well in advance. And so, in 1985 when I was twenty-one, I joined the Hindustan Times and,' she says with a smile, 'more than 25 years later I am still here.'

But I suggested to Shobhana that surely by spending all this time commenting on a newspaper owned by her family, it was obvious she would be asked to join it. 'You know, strangely enough, it wasn't. I never ever thought: I want to join the paper. I simply felt that I was talking to my father everyday and telling him that I had observed we missed out on a particular story or that we had a great scoop with some other story. I just thought that I was feeding him with my opinion for whatever it was worth and, not for a moment did I think that this was the first step to actually getting directly involved. Because girls weren't involved in the family businesses, so why would I have thought otherwise? I thought that I would just be at home with my children and perhaps start my own business. As to my father's businesses, I never thought of going into them.'

Our conversation then turned back to Shobhana's childhood in one of the most famous of all Indian business families. For readers who are not familiar with India, it is perhaps worth mentioning that Shobhana's maiden name is Birla. Her grandfather, Ghanshyam Das Birla (known as 'GD' Birla) and her father, Krishna Kumar Birla (known as 'KK' Birla) were major industrialists, but the family's business roots go back far longer. Shobhana's father talks about this in his autobiography, *Brushes with History*[2] in which he explains that the Birla family belongs to the Vaishya caste and are Maheshwaris[3] and that the family tree can be traced back to Jaimal who was born in the early 1700s. While it seems several of those early generations of the family were successful at business, KK traces the modern success of the family back to 1860 when his great-grandfather, Shivnarayan started what became a very successful trading firm in Mumbai, although it really took off in terms of success when KK's grandfather, Raja Baldeodas joined the business in 1879. The principle of futures trading which Baldeodas adopted was to move with the market, never against it. Thus, in case the trend was bearish, one should sell; if bullish, one should buy. 'Never swim against the tide', was the principle he followed, and this proved to be very beneficial.[4] By the time KK's father, GD, was born, Shivnarayan and Baldeodas had set up substantial businesses. The family at that time had two major companies in Calcutta (now Kolkata), Birla Jute Mills and Kesoram Cotton, along with sugar and fertilizer mills, heavy engineering, trading, and numerous other businesses.

It was GD who was one of the 'behind the scenes' supporters of the *Hindustan Times*, which was established in 1924 by the Akali family who were Sikhs from Punjab. Sikh nationalism was at fever pitch around that time as the infamous Jallianwalla Bagh massacre[5] had occurred only a few years before, and the Akalis wanted an English media voice to support the push for independence. It is understood that the Akalis raised money to establish the paper from Sikhs in the US and Canada. However, they ran out of money within six months of establishing the paper. The Akalis then sold the paper to Madan Mohan Malaviya, a conservative and well-respected nationalist with money raised from the Punjab National Bank and funds from unspecified sources. We now know a significant amount of the funds from unspecified sources came from GD Birla via Birla Mills. However, Malaviya too did not have enough money to fund the newspaper on an ongoing basis and so in 1927, GD and a number of other businessmen established the Hindustan Times Limited to acquire the newspaper. GD was the largest single shareholder and Malaviya remained the chairman until his death in 1946.

GD had to remain in the background in the beginning because the stated objective of the newspaper was to push for independence and the British could have retaliated by creating problems for the Birla family businesses. However, it soon appears he gave up any attempt to hide his support for independence. In fact, GD became quite open about his close friendship and support of Mahatma Gandhi. He had met Gandhi in 1916, not long after he returned from South Africa. Within a short space of time after that first meeting, GD became the principal financier of much of the Mahatma's social and political causes.[6] In a letter to Mahatma Gandhi in late 1927, GD wrote, 'Whenever you find any particular kind of work impeded for lack of funds you only have to write to me.

Even as it is, I shall be sending money. I can give more.' This was akin to an 'open-cheque' support of the struggle for independence.[7]

Whilst GD took a keen interest in the paper, he could not put a large amount of time into its management, due to his many other larger business interests. But Shobhana's father, KK was fond of politics and the newspaper industry and so in 1957, GD arranged for his son, KK to join the Board. And years later, in 1985, it was KK who inducted his daughter, Shobhana into the paper. With the family's close ties with Mahatma Gandhi and involvement in the freedom struggle, it is no wonder that Shobhana has lots of memories of her mother telling her all kinds of stories about the freedom struggle, and that in some way, set the ground for her closer involvement in public life.

'One of the stories my mother told me was how Mahatma Gandhi spent the last 144 days of his life until his assassination in 1948 in my grandfather's home, Old Birla House at 30 January Marg in Delhi [which was acquired by the Government of India in 1971 and now houses Gandhi Smriti]. My mother and aunts catered to Gandhiji's[8] needs, making sure he was comfortable with such things as his rather strict vegetarian diet. Meanwhile, my grandfather GD accompanied him to all the various strikes and marches. One of the other stories she told us was that Jawaharlal Nehru [who became the first prime minister of independent India and remained so until his death in 1964] was very fond of young children. When Nehru came to visit my grandfather at our home, there would often be a fight between my mother and aunts as to who would carry my eldest sister Nandini, who was then just a year or two years old, to meet Nehru. They knew this would lead to Nehru taking my sister on his lap and then spending time chatting to them, ignoring all of the important political and business issues he was really there to talk about. My mother continually told us these sorts of anecdotes. They all had to wear hand-woven clothes, because Gandhiji wanted Indians to only wear clothes made on looms. You certainly could not wear fabrics like the clothes I am wearing today; certainly no imported silks and chiffons. My mother loves chiding my sisters and me saying that the sort of 'spinning' we do at gyms to watch our weight is very different to the spinning she used to do every day in working a handloom to make the family's clothes. As you may know, many of the photos of Gandhiji are with him in front of a charkha. For him that symbolized nationalism: to say that we are Indian, we wear Indian and we buy Indian. But, of course, as I was only born in 1957 these are just stories for me.'

As to her father's involvement in politics, Shobhana has clear memories. 'My father was aclose associate of Indira Gandhi who of course became prime minister. At one time there were floods in Orissa and I decided I wanted to do something for the flood victims. I organized a little fete and asked my friends to make all sorts of handmade things, such as little notepads, diaries, calendars, and pouch bags. We managed to raise two lakhs, which was quite a princely sum then. I told my father about this and that I wanted to give the monies to the Prime Minister's Flood Relief Fund. My father said, "If that's so, why don't you come with me and give it to her personally rather than sending it through me?" And I, of course, never took him seriously. But apparently he did raise it with Indiraji and she agreed to meet me at the beginning of a meeting my father had with her. I had to travel all the way from Calcutta to Delhi to meet her. I can still vividly remember that moment. I felt extremely proud and happy and I went back and told all my friends that I had handed the cheque over personally and the prime minister had told me that money was going to be put to good use. These are small but important memories of my childhood which intersected with my family's involvement in politics.'

The Birla family was not just involved in business and politics; there was always a strong commitment to and interest in being of wider benefit to society, particularly in education where the family established and supported many schools and places of learning. Thus, for instance, when it became time to consider Shobhana's schooling, 'there was a school run by my uncles in Calcutta called Modern High School and which all the children in the joint family attended; except for me. My mother felt that I would get certain privileges in the family-run school. She took a very conscious decision and put me in Loreto – a school which had nothing to do with the family and where I was treated like any other girl.'

Shobhana laughed as I asked if she was the spoilt youngest daughter. 'Yes I was. I certainly was. There was a big age difference between my sisters and me; the oldest is ten years older than me, and the middle sister is seven and a half years older. Given that difference between me and my second sister, I feel I was clearly an afterthought, and I was quite pampered for that.'

During her childhood, Shobhana said her father was away from Calcutta on business much of the time, so that her mother was more responsible for her upbringing than her father. 'My mother was the disciplinarian at home, not my father. And, because of the age difference between my sisters and me, I have lots and lots of memories of the time I spent with my mother.'

When I asked if there were home teachers or a governess in early childhood, Shobhana said, 'I had many teachers coming home for private tuition in all subjects. It was very busy; we had a tight schedule but not one where I interacted a lot with people of my own age group. Interestingly, my governess was not English; she was an Indian Catholic, Sister Leela Johnson. She was with us for many years and actually joined the family when my eldest sister was three or four years old. In fact, she initially worked as a nurse for my mother when she was recovering from one of her many operations, before becoming a full-time governess. She taught us so many things about proper etiquette and grooming. I vividly remember her telling me it was not ladylike to blow on my soup to cool it; a lady should just wait until it cools. As my sisters were a lot older I quickly became her favourite and could get away with a lot. I loved her dearly.'

Shobhana also indicated her isolation from other children. 'In a sense, I grew up as almost like an only child because of the age difference with my sisters and as they, like most young girls of my generation, got married young. I think I was all of twelve or thirteen when my second sister got married. It was quite lonely for me during my formative years. It meant a lot of my time was spent with adults, listening to adult dining room conversations. I wasn't allowed to go out and play with friends. Maybe once in every couple of months, I could invite a friend over. It has changed so much in today's India. I have a little grandson who is four years old and he has such a hectic social calendar with his friends. It seems like his every waking moment is filled with activities. Every day I try and find out if he is free so I can see him. It is just so different from the life I led.' I sought to tease Shobhana by asking whether she at least had a dog to play with. She shot back: 'Yes, but he was not allowed inside the house!'

When asked if she had been a good student, Shobhana responded that she had been 'reasonably good'. She then explained how she had succeeded as a student in ways that would stand her in good stead for success in her business career, 'I wouldn't say that I was one of those who never studied, but equally I did not need to cram all night. I think the one trait I inherited from my father, and perhaps I got it at a very, very early age, was time management. I completely follow time management so, even when I was in school, everything was always very systematically slotted in – such as today I will study History and then do Geography tomorrow – and I would adhere to that. I was and am very disciplined. As a result I have never really had to slog too much. I have never been one of those students who had to be up all night drinking black coffee because I had an exam the next day. I was always able to go to bed without being stressed about the exam the following day. And my experience is that with good time management you get a lot more done. So this approach has always helped me.'

I asked about hobbies like sport, but there was no legacy of sporting habits from school such as tennis. When, as a keen golfer myself, I suggested she was missing out if she did not play golf, Shobhana laughed, 'I did give it a try, but either it means getting up really early or it means braving the heat and I don't like the sun. But,' she continued, 'I have become quite fanatical about my workout regimen and I have become focused on fitness and health issues.'

Then I asked Shobhana if there were any tricks she had maybe played at school, 'Many. I was getting into trouble all the time. Like bunking school with my girlfriends, avoiding classes, especially where we did not like the teachers and feigning illness and sneaking out of the sick room. But all these are stories about my life I would rather not talk about, because this is not what I want my grandchildren to know and follow.' When I laughed, she continued with a comparison between then and now, reminiscent of her previous comparison of her grandson's social life and her own as a child. 'It was relatively harmless and okay when I was growing up, but for my children I have been quite strict, no bunking, no getting out, no leaving the school boundaries during school hours, there has to be a certain element of security. But then don't forget that we grew up in a different time and times have definitely changed now. So whereas on a few occasions I bunked school and conveniently walked in again just before the car came to pick me up; if the same thing happened today, I would go ballistic because it is no longer a safe world like it used to be.'

After school, Shobhana said she went to Loreto College, a women's college affiliated to Calcutta University. While there, before she graduated and less than a month before her eighteenth birthday, she married Shyam Sunder Bhartia, who was twenty-two years old, and had just graduated from St Xaviers College, Calcutta University. It was an arranged marriage. 'At that time, I think almost everyone got married at the same age, so I don't think we really gave it much thought. It was kind of drilled into you that you get married when you are eighteen. And it wasn't just my family who expected it; the Marwari society at large expected it.'

I asked Shobhana the process of her arranged marriage. 'I had a chance to say "no" or "yes". I was given the opportunity to meet a number of boys and I had a chance to pick, but that's about it. It could be you have afternoon tea or you could meet over a meal or whatever and you get to spend some time together to make a very quick assessment of whether you feel compatible. You already know enough about the boy you are going to meet beforehand, in terms of what his educational qualification is, what the family does. You find out about the family: are they liberal or are they conservative? And then you leave much of the decision making to your parents, because how much can you decide in two hours of meeting someone for the first time?'

Shobhana then explained her move from Calcutta to Delhi. 'Both my family and my husband's family, the Bhartias were Calcutta based families. So logically Shyam and I started our married life in Calcutta. However, Shyam set up some businesses in Uttar Pradesh and, as he was a first-generation entrepreneur, he felt he needed to be "hands on" and could not operate from a distance. This meant a move to Delhi, which was much closer; still three hours away, but much closer than Calcutta. We relocated not long after I had my second child. Delhi was a new beginning for both of us.' One result of the move was that Shobhana was able to see more of her father. I asked her whether she had seen more of her father when she became an adult. 'Absolutely, much more of my father when I became an adult, much more of my father when I moved to Delhi and particularly because my father was a nominated member of the

Rajya Sabha, India's upper house of parliament, for three terms from 1984 to 2002. And then, when I joined the *Hindustan Times* in 1985, of course I saw a lot of him because I was working under my father.' [Like her father, Shobhana served as a nominated member of the Rajya Sabha from 2006 to 2012.[9]]

'The *Hindustan Times* was never really thought of as a business by my father; it was much more of a cause. My father's business focus was on his other industries, whereas the *Hindustan Times* was supposed to play the part of a sort of social responsibility. It was not seen as a media business ever and the bottom line was something you did not look for or speak about. To my father, the thought that the paper should be benchmarked against others is something that he would never have considered. For him, the Hindustan Times was still the media vehicle that was used for the Independence struggle. He remained closely associated with the *Hindustan Times* and was the chairman of HT Media Ltd till he passed away in 2008. Strangely, in his last few years, I think the newspaper was the one area that he was very engaged in, because my father has always had a very keen passion for public life. I think for him, it was a platform to bring out a change and play a meaningful role in the way things were happening in India.'

Shobhana briskly summarized her formal positions within the *Hindustan Times* since she joined in 1985. 'I joined as a director in 1985, became an executive director in 1989, vice chairperson in the late 1990s, and chairperson when my father passed away.' I asked whether there had been any big differences of opinion with her father during this time. 'Very often. One big one was on Mumbai – I felt we should have entered the Mumbai market years before we actually did, whereas the then management told my father that we would "bleed" profusely if he did and it was thus not a wise investment. The *Times of India* had a complete monopoly and by delaying our entry into Mumbai and giving them a free run for so many years. I felt it was absolutely wrong and we had huge heated arguments on that. We also had some arguments on our entering the electronic medium. I started a television channel. Unfortunately it was one of the stories of "too many cooks spoil the broth". Apart from Hindustan Times, there were four other partners – including Pearson of UK, Carlton of UK, TVB of Hong Kong, and Schroder of Germany. There were just too many partners and in due course we had to shut the venture down. But when I started, it was way ahead of its time. It could have given Hindustan Times a great "first mover" advantage in the market and I am confident it would have been a "rip-roaring" success by now. But there wasn't enough alignment amongst the partners. I had a lot of arguments with my father over this venture as I felt we were not giving enough attention and focus to the channel and, when it started to fail, I thought the Hindustan Times should have completely taken over and driven the business ourselves. This was one argument I lost with my father but,' she says with a grin, 'I had my victories too.'

Shobhana described her own role at the Hindustan Times in what could perhaps be termed as the transformation of a 'passion' into a 'business'. 'I started trying to benchmark the Hindustan Times with the best in the world. But then I realized there were many problems here in the newspaper business; we had very strong unions in those days and it was very difficult to try and achieve very much. You had to do things in a particular way. Making any kind of changes was not as simple as it looked. It was not like a textbook case. It was easier said than done. Even in Delhi [as opposed to Calcutta], we had very strong newspaper unions. So it made life quite difficult, and when I wanted to reposition the paper to make it more contemporary and change its profile, achieving this was a Herculean task.

'My dream was to make the Hindustan Times one of the best newspapers in the world. For the reasons I mentioned, I thought there was no point having benchmarks in India. I thought of the *Washington Post* as a great paper and wrote to Katharine Graham who was its chairperson. This would have been not long after I joined HT in 1985. I was surprised when she replied that she would be happy to meet me and facilitate my spending time with them to understand what they did and how they did it at the Post – things like the instruments and tools that they used for circulation, how they measured productivity on the editorial side and what was the interaction between the various facets in terms of advertising and brand building. I met Katharine Graham or Kay as she eventually invited me to call her. As you probably know, she was the "grande dame" of the US newspaper industry and had a reputation of being absolutely terrifying. Even after I arrived in Washington, I got "cold feet" and nearly turned around and went home. I was just 27, the mother of two small boys and a novice in the industry. What was I thinking in contacting her? To my shock and surprise, she was extremely encouraging and supportive. She even allowed me to sit through some editorial meetings in the evenings. Ben Bradlee, who was a famous journalist, was editor at that time and he let me sit in on meetings when they were finalizing the pages for the next day's edition. It was fascinating. This started a long relationship between the *Hindustan Times* and the *Washington Post* and Kay allowed us to bring to the *Hindustan Times* for 6 months on secondment, her executive editor who looked after design. He gave *Hindustan Times* a completely new and a modern look, changed the font, changed the design and overall made the paper a more contemporary, modern product.'

What I did not find time to ask Shobhana was whether, during her long association with Katherine Graham, they had ever compared notes on possible perceived similarities of their upbringings and positions – such as each of them being a younger child, each being a child born into a family with considerable wealth, each having a similar childhood with fathers' absent on business and with private tutors and governesses, each going to the private school for ladies (surely 1970s Loreto House in Calcutta might have closely resembled 1930's Madeira in Virginia – even if the Indian school foundation in 1842 considerably antedated the American in 1906), each going to university, each marrying young and having children, each unexpectedly entering into publishing, each being inheritors of family owned businesses, each facing similar problems, such as managing the unions, modernizing the newspaper, and overseeing the introduction of outside capital. Even if they never spoke about the similarities, I am pretty sure Katherine Graham saw them and wanted to take Shobhana 'under her wing' and protect her from many of the injustices she felt she suffered as a woman at the top of the US newspaper industry.

And what about the opportunities for women in Indian business today, I asked Shobhana. 'I feel that it is a shame, if we expect to sustain our rate of growth, we think that it can be done without taking into account 50 per cent of the population. And you know India has 68 per cent of its population under the age of thirty. We keep talking about the demographic dividend that India has, as China is ageing, the United States is ageing, but India is a young country. But even if it is a young country, there are so many challenges as well and, unless we actually ensure that this 50 per cent of the population, which is female, also become partners in the growth story, I think it is going to be a huge wasted resource. I try to encourage women wherever I go to try to hone their talents. You can be an employee, you can be self-employed, you can join a non-governmental organization, you could go in for charitable work, you could go in for any of the arts and crafts and performing areas, but I believe women need to put their energies to productive use. Many women used to face issues in terms of attitudes towards them and the family support that is required, but all that is changing now, and people are much more receptive. I still think we have some obstacles that we need to overcome. For instance, if I am a young professional, I will still have issues if it is a nuclear family, because what do I do with young children? We don't have enough infrastructure in the form of crèches and places to leave children while we are working. We don't have enough employers who are aligned to taking a more sympathetic view and, for example, giving women a six-month maternity leave. At the moment, if I want to now raise a family, I will probably have to quit my job. There are of course a number of companies who are gender friendly places to work but there are many more that are not.'

This response led to the obvious question about the position at Hindustan Times. 'I believe we are sensitive when it comes to trying to provide a conducive work place for women. For instance, we definitely have the security of women in mind. As you know, there are late shifts in a newspaper and, if you have a man in a late shift who goes home at 10:30pm after setting the front page, he will find his own way home. But if I have a woman who is also doing the same role, then we provide a car to take her home. She shouldn't have to feel that she is only good for a 10-6 job, because then the scope for her career growth is limited. In my opinion, you need to create an environment which is actually a more level playing field for women.'

As a related question, I asked Shobhana whether these days daughters could expect to inherit. 'Well, in my case, my father only had daughters and we inherited. I only have sons but I can assure you that if I had daughters they would be treated equally. I am aware that a number of the larger business families are creating constitutions to deal with matters like this, as well as a whole range of issues such as who can speak for the family and whether family members can work in management. We are actually right now looking at this for my family but, at this point, no decisions have been made and we are just learning what is involved and the pluses and minuses.'

I really enjoyed my meeting with Shobhana and, given what I knew about her illustrious family history before we met, I was pleasantly surprised to see she did not seek to trade on that in any way. She was refreshingly modest, clear, and articulate and seemed very 'happy in her skin'. My first impressions were definitely proven to be correct.

---

[1] HT Media (http://www.htmedia.in) which is dual listed on the Bombay and New York Stock Exchanges, owns the *Hindustan Times*, one of the oldest and largest English circulation daily newspapers in India, as well as numerous other media businesses, including *Hindustan* (a leading Hindi language daily), magazines, and FM radio stations.

[2] Krishna Kumar Birla, *Brushes with History: An Autobiography*, Penguin Books India (Viking), 2007.

[3] Maheswaris are a minority community of Bania originating from Rajasthan. They are a sub-group within the Marwari and Mewari communities (the former of which have been extraordinarily successful in business and a number of Marwaris are subjects in this and my other book on Indian life stories. Other well known Maheshwaris who are covered in my books are Rahul Bajaj, Kishore Biyani, and B.K. Jhawar.

[4] Krishna Kumar Birla, *Brushes with History: An Autobiography*, pp.4-5

[5] The Jallianwala Bagh massacre (also known as the Amritsar massacre) took place in the Jallianwala Bagh (Garden) in the northern Indian city of Amritsar on 13 April 1919, which happens to be 'Baisakhi', one of Punjab's most important festivals. That day, 50 British Indian Army soldiers, commanded by Brigadier-General Reginald Dyer, began shooting at an unarmed gathering of men, women, and children without warning as Dyer thought the gathering was a precursor to a major insurrection. Dyer ordered soldiers to reload their rifles several times and they were ordered to shoot to kill. Official British Raj sources estimated the fatalities at 379 and with 1,100 wounded. However, the casualty number quoted by the Indian National Congress was more than 1,500, with roughly 1,000 killed. Dyer was removed from duty and forced to retire by the House of Commons, but sadly many British at that time supported his actions.

[6] *History in the Making: 75 years of the Hindustan Times*, The Hindustan Times, 2000 p.16.

[7] ibid p.20.

[8] '-ji' at the end of a person's name is a Hindi word being a sign of respect or admiration

[9] Just as her father, KK, was nominated by Rajiv Gandhi for appointment to the Rajya Sabha, so it was that Sonia Gandhi who nominated Shobhana. The nominations are reserved for eminent people from the fields of literature, the arts, and social service. Shobhana's nomination was set to be challenged in the Supreme Court on the basis she was a 'media baron' rather than a journalist. However, the challenge did not even get past the initial pre-trial pleadings, as it was determined that 'social service' should be construed widely and that Shobhana would be covered by this.

But also if your mind is still working and you see what is happening in the world, you immediately want to know more about it and find alternatives and answers. I mean, who retires? Only those who have jobs and are working for somebody else, they retire. But, for me, everything I do is a continuation of my lifetime's work.

ELA BHATT

Founder, Self-Employed Women's Association of India[1]

For those who know or know of her, they will agree that Ela Bhatt is certainly not a traditional business leader. But, for me, there is absolutely no doubt she is a leader in many senses of the word and her impact in assisting poor or disadvantaged women to become organized as small-scale entrepreneurs has been so profoundly successful that it warrants her inclusion in this book several times over.

I met Ela in her modest home in Ahmedabad to which she had just returned early that morning from a trip to Delhi. When she entered the living room, I was thrown off balance a little; on the one hand there was this sprightly, smiling, and unassuming septuagenarian looking like anyone's grandmother but, on the other, she was someone who I knew had 'steel' in her make-up in order to have succeeded against all 'odds'.

Ela told me: 'I was born here in Ahmedabad on 7 September 1933. I grew up in an atmosphere of nationalism. While I was in school, our country was fighting for its freedom and, during that time, I saw my maternal grandfather and my mother's brothers all in jail. My family's name is "Bhat"; we are Nagar Brahmins and therefore believe in the importance of education. This was especially so because my mother had missed her own education. Her schooling had stopped quite early; she had only studied up to sixth standard. She had been very keen to continue, but some elder relatives in the family were against this and just wanted her to wear a sari and get married. But my father was a born teacher, so when they got married and there was a lot of time, my father would sit with her every evening and help her study. Eventually, my mother reached the point where she was ready to complete secondary school. And luckily for her, there was a university in the locality at that time – one of the first of its kind – where you could come from outside the normal school environment and take the exam. She passed her school graduation and then spent three years doing her university studies by correspondence, graduating in something like geography and Sanskrit. That said, she was very much a housewife, mother, and my father's wife, but she also started participating in the women's movement. She became a member of the All India Women's Conference, which had been founded in 1927, and later, was elected as the President of the Gujarat circle.

'My father was also born in Ahmedabad and became a lawyer practicing in nearby Surat where I was brought up. Eventually, my father was appointed to the bench; first as a District and Session judge and then to the High Court from which he later retired. While he was a judge, he was transferred to different districts, including Bombay, but my mother and I stayed in Surat, where life was very easy going. Surat is well known for its easy going life and its good food.' Ela adds with a smile, 'There is a proverb that if you want to die you should die in Banaras (or Kashi, as it is also called) but, if you want to eat, you should go to Surat.

'I have two sisters; one six years older and one six years younger. My elder sister married young and started a family and so I think my father had his heart set that I would become a lawyer, as my paternal grandfather was also a lawyer as were all my uncles on my father's side and many of my cousins.

'My early childhood years were a little different as my parents were very ambitious for me and spent a lot of time teaching me, even before I could enter primary school at the minimum age of six years. As soon as I was six, my father took me to a school where I undertook the standard entry test. Because of all they had taught me, I was able to start in fifth grade. However, there was a drawback as I was always with girls who were much older than me which made it very hard for me to develop friendships, or even play games with them. I also felt that the other girls would not take me seriously and became more and more shy.

'This was a neighbourhood school, called Sarvajanik High School for Girls, a good school and had good teachers. It was a normal school – there were not so many missionary schools in Gujarat. And it did not discriminate, so there were adivasis[2] and other "backward classes"[3] attending. We were taught in Gujarati but my parents always taught us English at home. My father particularly was fond of Shakespeare and other stalwarts of English literature. As he was a litigation lawyer, he had long vacations when the courts were in recess and this, of course, continued when he became a judge. This meant he had lots of time to spend with me during those vacations. Also, as soon as the school year was finished and the results were out, the very next Saturday when he was free, we would go to the bookshop near our home and get all the books for the next year. During the vacation, my parents would make me finish them all so I had very little time to play or have fun like normal children. I think that I was the most attended and groomed of the three sisters by my parents. My younger sister was six years younger and, by the time she got to school age, my parents had more work to do and were busier and had less time to spend on her.

'My father admired the British for their education, discipline, culture, and their legal system. But, on my mother's side, they were all nationalists and, because of this, in and out of jail. My maternal grandfather was a doctor. Just as my father's family had many lawyers, so my mother's family was mostly doctors. My maternal grandfather was the leader of the non-violent nationalist group, which planned to "steal" salt from the Dharasana salt farmers in Gujarat in May 1930. They had advised the government they planned to do this and Gandhi was arrested before the march started. Those who marched on were told no matter how much they were provoked or beaten by the police they should be non-violent and not fight back.

'The worst time for my grandfather was when he was in Visapur jail for about eighteen months. As a leader of the movement, he received the most vigorous punishment. But he was so principled that he would stick to every rule. For example, he would not break the jail's rules that you were not allowed to write to your family and were not allowed to eat food brought from your home. His wife, my maternal grandmother, was also a very strong person who held the fort while my grandfather and their two sons were in jail. Their wives often came to stay with us during those periods. My mother gave solace to them, but I think that in her heart, so many things must have been burning. I wish that I had found time to talk with her about it.

'Not only was my mother ambitious for me, but she was very skillful, efficient, and organized – every vessel in the house had to be accounted for – she would not tolerate even a spoon out of its place. She found it very hard to tolerate the errors of others and this meant that my sisters and I were often not good enough for her and did not have an easy relationship with her.'

Ela Bhatt graduated from school at the young age of fifteen and went to study for her bachelor's degree at MTB College in Surat. She was sixteen when she first met and fell in love with Ramesh Bhatt (whose family name is the same as Ela's but with an extra 't'), a fellow student who was only two years older. Ela describes their meeting in her book, *We are poor but so many*:[4]

> Ramesh opened my eyes to the world. It was 1949, and I was a shy and studious university student, who admired Ramesh from a distance. He was a fearless, handsome student leader and an active member of the Youth Congress. He was collecting primary data on slum families for independent India's first census of 1951. When he invited me to accompany him on his rounds, I timidly agreed. I knew my parents would disapprove of their daughter wandering in dirty neighbourhoods with a young man whose family one knew nothing about. The Maynafalia slum of Surat was not far from where I lived, but it could just as well have been worlds away. The air smelled of fish and fecal matter. The one-room houses common to the area

had mud floors, no windows, an appliqué of tin strips for roofs, flimsy jute sacks served as room partitions. Tiny backyards functioned as the common bathing, washing, and defecating grounds. The dirty water irrigated papaya trees and red canna lilies; both were sold in the market for income. Mosquitoes and flies settled on every object in sight. The men and boys fished in the river; the women sold the fish. In the morning, they ate millet bread with chillies and garlic, and in the evening, they made a meal of boiled vegetables and any unsold fish. Their children, who cried a lot, were named after biblical movie characters – Delilah, Rebecca, Samson. The women invariably wore fresh flowers in their hair.

Ramesh was completely at ease in this environment, listening and laughing and teasing and gathering data from the slum dwellers like a nosy new neighbor. I, however, had never seen anything like this at such close quarters, and I was uncomfortable. I was paralyzed and passive, frustrated with my inability to step out of my shell. All the same, learning about "how the other half lives" was a liberating experience, and it made a deep impression on me.

Ela had been correct in her original apprehension of the opinion of her parents about Ramesh. 'My parents did not approve of our marriage for a long time, so we waited as I decided that I was not going to get married without my parents' blessings. It was largely a "class" problem in their eyes. Ramesh was also a Nagar Brahmin, but his father was an impoverished village Brahmin who had become an industrial mill worker in Surat. Ramesh lost his mother when he was only five and his father was already elderly and, as the mill had closed down, Ramesh was working several jobs at the same time as well as studying. Not only this, but living in his father's small home was his father's sister, a child widow who took care of the family. So Ramesh grew up in that environment, but he was brilliant and handsome.

'According to me, Ramesh was outstanding in every way', continued Ela and even after all these years I could feel the intensity of her love for Ramesh. 'He was already famous; he used to write a column in a newspaper. In Congress circles, he was known as a Gandhian student leader. But, in the beginning, for my parents who had not met him, their position was that "we did not educate you for this". My parents were not so rich, but socially they had a high status and wanted me to marry someone of equal status. And my father was right when he said to me: "Have you seen poverty? How are you going to spend your life in poverty? You know getting married is not an ordinary thing; it is not just romance". To prove to them that I was serious about Ramesh, I left home to spend one year in a village of landless labourers in Gujarat.

'Of course I could survive for this short period because of my caste, my language and my education as I was of course not actually poor. But, at that time, to go into the villages was seen as a career too. Gandhi had said that once you were educated, once society had spent on you, then you should spend your life in rebuilding the nation. And our nation is its people —especially the people in rural areas who are hard working, honest people and they need to be given a chance to move forward so that when they do, our country develops too. And our teachers were also like that; they told us to go to the villages, to live and work there, and our whole generation at that time thought and planned like that. For my future as a good Gandhian, a year in a village could be seen as a good education. But at that time, I did not see it like that; my only motive was to prove to my father that I could live in poverty.

'I lived with a family in a village in the south of Gujarat. But of course when they met me they thought something must have happened with my family, as I did not know how to do many daily chores such as drawing water from the well and starting the *chulha*, a cooking stove. I honestly worked as a farm labourer so that I had my own money. I really wanted to live on that income but I had a lot of extra support by being a Brahmin. People would say to me, "Today is my grandfather's anniversary, so if I feed a Brahmin then I will get lot of good luck." My parents did not come and visit me for the whole year I was there. They were so angry. They knew where I was, but I think they wanted to test me. Ramesh also left me alone to prove myself.

'So I experienced life in the village for a year but frankly, I was not really ready to learn much from the experience at that time. I was ready to do it but it was not for the sake of learning; it was more to prove a point. I learnt more about the reality of poverty in India when I went around with Ramesh for the pre-census testing.'

Before Ela and Ramesh were married, she studied for two years at the Sir L.A. Shah Law College in Ahmedabad, and received her degree in Law in 1954. 'Ramesh also trained as a lawyer at Gujarat University. That was the university started by Mahatma Gandhi in 1920, when he gave the call that Indians needed to leave the British education system including its universities and colleges. This was an alternative education Ramesh felt the country would need when it became independent. Ela added that she is now one of the trustees of that university.

'Ramesh got a job at Gujarat Vidyapith to teach economics. He could have been a good lawyer but he was proud and wanted to avoid the impression that boys like him might get married to a well-to-do girl like me because of the money. And that, as my father was a lawyer, he would expect to be immediately absorbed and adopted into my father's legal practice. In fact, because he was such a proud person, for our marriage too he didn't take anything from my parents. There is no dowry for a Brahmin marriage, but each family usually makes gifts to the son-in-law or daughter-in-law. But we decided not to take anything and we got married in khadi – in hand-spun, hand-woven cloth. Since then, for all my life I have been wearing khadi.' Khadi was also an integral part of Gandhi's Swadeshi movement and an icon of the freedom movement and Gandhism.

'My parents finally approved the marriage and we were married in 1956. They eventually saw that there were good things about Ramesh, that he was a good man and that their daughter would be happy so long as he was there – and then he had also been trained as a lawyer so they thought that, whatever happened, he would be able to provide for us.'

I asked Ela if she had found the early years of her marriage to someone from a different background difficult. 'It was difficult. I had been living in my father's high court judge's bungalow in the Shahibaug district of Ahmedabad. Then I came to live with my husband in one small room for a professor's family. He soon moved to another college where we had a rented room and we did everything ourselves without any help. I learned from him how to do housework and, as part of the housework, the correct system of recycling and saving things and all of our Indian traditional ways – and also the ever important issue of budgeting. I also learnt from my aunt-in-law who lived with us. She was my husband's responsibility after his father died because she had been a child widow at twelve or thirteen years of age – she was his father's elder sister. By the time we married, she was already old but still strong; she lived a very traditional and simple life. I don't think she ever liked me as I took her nephew away from her, but she lived with us until she died; in fact she died in this house where we are meeting.'

In 1955, shortly before Ela married Ramesh, she joined the legal department of the Textile Labour Association (TLA) – the textile workers' union which was started by Anasuyaben Sarabhai in 1920 and then supported by Mahatma Gandhi. She adds, 'At the time I joined, it was one of the strongest trade unions in India. It also had active political connections with the Congress Party and its government. I continued to work there until 1981 when they threw me out.'

Ela continued to talk about the genesis of the Self-Employed Women's Association (SEWA) that she created out of nothing. 'Over time, I became a skilled labour lawyer who knew how to use the legislation and the power of the union to protect textile employees. But gradually my mind was changing because I became aware of vast numbers of people who were not protected. In 1968, textile mills started to close down as the industry was in a global slowdown due to changes in technology and fashion demands. Thousands of workers became jobless. The leader of my union asked me to go to their houses to see what they were doing for survival. We did not know what was happening at their homes. I saw that it was the women who were running the homes and earning money and feeding the family. They sold fruits and vegetables in the streets, stitched in their homes at piece-rate for middlemen, worked as labourers in wholesale commodity markets, loading and unloading merchandise or collected recyclable refuse from city streets. And women who were engaged in these kinds of economic activities were not covered by any labour legislation; there was no protective legislation for them. And so my consciousness arose about these women because, before this, the problems of women workers had not been on my mind. I had been from early childhood very conscious about justice, but not about these women and their working conditions. Two things occurred to me, firstly that, if India was to have a proper labour movement, then it is these workers who should be in the mainstream of the labour movement, because they were over 80 per cent of the workforce in India. The other thing was that, if we included these women in the labour movement, then it would be necessary to include poor rural working women, as well as poor urban women, and that their issues would need to be addressed.

'I began to realize the needs of these women in the context of my work for the labour movement, and I think also that it was because of my Gandhian background that I considered things in a holistic way. As my experience was of organized unions, I asked myself why we could not have unions for the workers in the informal sectors. While I was still working in TLA, I started the process and, in 1972, the Self-Employed Women's Association (SEWA) was registered as a union. Although these women were in the "informal" sector, I chose the term "self-employed" to make it more positive. I saw problems of definition between the formal and the informal, and between the marginal and the mainstream – these women were not "marginal" or "peripheral" to anything; they were simply "self-employed". All of my work in establishing SEWA was done with the blessings of TLA leaders – especially its then president, Arvind Buch – and with their support. In TLA, we followed the Gandhian view of labour and that was always a completely holistic view, so that a labourer is no different from a lawyer and a lawyer is no different from a politician and we are all equally important parts of society.

'It was not an easy thing in 1972 to register as a union. The Labour Registrar conceptually argued that these women could not call themselves a union, because they had no regular employer and therefore nobody against whom to protest. I responded that the women did not have to be against someone else; they needed to come together for themselves. I said the first thing was that the unionizing was for the solidarity of the workers themselves, to bring their strength together and to play an important and significant role in nation building and the country's affairs. They told me, "Oh that is all big talk." But I kept arguing that labour issues were not necessarily about one single employer and that there would likely be certain policies and laws against which the women would want to protest. The registration was refused several times. I was told: "You know this type of union is not conceivable; it is not possible." But we persisted and went to Delhi, as a result of which the Delhi Registrar gave orders to Gujarat to allow our registration. This process of registration took about nine or ten months.

'Once SEWA started, we looked at the problems faced by these women who were self employed and working on their own. We spoke to them of their problems and, again and again, it came out that heavy indebtedness was one of their major problems. Many of these women had to pay a heavy rent for the means of their production – their pushcarts or sewing machines or whatever – and secondly the moneylenders charged very high rates of interest, up to 10 per cent per day. We had to find a way to solve these problems. This was at the time when Indira Gandhi was making big statements about helping the poor and going to the poor. As she had already nationalized the banks she was able to issue a directive that the big banks had to go out and find small borrowers. But the banks did not know how to reach these small borrowers. We were well placed to do this so we approached the Bank of India. But the bank did not like our women; they did not like the look of them. These women would always go in groups of two or three, lurking in the shadows and then moving about here and there. They were the most unwelcome kind of customers. We were discussing what we could do at a meeting of our members when Chandaben, one of our members, asked why we could not establish our own bank. I had never thought of this and, like a good Brahmin, I never touched somebody else's money. I responded to her, "But we are so poor," to which she responded "but we are so many" and which years later became the title of my book. I told Chandaben we would need share capital and she said with our membership we could collect the necessary capital in six months. So we did that and went for registration as a cooperative bank. At that time, there were only about five thousand SEWA members – now there are one million, three hundred thousand.

'Again we had a problem with the registration – with a different registrar; this one was the Registrar of Cooperatives. He asked how one could have a bank with people who could not even sign their own names. I said that was arguable, but that these were people who dealt with money every day so that they knew the worth of money. They certainly knew what an interest rate was. But he kept saying, "No, you know that they are not reliable. They belong to this caste or they belong to that caste. They are all slum dwellers. They are migrants. So, any day, you know they will move away and I tell you that these people will never repay. You will have to commit suicide; you will not be able to show your face in public."

'Ultimately the whole thing came down to the fact that they could not sign. I suggested a thumb impression as an alternative but that was not accepted. So I suggested a photograph instead, which was accepted; this became the first time photographs were used for banking in India. Now it has become common. The woman would stand with her name written on a slate and a photograph would be taken. Later on we had problem with that too; some women said that they were not going to stand like that as it looked like they were in police custody. Finally, the photographs were used, with a copy of the same photograph on the ledger book and on her passbook. SEWA Bank was registered in 1974 and now has 500,000 members. We have distributed a dividend every year from the second year. The Registrar, like me, was a Nagar Brahmin and after he retired he wrote a book about his own life and how he was proved wrong.'

I asked Ela to talk a little more about SEWA. She told me that this is treated in detail in her book.[5] Ela's assistants found me a copy and I strongly recommend the book to any reader wanting to understand SEWA better (and which is now available as an e-book on Amazon) and the extraordinary leadership role played by Ela. But Ela did talk about one experience that is also covered in the book.[6] It involves the case of Lakshmiben, a vegetable seller in the Manek Chawk market for more than 40 years. 'Lakshmiben earned around 10 rupees per day but was often fined 12.5 rupees for being an unregistered seller in the market. This was unsustainable and manifestly unfair; particularly in 1981 when I decided to make an issue of it. There had been many demonstrations and riots that year in Ahmedabad on matters such as reserved seats for scheduled caste and tribes. As it happens exactly at this time, I received an invitation from Justice P.N. Bhagwati, who was a Supreme Court Justice and Chair of the free Legal Aid Committee, to attend a seminar in Delhi. I responded in a very direct way that my attendance would not mean anything while so many laws were anti-poor and gave the example of Lakshmiben. We were extremely fortunate because Justice Bhagwati turned my letter into a public interest petition. We filed a petition in the Supreme Court against numerous parties in the state of Gujarat and the upshot was that the court ordered that all SEWA workers in the market were to be protected.'

Ela Bhatt had spoken, with some lingering bitterness, earlier in the interview about being thrown out of the TLA in 1981 and I had not pursued the matter as she told me this was fully treated in her book which I subsequently read and found the following passage,[7]

> In my enthusiasm to develop SEWA, I had failed to notice a growing crack in the foundation of SEWA's relationship with the TLA. SEWA's growing numbers and its uniqueness as a women's organization drew a lot of attention. The TLA considered SEWA its offspring, but found it difficult to control the pace and direction in which it was going. I did not realize that the TLA's attitude toward SEWA, too, was changing.
>
> What I did notice was that the TLA had very little room for new ideas and a dwindling ability to face new challenges. It had become a top-down organization where the leaders had stopped listening to each other and, more importantly, to the members. Despite the looming changes in the textile industry, there was no real attempt to equip the workers to adapt to changing economic conditions. It was sad to watch the growing rift between the laid-off workers and the shrinking union. SEWA, however, was preoccupied with learning about the various ways in which families of the textile workers were coping and adapting and was trying its best to help them in their efforts.
>
> Tensions came to a head in early 1981 during a period of bitter caste-class violence [as mentioned by Ela above in relation to the case of Lakshmiben]. The furore started when the Chief Minister of Gujarat proposed reserving two seats in the medical post-graduate course for scheduled caste and scheduled tribe students, commonly known as dalit (the oppressed) and adivasi (indigenous people) who have for generations formed the poorest of the poor. India's constitution provides for reserving a certain quota of seats in formal education institutions, government jobs, and elected bodies for them. The Gujarat government wanted to increase this quota at the state level. Competition for medical school entry is fierce, and upper-caste medical students and their allies vehemently opposed the plan. The issue flared up and took on a broader political dimension.

Incidents of violence broke out between the upper castes and the dalits. Most of the dalits, poor slum dwellers, became the victims of violence, losing both lives and property. The police clamped a curfew over the entire city.

SEWA could not remain silent while our dalit members were being attacked in their homes and on the streets. Because of the violence and the curfew, the daily wage earners and the self-employed in the city had no work, and therefore no income; consequently, they were starving. From SEWA's perspective, discrimination against dalits was rampant in all walks of life; those who had overcome so much adversity to become medical students certainly deserved support. Despite pressure from their dalit members in the mills, the TLA leaders thought it wise, for political reasons, to take no sides. Despite the curfew, all the mills in Ahmedabad continued to operate under government protection, while workers in the informal economy starved. I called a meeting of the SEWA leaders. First, we prayed for peace, and then we passed a resolution to appeal to the citizens of Ahmedabad to restore peace. Communal harmony was a union issue, a cooperative issue, and a feminist issue. It was fundamental to our existence.

Many upper-caste medical students felt that as a Brahmin, my sympathies should have been with them, and not the dalits. They directed their anger toward me in the darkness of night. A band of young rioters gathered outside my home, pelting it with stones, breaking windows, and threatening to set it on fire. It was the most traumatic experience that Ramesh and I had ever faced; but there was more to follow. On 1 May 1981, the TLA leadership asked me to resign and move SEWA's offices away from their headquarters. I had expected strained relations with the TLA leadership, but I never imagined for a second that they cared so little for SEWA. I felt hurt and betrayed. Never had I conceived of SEWA operating outside of the TLA, and I didn't think we could survive without their support. "Well, consider this a blessing", Ramesh said very quietly. He had long seen a break with the TLA as inevitable, but he had kept these thoughts to himself. I was not so sure.

After I had calmed down, a different picture began to emerge in my mind. I began to realize that women workers would always be of marginal importance to the TLA—their numbers in the textile mills had declined from forty percent to four percent in 50 years. In the process of modernizing the textile mills, union and industry had both agreed that women were dispensable—the mills found women to be "expensive" —whereas the TLA's attitude was that it was better for women to be homemakers and for men to earn the higher wages. There was an unspoken boundary beyond which women were not allowed to step or speak. Certainly, the TLA would never have allowed SEWA to move in the direction we have since taken. They would never have approved of us setting up large numbers of production cooperatives, or building women's networks that crossed geographical, political, and ideological boundaries. They would never have put modern technology in the hands of the women, nor would they have believed that poor women could manage an annual turnover of crores of rupees and enter the global market.

Ela was elected general secretary of SEWA at every triennial election until she retired from her active leadership role in 1996. She also stepped down from the Chair of SEWA Bank in 1998. I mentioned that she was still on the board of CSE (Centre for Science and Environment), run by Sunita Narain who is also covered in this book. 'I have sent my resignation to them several times, but they do not accept it.'

We turned our conversation to her family. Ramesh and Ela have a daughter, Ami born in 1960 and a son, Mihir in 1961. 'My daughter is a China specialist. She went to JNU (Jawaharlal Nehru University) in Delhi and there she took up Chinese studies, which was very rare at that time. She found she had an ability to learn other languages whilst she was at school. Each year, the children would do a project in a different part of the country and Ami found it easy to pick up the different languages. Her school principal and Ramesh encouraged her to pursue languages at university where she began to study Chinese. The choice of Chinese was very rare at that time; eventually she continued her studies at Peking University for six years. She married an American and now lives in the US with her husband and two children who happily I see quite often.

'My son, Mihir, trained as an architect and then as a planner. He got a master's degree from MIT in city planning and, when he came back to Ahmedabad in 1989, he founded the All India Disaster Mitigation Institute. He has two sons and I am very lucky that he lives with his family in the house next door.'

And what about Ramesh, I asked. 'He continued teaching for many years until Ramnath Goenka, who owns the *Indian Express*, asked him to become its General Manager. It was from this role that he eventually retired. In retirement, he established the Foundation for Public Interest. Sadly, Ramesh passed away in 1993 at the age of 62. He went for his usual morning walk and then on the way home he had what we now know was a heart attack. But rather than call the doctor or ask for a lift home, he just sat down for while and then got up and walked home. Once he got home he did not say anything to me but did his normal ablutions, which was to shave in the backyard and then take his bath upstairs. We then had breakfast together and after which he said that he was going upstairs to rest. This seemed very strange to me so I went and asked him if he was feeling well. When he told me what had happened I immediately called the doctor who advised me to take him to hospital. The doctors in the hospital started to do tests on him. Ramesh was very relaxed and in no pain and chatted with me noting that the hospital staff were preparing lunch and asked me what time it was. I told him it was fifteen minutes to twelve; by twelve he was gone. It was so sudden.

'I would also like to tell you about the day I retired from SEWA. The last day was quite dramatic. It was the day that a new executive committee was to be elected. I told everyone that I was not standing for election as General Secretary and the elections proceeded and by the end of the meeting I no longer had a role. To be honest, I had hoped someone would stand up and say a few good things about me; but there was nothing. After the meeting I came downstairs to my office and sat in my chair for the last time, but everything inside of me felt empty. I picked up my bag and left the office and got in my rickshaw. But there was a lump in my heart. I knew perfectly well that my SEWA colleagues were stunned and did not believe I would really retire and that they did not have the words to say anything at that time. I knew all of this but still I felt bad.

'I could not cry. Then I came near my house where there is a music school on the left of the road. So I saw that and asked my driver to stop the rickshaw. I went in and upstairs into the school and the students said "Oh, hello Elaben."[8] There was a lesson in progress so I just sat there and waited for it to finish. The teacher then came over to me and asked if I wanted to join a class. I told him I would, and so he asked me to sing a few things to find out my level. The following week I joined the music school.

'But the point of the story is that I always used to tell my husband that I wanted to learn music. He had a standard boring answer: "Ela, there is a time for everything, there is a time for everything"; he was neither encouraging nor discouraging. But it is true the time did come. Music has become my passion; if I had not spent all those years at SEWA, I am sure they would have been spent on music. I love classical Indian singing. That can be in any language, but the term is used to refer to singing in a way that uses the "swara" or the basic notes of the scale in Indian classical music in a systemic way. I still take lessons three days a week. During my days with SEWA, I only had time to sing our bhajans – our devotional songs – either in a group where everybody is singing or people would ask me to sing. We learn these songs in our childhood. My teacher is very patient because I do not have enough breath to be a real classical singer. But I am not singing for anyone other than myself. However, I would tell anybody that singing is very good for the health; if you sing for one hour, you use so much "pranayama" that your breath is rhythmic and it is wonderful for your natural energy.'

Although Ela has cut down on her formal roles at SEWA and elsewhere, she is still very active. 'I am supposed to have cut down on my travels but some things you just have to do. It becomes like a dharma. As you know, I have just come back from Delhi where they wanted my input at the Microfinance Summit. Like many people, I am even busier today than before I retired. But also if your mind is still working and you see what is happening in the world, you immediately want to know more about it and find alternatives and answers. I mean, who retires? Only those who have jobs and are working for somebody else, they retire. But, for me, everything I do is a continuation of my lifetime's work.'

For me, hearing those words spoken with a gentle passion seemed a fitting time to end our meeting. I am now in my 60s and it is inspirational to meet someone like Ela Bhatt for whom her love of life remains as strong in her eighth decade as it clearly did from the time she was a small girl.

[1] The Self-Employed Women's Association (www.sewa.org) was founded in 1972 as a trade union of self-employed women.
[2] Adivasi is a general term for ethnic groups who claim to be from the indigenous population of India. Adivasi societies are present in a number of states including Andhra Pradesh, Gujarat, Bihar, Madhya Pradesh and Tamil Nadu.
[3] The Central Government of India has legislation to help underprivileged or disadvantaged minorities in India and which includes Scheduled Caste, Scheduled Tribe and 'other backward class'. The groups can obtain preferential treatment for such things as education.
[4] Ela R. Bhat, *We Are Poor But So Many: The Story of Self Employed Women In India*, published by Oxford University Press Inc. 2006 and reprinted in 2007 and 2011 pp. 5-6
[5] *Ibid.*
[6] *ibid.*, pp.87-88
[7] *Ibid.*, Introduction
[8] 'ben' is Gujarati for 'sister' and is commonly used as a suffix for women's names – hence Ela-ben. It is widely used in SEWA and creates a 'sisterhood' amongst its members.

> We were the first to invest in a Dolby sound system. But it was not just a question of an English language movie with a great sound system because there were other differences too, such as a clean place to watch the movie, a staff wearing clean uniforms, and the overall experience was colourful.

AJAY BIJLI

Chairman, PVR[1]

The suburb of Vasant Kunj, where I was to meet Ajay Bijli, is a thirty minute-drive from the centre of New Delhi. I reached Vasant Kunj by taking a wide, multi-lane road and was surprised when a huge modern mall sprung out of nowhere. And at the top of the mall, Ajay's PVR Cinemas, has a premiere multiplex facility. Those not familiar with modern India might be surprised that many of these malls are world class and include all the brands and shops that one would expect to find, right from McDonalds through to a number of well-known Indian retailers such as Pantaloon and Raymond. The cinema complex itself was equal to, if not better, than any I have seen in the West. Ajay and I met in the coffee shop of the complex and, from its restaurants and bookshop, I could plainly see the experience of going to the cinema was intended to be much more than just watching a movie.

I began the interview with Ajay Bijli, as I usually do, by asking about his childhood and about the family he was born into. He told me his grandfather, Lala Sain Dass, a Punjabi, had started Amritsar Transport Company (ATC), a trucking company in 1939 and that was the principal family business for many years. 'My grandfather was very passionate about the trucking company; probably as passionate as I am about PVR and its cinemas.' On his grandfather's death, ATC was left entirely to Ajay's father, who was the youngest son, 'My grandfather had three sons and one might have thought the business would have been bequeathed differently, but it seems my grandfather felt that my father was the "blue-eyed" boy who could take the family legacy forward. My grandfather was quite an emotional person and later in his life used to frequently change his Will. The story in the family is that if my grandfather got upset with one son, he would then take him out of the Will. This happened shortly before he passed away and the upshot was that my father got everything.'

Ajay told me how his father had moved from Amritsar to Delhi in 1961, because ATC had outgrown its Punjab origins. 'He wanted to expand. Because Amritsar was a small town and Delhi was the capital of the country, he was very keen to move his base there and take the company to another level.' This was not a joint family move but just Ajay's parents. So it was in Delhi that Ajay was born in 1967, followed five years later by his brother Sanjeev Kumar. They were to be the only children. Looking back, Ajay can see he was over-indulged as a child, and that this indulgence was partly explained by the age gap between his father and himself 'because I was born very, very late'. Indeed, by the time Ajay reached the same age, as his father was when he was born, Ajay was already the father of three children, the youngest six years apart from the oldest.

Ajay's father died in 1992, but the family still lives in his father's old family home, including his mother and his brother: 'We all live in the same old family house in which my brother and I were born. Over the years, we have made little changes here and there. For instance, my mom is still in the room that she shared with my dad, but I had to renovate the house a little to accommodate my kids and Sanjeev also did some remodeling. Sanjeev and I make it a point to meet mom every single day for breakfast when we are in Delhi. We go to work in separate cars because we both have to think through what needs to be done every day, but we pretty much complement each other and are comfortable with each other's company.'

So Ajay grew up a 'Delhi boy'. He went to Modern School, a distinguished co-education private Delhi school. He describes his childhood as 'wealthy' rather than 'middle class'. 'As the first son of a dad who had done well for himself in business, I was a very pampered boy. My mom tells me that all the aunts and the family generally saw me that way. Dad really indulged me.' Ajay elaborated on the nature of these indulgences: 'simple things, whatever children want, whether it was toys or clothes, all that sort of stuff. Ever since I was a kid, I would travel first class with dad, which was a big thing at that time. Then, when I was sixteen or something, and in Delhi in those days you could get a car licence very easily, the first car I got was a Volvo. I would take it to school. Then I went to college, and got a Honda. So, he didn't spare any expense in making sure that I was very well looked after.'

Despite the indulgence, Ajay Bijli was a good child and student, 'I was always a very serious person for some reason. Somehow, in the way my parents had brought me up, there was a message underlying somewhere, that I needed to be a conscientious person. I could have all the fun, all the indulgence, but at the same time I knew they expected me – but not in a high pressured way – to be a good student. I knew I wanted to make my parents proud.' Later in the interview, when I returned to the question of why his grandfather should have taken the unusual step of favouring his father, the youngest son, Ajay replied, 'Because my father was a conscientious person. He was very obedient. He was a good child... not flamboyant at all. He was at the same time very positive, very optimistic, and also very correct. So, these are the values that I imbibed from him over a period of time.'

There was an indication that any parental over-indulgence had its limits after Modern School. 'I wasn't very happy with my college education at all. There was a small struggle with my dad after school because I had got good grades and wanted to go abroad and study. I wanted to do an MBA. But he wanted me to stay in Delhi. I joined Hindu College, part of Delhi University, because my dad wanted me to do a Bachelor's degree in Commerce, which for him was an all-important business degree. St Stephens' only had Economics and was therefore unacceptable to him. The top college, Shri Ram

College of Commerce, was "not on" as I fell short of their cut off by a couple of percentage points. The second best college for business was Hindu, but I didn't like it at all. I was generally very happy with my life, but was a little disillusioned that I was not getting a very good education. But I just went along with the flow. I played basketball and a lot of other sports for the three years I was there so, all in all, life was fine. Surprisingly for me, I topped the final year in my class and received a first division honours degree, but to be honest, there were only 35 students so this achievement needs to be taken in context,' Ajay says with a chuckle.

When I asked whether he went to the US to study after this degree, Ajay replied: 'No, not immediately [much later in life he completed the Owners' President Management Program at Harvard Business School]. In 1988, my dad asked me to join the business whereas I wanted to do an MBA. He was very emotional about it. I was "the apple of his eye" and he just didn't want me to go. In fact, my parents were paranoid about it as they thought if I went I would not return. They wanted me to be in front of their "eyes" all the time. So I gave up and said "fine". They said "what do you want to do, you are smart enough already, join the family business. It is okay if later on you want to do something like get married."' In contrast, Ajay's brother, Sanjeev took his first degree in finance and accounting from Salford University in Manchester (where there were some cousins living) and then graduated with an MBA from Imperial College, London. But Ajay joined the family business to just please his parents.

However, his parents were more indulgent about his marriage. When I asked if he had been a 'good' boy again with an arranged marriage, he responded, 'No, in this case, I wasn't very compliant. Because I was in a co-ed high school, I was surrounded by girls all the time, and I fell in love with my future wife at school, between 1984-1985. She was a year senior to me, but I liked her instantly. But I have to say,' he adds laughing 'she didn't take to me instantly. She left Delhi after finishing school and went to Bangalore to do her studies to become a doctor. When she came back from her studies, we met up again through some common friends, and that's the time she also got to like me.' When I asked about the attitude of his parents, 'Actually, it is very funny. Whilst neither my dad nor mom had the education they provided for my brother and me, they were very liberal in most of their views. Their view on my marriage was something like "now that we have come to Delhi, which is a much more liberal society than Amritsar, and we have put him in Modern School, we too have to adopt more liberal thinking." So, for them to then think conservatively and expect me to also be like them was not possible. So I am really grateful to them. They were very open. They said, "fine, if you have met a girl and you like her and whatever, just go ahead." My dad was just very relieved that his son was settling down and was not somebody who wanted to run around and have too many relationships.' So Ajay Bijli got married in 1990, at the age of twenty-three, to Selena. Two daughters were born in 1992 and 1994, followed by a son in 1998.

Ajay Bijli joined ATC in 1988. He spent two years in the trucking business, 'But I just wasn't really there. It was an old company with very established personnel and with set processes and ideas. For me to try and persuade them to do things differently was impossible. I was determined from the beginning that I must "add value" when I joined the family business. I really did not want to be one of those sons who join the family business and then just "coast". I was very frustrated.' In 1990, Ajay was able to relieve this frustration by becoming involved in the single cinema screen business owned by ATC, and which is the beginning of the PVR story.

Two years later in 1992, at the age of twenty-five, there occurred what Ajay Bijli called 'the turning point of my life' – the sudden death of his father at the age of sixty. 'It was actually unexpected. He was a little heavy but he was not at all unhealthy. One day, when we were stuck in a traffic jam, he had a little pain in his chest. We immediately went to a nearby hospital but nobody seemed to be able to help. It was a horrendous experience. By the time we reached a hospital which had proper facilities, it was too late. As I was in the car with him, it made it even worse for me. He really needn't have passed away. If he had been handled promptly and efficiently, it wouldn't have happened.

'I was very immature at the time my father died. I was running a single screen cinema. The guidance that a father would normally provide over time to a son or daughter joining a family business didn't happen. I must say that I took him for granted. I took it for granted that he would always be there. There followed a huge struggle for survival and a lot of people appeared out of nowhere to advise me of what to do. Looking back, in most cases, the advice was useless.'

He asked his mother what he should do. She knew he was passionate about the cinema business, but the trucking business had become very large and could not be ignored. 'My mom told me to try to manage both businesses. There was just one unit for cinema and there were 100 or so outlets all over the country for the trucking business; this was where our "bread and butter" came from.'

And so Ajay went back to the trucking business. 'Whilst I was doing an okay job, I have to admit it was not a very good job because my heart and soul wasn't in it. But somehow, I got the respect of the management and workers, and the business remained profitable.'

Then in 1994, Ajay had another setback because one of their big trans-shipment warehouses caught fire in the middle of the night. Luckily, there were no casualties, but everything was destroyed. 'This really demoralized me and I felt the trucking business was just too hard. There were lawsuits right, left and centre because goods had been damaged and we had to pay up. My family tradition has been very ethical; to always do the right thing. The warehouse was underinsured. It wasn't insured according to the value of the goods that were stored. Whatever money we had, I paid. My mom said in her wisdom that if my dad was alive, he would have paid everybody to ensure the customers did not lose trust.

Ajay became more and more disillusioned. 'My mom's brother, my uncle used to work for my dad, so I went to him and said, "Can you please look after the trucking business for now, revive it or whatever? I will come once a week and spend time with you and once a month we can review the accounts, but I want to go back and run the cinema business." I told him that I felt there was potential to take the cinema business to another level altogether.' And how right Ajay was!

With 5 to 10 per cent annual growth, the ATC continued to grow such that it became one of India's leading transport companies with 65 offices and 300 destinations across India.

But Ajay was not entirely happy about his relationship with ATC. 'The trucking business is still there. I am not very proud of the way I have handled it. Certainly it is big but perhaps it could have become bigger if I had paid full attention to it. Fortunately for the family, my uncle is very passionate about the business as is one of my cousins. I have always found it a very complicated business, and still do. So, I really need to take time out and decide what needs to be done with that company. There are huge emotional linkages to the business. Every time I bring up topics such as we need to sell the business or take some other drastic action, it is very difficult to hold a rational discussion so deep are the emotional ties for some of the family members. It is something that needs to be addressed and I feel guilty for not addressing it properly, because most of my time gets spent in my multiplex cinema business.'

I asked Ajay how a trucking business ended up owning a cinema. 'My father used to get involved in arbitrating disputes as he loved solving problems. Although he was not a very well-educated businessman, he had an aura around him. Delhi business families used to come to him for help and advice. For example, if brothers or partners were fighting or having some sort of dispute, he would try and help them resolve it amicably. One day, there was a dispute by a dozen or so people who owned a cinema property. Dad apparently suggested many solutions that were all rejected. In frustration my father suggested to them the only way to resolve the dispute would be for him to buy the cinema. And so, the Bijli family became the owners of the Priya cinema in Vasant Vihar.'

Ajay then spoke of his own involvement in the cinema business, 'So it just happened that when I finished college and I got a little restless in the trucking company, I spoke to dad. I said listen, you know, there is this cinema that we have got, everybody knows that it belongs to the family. It is in a great area, you know, demographically. The catchment area is full of people I think have the propensity to watch movies, because there is another cinema in the same catchment area which does very well, and they play Hollywood films. And I had just come back from my honeymoon – I got married in 1990 – and I had seen a multiplex in Orlando. I was really fascinated by lots of screens under one roof. If the quality of sound and projection system is very good and if it is a hygienic atmosphere, people will come and watch movies. But in our case, the sound wasn't good, the projection wasn't good, the whole place was very dilapidated, but the catchment area was very good. My dad said, "Fine, if you want to give it a shot, you do that, but this is really not our main business, and you know ticket prices are controlled in India?" At that time, you couldn't charge more than Rs 12 (about

USD 0.25 today). This is pre-1991. It was perceived to be a "poor man's" entertainment and accordingly the government sought to control the industry. He told me that is why he had not invested in the business because there was no upside. We could buy whatever we wanted – Dolby systems, better seats, better sound and projection systems – essentially all that was available and we had seen in developed countries. But, the government ceiling and the revenue generated would not justify our investment. I responded that I may be able to balance the low prices with high occupancies and asked him to "let me just give it a shot." I said, "I am not going to take too much money from you. I am going to invest a very modest amount." In 1990, when I was just twenty-three, my involvement with the cinema business really started.'

Ajay set to work with the single-screen Priya cinema. 'I basically souped up the traditional silver screen cinema. I didn't have any movies but knew that without them I would be finished. I decided to try and get Hollywood films, because in Delhi we had about 62 cinemas halls at that time and most of them were playing Hindi movies. So that looked like a differentiating positioning for the cinema. While the cinema was getting renovated, I took a flight and went to Bombay because that is where all the US studios such as Warner Brothers, Columbia Tri-Star, Sony, and MGM had their offices.

'I went to the studios and told them they should supply me with films as I had no content. I asked them to add me as potential distributor in Delhi to which they predictably responded that I had no experience or background in English movies. I pleaded that they give me an opportunity, just a little opportunity and a good film and I am going to make sure that there is transparency, good customer service and I am sure people will come. God was kind to me as I got *Tango & Cash* as the first movie to screen. I took the advertising posters for the movie back to Delhi and pasted them up everywhere. The response was great.

'We were the first to invest in a Dolby sound system. But it was not just a question of an English language movie with a great sound system because there were other differences too, such as a clean place to watch the movie, a staff wearing clean uniforms, and the overall experience was colourful. I was very much into colour; I observed both Indian and Hollywood films are typically very colourful and vibrant, so why should the cinema halls look grey, dark, and dingy? This belief in the importance of colour is something that became part of the PVR's philosophy.

'Unbelievably too, not long after starting up, the Federal Government announced partial decontrol of cinemas. It was not a question of my dad or me lobbying the government. It was just that cinemas were closing down, and the producers were saying, "Listen, something needs to be done as there are so many restrictions and archaic laws affecting the industry. At the very least you can decontrol ticket prices." Partial decontrol meant that for 20 per cent of the tickets, you still couldn't charge more than 5 rupees, but for the balance of 80 per cent, you could charge as per the market dynamics. Every six months, one could make a case to the government to allow you to increase the prices. So that became a big boost.'

I asked how this 20 per cent worked: 'How it worked was that they allocated the first rows. So, if your seating capacity was say 1000, around 200 of your seating capacity had to be sold at 5 rupees. So every cinema exhibitor put that 200 into the first rows at 5 rupees because there is a front row syndrome anyway – nobody buys the front rows, unless you are really running packed. So, that's how it worked. That remained for a very long time up until 1998. Everything else had opened up some years before, but cinema was always considered to be a staple entertainment for the masses. It was always viewed not as an industry but as an idea that unites India. It is a place where there should not be any segregation between the socioeconomic classes. However, the middle class by and large did not want to go to the cinema because they typically associated it with dirty, unhygienic premises. But slowly the position changed.

'In 1992, only one year after the refurbishment, the Priya cinema was doing very well. We started having queues, we had full houses, and it became one of the top grossing cinemas in the country.' But 1992, as noted above, was a significant year for other reasons as Ajay suddenly lost his father and had to turn his full attention to the big family trucking business. It was not until 1994 that he was able to return almost full time to the cinema business. In the meantime, producers and distributors, like Warner Brothers and Universal Paramount, saw the success of Priya and made contact with Ajay as they saw him as a potential ally in opening up

India to the Hollywood market. 'They put me in contact with an Australian company, Village Roadshow.

'Village Roadshow was growing rapidly in Asia through establishing joint ventures with local cinema operators. There was Golden Village in Singapore, Tanjong Golden Village in Malaysia, and Entertain Golden Village in Thailand. But Village Roadshow was finding it difficult to find a partner in India. I took a flight to Singapore where they had a regional office and met John Crawford. The main family behind Village Roadshow was the Kirby's, Robert Kirby and his dad, Rick Kirby. John was the delegated authority for Asia. We met for lunch in Singapore and just hit it off. Literally, on the back of a drinks' coaster, John started doing some numbers, asking me what ticket prices were, what the occupancy was, whether there was the entertainment tax and so on. By the end of our lunch, John said, "We have got a business here." He suggested we look at a joint venture to which I agreed. He came back in a very simple 10-12 page agreement. It was 60:40 in my favour which I found extremely generous as I could not match their financials. It was a partnership of unequals, so to speak, because there was no way I could have funded the growth in equal terms. There was a clause that equalization would happen in seven years or if the joint venture company was listed. But before that, let it be 60:40 and we grow the business.

'Village was aware of the complexities of the business in India and relied on me to handle them, as they knew it would be impossible for a foreigner to do so. Do you realize that the cinema business was subject to different laws in every state as well as being subject to Federal taxes? There were, for example, different building by-laws, different state cinema legislation, different controls on ticket prices and different censorship regulations. It was like building a business in 25 different countries, all under one roof.' Priya Village was born in 1996 between Priya with one screen in Delhi and Village Roadshow as one of the largest global players.

Village immediately wanted Ajay to turn Priya into a multiplex but he persuaded them to allow him to look for another site as Priya was running with over 80 per cent occupancy and Ajay knew it would be out of action for a considerable time if they renovated it. Ajay found another single screen cinema in Saket in south Delhi, and set about converting it into a multiplex. 'It took us 14 months as we had to rewrite the building bylaws and a lot of other things. We nearly went mad trying to convince the government that, yes, it is possible, to have under one roof four cinemas with four projection rooms, one common box office and one common confectionary stand. We also had to explain that with the right exit and entry points it would be a safe cinema. Finally, in 1997, PVR Saket opened. It was madness with huge queues and both my wife and I had to help selling tickets. At that time, the maximum price for a ticket was about Rs 30. We decided to charge Rs 60, so people would come to the box office and ask "Can I watch four movies with Rs 60?" We had to keep explaining, "No, Rs 60 is the price for one movie, but there are four auditoriums, so you can choose which movie you want to see." And we didn't at that point have computerized ticketing, so it was very difficult. We had pink, green and yellow slips to differentiate the different movies. Village Roadshow was very happy with the result and asked me to aggressively grow the business but I managed to persuade them that it is not a simple matter to grow this business in India. But we did find and convert two more single screen sites in Delhi.' By around 2001, PVR had 12 screens, all in Delhi.'

During this period, his younger brother Sanjeev joined the business having finished his studies. In order to learn the business, Village arranged for him to spend time at their cinema complex in Hobart in Tasmania, Australia. I must admit, I was shocked as I could not think of anywhere on the planet less like India, and certainly Delhi. Ajay laughed and said Sanjeev felt the same. 'However, it gave Sanjeev an excellent grounding in how Village ran a cinema. Sanjeev gained experience in all facets of the business including programming, marketing, and even working behind the confectionary counter, selling popcorn and Pepsi. So Sanjeev has been involved almost since the beginning. In terms of personality and interests, we compliment each other and both follow the principle our dad taught us of respecting the views of others.'

In 2001, not long after 9/11, Ajay received a call from Graham Burke, the managing director of Village Roadshow who was very close to the Kirby family. 'He said, "Ajay, I know you are a good partner and you fit all the criteria that we need in a partner. You are honest and enthusiastic but my Board has just taken a decision, we need to scale down our global operations and we wish to withdraw from our Asian joint ventures, including the one with you." I was shocked and made a number of trips to Melbourne to try and persuade them to change their minds, all to no avail. They were polite and courteous but I found that once they had made their decision, that was it.'

What made it even more frustrating for Ajay was that this was the time when a number of malls were being planned and built throughout the country. And all of them wanted cinema multiplexes as an important foundation tenant. 'Under the joint venture, we started signing leases. But the malls were still not built. They were all at that stage just land. Whilst we still had at least three years to finance the fit outs, we still had to finance the lease term by paying a deposit to secure the lease. There would at that time have been exposure upwards of USD 20 million which would have been simple for Village to finance but impossible for PVR on its own.

'But the Village Roadshow people were very considerate to my situation. They said, "Listen, Ajay, you take your time. You find another partner who can buy our 40 per cent stake or you go to a private equity firm. We are not in a hurry but we don't want to spend any more money." Robert Kirby and I had become good friends and had a common interest in cricket. In fact, the moment I finally realized our joint venture was over was while we were watching a Boxing Day test together at the Melbourne Cricket Ground.'

Ajay decided he had to find an Indian solution to acquire the Village shareholding. He met with a family friend, Sunil Mittal of Bharti Airtel who is a well-known and prominent businessman. He was clear in his advice and suggested Ajay meet with private equity bankers and offered to put him in touch with some. 'Over a period of some six months, I met with these firms and provided my financials and views of the future. Renuka Ramnath, who headed ICICI Ventures at that time, loved the story. ICICI had just established the India Advantage Fund, which was focused on the India consumption story, and on businesses involved in retail and consumption patterns. Having satisfied herself on our financials, Renuka told me she wanted to meet Village Roadshow to find out what I was like as a partner. Fortunately, Robert Kirby must have given good feedback so we passed this test too. Actually it was a life lesson to me that it is extremely important when one has a partner to work hard to understand the partner's viewpoint. Clearly, I could have "lost it" on hearing Village wanted to withdraw and the joint venture could have ended acrimoniously in which event no doubt Robert's feedback to Renuka might have been somewhat different. By putting myself in Village's "shoes" I eventually understood where they were coming from.'

On her visit to Melbourne, Renuka saw a number of big shopping mall multiplexes such as the Crown and Jam Factory. 'This convinced her of our business model, and on her return to India, she advised me that ICICI would fund PVR and provide me with funds to acquire Village Roadshow's shares for USD10 million which was exactly what Village had invested. This was extremely fair of Village as they did not ask for any valuation of the shares, which would certainly have been higher. ICICI then acquired Village's 40 per cent from me and injected Rs 40 crore, which is about USD10 million at that time, in the company. A lasting link remains with Village Roadshow in so far as they have allowed us to continue with the PVR brand in its short form.'

With the access to funds, PVR opened 7-plex cinema in MGF mall in Gurgaon and paid back its debt in three years. An 11-plex opened at Bangalore and paid back its debt in two years. Ajay remembers: 'It was madness, there were huge lines and over 2.4 million tickets were sold in the first year. We have kept photos of the crowds.' PVR also opened in Bombay and Hyderabad.

The year 2006 was another milestone as ICICI decided it was time to exit as the financials were good and the future looked bright as there were another 100 screens signed up. 'We decided to list PVR and ICICI sold down to 10 per cent and made a healthy multiple of five times on their invested capital. My family also reduced its stake to around 40 per cent. We operate now about 158 screens in 38 properties across India. And we have about 350 new screens signed up. We are growing by about 50 new screens a year.'

When I asked if the future growth would take place in tier-2 cities, Ajay replied, 'Actually there is huge growth left in major cities like Chennai, Bangalore and Hyderabad as they are slowly making their laws more consumer friendly. That said, believe it or not, in Chennai there is still a control on ticket prices. Given this, PVR does not need to go to tier-2 or tier-3 cities as quickly as one might think. Also in tier-1 cities, more and more quality malls are being built giving us significant expansion opportunities in cities which we already understand.'

I mentioned to Ajay that the Vasant Kunj mall seemed a retail experience as modern as any in Australia or Singapore. He enthusiastically agreed, 'Absolutely. This is basically an indulgence that I had been very interested to do for a very long time. I have seen these little things happening everywhere outside India. In London, I like to go to Electric Cinema in Portobello Street which has a restaurant and brasserie as well as a cinema. Then I saw something else in IFC Mall in Hong Kong that has a bookstore and a cinema. This Vasant Kunj PVR experience, even though it is only a 4-plex, is an indulgence that combines all these features.'

Many successful businessmen are reluctant to talk about their failures but Ajay was eager to talk about one of his. 'In 2005-2006, we started a film distribution business called PVR Pictures. We started distributing films from MiraMax and smaller studios that were not represented in India, such as Focus Films and Intermedia. This business became quite successful because all our cinemas were demographically in catchments where we could play Hollywood films. However, Indian producers started approaching us to distribute their films as well. We started doing this, but it is more risky as Bollywood producers wanted us to pay upfront for the rights, whereas with Hollywood distributors, provided they trust you to be transparent, you play the movie and, whatever the box-office revenues are, you deduct your commission, and repatriate the money to the producers. Anyway, we indulged a little bit but we didn't lose any money.

'Then, in 2007 we took a big step when I met Aamir Khan, a very famous Indian actor/producer with a tremendous reputation and for whom I have the deepest respect and admiration – I was, I guess you would say, a devoted fan. I met him at the premiere of one of his movies and told him I was very influenced by *Lagaan*, one of his more famous movies. I told him I would love to make a movie with him if he had a script he thought I might like. Two months later, I got a call from him and he said – and this call was certainly another turning point in my career – "Ajay, I have got these two scripts, are you sure you want to co-produce a film with me and then distribute it?" Of course I agreed and we entered into an agreement to do two films and both did phenomenally well. One of them – *Taare Zameen Par* – was nominated for a foreign film Oscar. It is a very sensitive movie about a dyslexic child and his teacher. If you ask anybody what is his or her favourite Hindi film in the last ten years, it will probably be this film. We then made a teenager game-changing movie with Aamir's nephew – that was a fun movie. It again did very well. So Sanjeev and I thought this was a good business to be involved in. Here we were moving along, chugging along, running a good company, with cinema exhibition as the core, and we got diverted into doing movies, which are very volatile, very unpredictable.

'Anyway, even our investors got excited. They seem to have thought, these guys are not only good at making cinemas, they are also very great in making movies now. JP Morgan invested USD15 million into PVR Pictures which was a 100 per cent subsidiary of PVR Cinemas. And Renuka put in another USD15 million based on her earlier positive experience with us. We were armed with USD30 million to make more movies. And this is where we goofed up. We made four movies with that money and all of them bombed. We closed down the business in 2011. Fortunately, we had only spent 50 per cent of the funds, so we were able to return some of the funds invested. But our share price took a beating and collapsed by 50 per cent as once the subsidiary's results were consolidated back in the parent company the return looked poor. Sanjeev and I decided that the film business was just too risky for us at this point. So, we regrouped and spoke to our investors and we said, listen, it is not meant for us and bought them out. Immediately, our share price recovered. Certainly the Hollywood studios and new media players like Warner and Universal have diversified and got involved in all aspects of the movie content business but my conclusion is that this is too early in the PVR story or may never be relevant in India.

Ajay also talked about another attempt at vertical integration. 'Touch wood this has been successful. In 2008 we created a joint venture, PVR blu-O, with Major Cineplex Group, a Thai company to open ten-pin bowling alleys. Major Cineplex has successfully combined bowling centers and ice skating rinks with its cinemas and I wish to do the same in India. The idea is to create a destination factor. But we have learnt our lesson from our failed attempt at producing movies so I am sure we will move slowly and carefully and keep our focus on exhibiting movies.'

As our meeting drew to a close we chatted about who I was interviewing for this book and that I had interviewed Kishore Biyani for the first Added Value book on Indian business leaders. Ajay noted I had found it hard going. He laughed and said that he and their mutual friends jokingly tease Kishore by telling him he is 'the half sentence man'. 'We are good friends and interact frequently as both of us are major tenants in malls; he with his Pantaloon and other brands and we with our cinemas. From time to time we sit together on panels at retail conferences and very often Kishore's responses will be incisive but so short that he forces the other panel members like me to complete his sentences.'

By now it is the middle of the day on a Saturday, and the mall is coming alive with shoppers and, from the spot where I am sitting with Ajay, I can see young couples browsing in the complex's bookshop, sitting down for a meal and, of course, forming lines at the cinema ticket office. I can see that Ajay is also observing the crowd, and decide it is time to leave him to focus on the business. As I return to my hotel I cannot but reflect, both as an Australian and as a lawyer, on Ajay's overall positive experience with Village Roadshow even though their joint venture ended unexpectedly for PVR. Ajay's view that if a joint venture is to end, it is important to try and do so amicably made a lot of sense to me. And as I complete this chapter many months later, this advice still resonates strongly.

---

[1] PVR Ltd. pioneered the multiplex cinema business in India by establishing the first multiplex cinema in 1997 at Saket, New Delhi. In late 2012, PVR acquired a majority stake in Cinemax India that, together with other organic growth, has catapulted the group to being India's largest with more than 400 screens across 93 locations and with a seating capacity of over 100,000 seats. By way of comparison and, as an indicator of the likely growth ahead, the USA has around 40,000 screens across 6000 locations.

> It is our philosophy – and that philosophy started off way back – when we have somebody to invest with us, we will always leave something on the table for our partner. There is no fun if I try to take all the "cream" myself. You will be unhappy and, if you are unhappy, you will make damn sure that I am also unhappy.

ANAND BURMAN
Chairman, Dabur[1]

I met Anand Burman in his office in Delhi. Perhaps in keeping with Dabur's profile and image, the fit-out is conservative and tasteful but certainly not contemporary. Works of art are strategically placed in the reception area and his office and the only piece that I could not identify turned out to be an elaborate wooden cigar humidifier made for him by one of his friends. Beside his desk on the wall is a beautiful photograph of his mother who passed away some years ago.

'First of all, I would like to explain to you the origins of our family name, Dabur. It is very simple, not rocket science.' Taking a blank sheet of paper from his desk he started explaining. 'In English, when you write "Doctor" as, for instance Doctor Burman, you write "Dr" as the abbreviation for it. In Hindi it is *"Da"* not "Dr.", – and Anand wrote Da on the paper in front of us. Then beside the Da he added 'Bur' as an abbreviation of Burman, to produce 'Dabur'. 'So it is as simple as that, "Dabur" is the abbreviation of "Dr Burman" who was my great-great grandfather S.K. Burman who founded the company in 1884 and whose picture is over there; the chap with the rather thick mustache.

'His family was in the silk garment business near Murshidabad in central Bengal. At the time of the Indian Mutiny in 1857, most of the family members were massacred by the British; his aunt and he were the only survivors. They moved to Calcutta to stay with other relatives and S.K. ended up at medical college in Calcutta and, a few years before 1884, started practising medicine. If you were to do a rewind to that era, there was no medicine as you and I know it today; probably the only commonality from that time would have been aspirin, and even that was not widely available. Alexander Fleming with the antibiotic, forget it; penicillin forget it; none of that stuff even existed.

'The standard formula medicines at that time were mainly what they called "patent" medicines whereas traditional Indian herbal medicines were called "Ayurvedic". The Ayurvedic medicine trade was very disorganized and fragmented with Ayurvedic physicians making their own products. There was no company producing standardized Ayurvedic medicine. My great-great grandfather set out to change this; firstly by identifying common ailments and developing his own patent medicines to treat them. Some of them are still in the market today after more than a century. Years later, he branched out into Ayurvedic personal care products for skin care, oral care and so on.

'Whatever savings he had he put into the business. It was all pretty simple stuff. He had a couple of people to make the medicine and as his reputation for effective drugs grew, the business grew. At that time the company was called S.K. Burman Private Limited. In the late 1890s and early 1900s he actually used to distribute medicine by mail order which we subsequently stopped back in the 1920s. I guess what goes around comes around. He had two daughters and one son, Chunni Lal Burman. C.L. was not a doctor; he was very content to live the life of a businessman as he inherited a successful business from his father.'

As Anand drew the third line of the family tree, he continued, 'C.L. had three sons: Puran Chand Burman (PCB), Amar Chand Burman (ACB), and Ratan Chand Burman (RCB). ACB passed away at a young age; he was married then but had no children.' Anand drew a circle around ACB's name and crossed it out. 'PCB became the builder of the back end of the business such as the formulation and manufacturing of the products. RCB, on the other hand, was responsible for the front end of the business, such as sales and marketing, dealing with the agents and making sure that the finances were all in order. It was a good team and the business grew rapidly.'

Anand Burman started to draw the fourth generation. 'PCB had two sons: Ashok Chand Burman and Vivek Chand Burman. Ashok, my father, has passed away. RCB had three sons: Gyan Chand Burman, Pradip Burman, and Sidharth.' With a smile Anand says, 'After Gyan, we decided to drop the CBs going forward as it got too complicated and repetitious. So there were five in the fourth generation.

'And it was during this fourth generation that the business really exploded in growth – we are talking from the 1980s onward – although my father Ashok, who was the eldest of his generation, had been in the business since the 1950s. So we are talking both pre- and post- the "licence raj". But we never had any issues with licences because it was an ongoing business, so that we had a COB licence – carry on business license – which allowed us to keep going without any of the controls of the licence raj. It would have been a very different situation if we had decided to set up a new steel or cement plant. All manner of licences would have been required. Even for pharmaceuticals if you were already in existence when the licence raj started the COB licence protected you.

'This gentleman,' – Anand says pointing to a painting of Vivek on the wall – 'was the marketing whiz at that time. And this gentleman,' – he says pointing to a photograph of Gyan – 'was in charge of the manufacturing and production in the entire back end. He passed away in 2001. Pradip was in charge of engineering, Sidharth was in charge of finance, and my father Ashok was in overall charge of the business. He was the chairman and the forward thinker. He passed away in 2011 at the age of eighty-one.

'So now let us come down to the next generation.' Anand Burman drew in himself as the oldest of the fifth generation. He added, 'I am not putting names of any women yet as I am an only child; Vivek has two sons: Mohit and Gaurav; Gyan has one son Amit and a daughter, Gauri; Pradip has a son, Chetan, and a daughter, Devika; and Sidharth has a son, Saket, and a daughter Sumati. I am turning sixty-two this year [2014] whereas Saket as the youngest is only around his mid 30s – a spread in my generation of almost 30 years.

'Then there is one more generation to deal with and that is the sixth generation. I have a son, Aditya and a daughter, Anisha; Mohit is not married; Gaurav has a son, Bodhi and a daughter, Aria; Amit has a son Adhiraj and a daughter Diya; Chetan has a son, Kamran and a daughter, Ishana; and Saket is not married. In my son's generation, he is the eldest, and is the only one who is married. He is married to Shivani, and has a daughter, Ariana. She is the start of yet another generation of the family. You will note that so far I have not written down any of the girls' names as traditionally they would not be included or involved in the family business. We are, however, in line with modern thinking and fairness, considering including daughters in the future. It is clear in my generation they are not included, but for the generation after me the answer is not yet clear. We have a family constitution but it does not currently deal with this matter; it does not specify either one way or the other; so it is left open-ended purposely.'

I asked Anand whether they lived as a traditional joint family. 'Perhaps I should start with how we live. My father until he passed away, myself, my son and our families all live in the same house. Vivek and his two sons, Mohit and Gaurav and their families all live in the same house, but Gaurav spends a lot of his time in England. Gyan and his son Amit and their families all live in the same house. Pradip and his son Chetan do not; they live separately. And Sidharth and Saket live together in Dubai. So to answer your question, no it is not a joint family in the traditional sense of the word. However, if you looked at it in terms of ownership of the business, it is more traditional.

'As far as the decision making in the business is concerned, let me tell you what we went through in the 1990s. We were until then very much a joint family in terms of the role allocations just as in the previous generations where one son looked after the back end, another looked after finance, and so on. This was exactly how it was when I joined the company in 1980. I had finished my Ph.D. in the US and came back and joined the family business. I mentioned earlier the roles of everyone in my father's generation and they had to find a new role for me which was looking after our portfolio of products.

'So everybody in the family had a role to play until the 1990s. The company was growing fairly rapidly and we were all having a great time and as the company grew we each did our own thing with everybody with their "shoulders to the wheel" in their respective areas. And then we began to have a lot of issues. The main issues were management related such as sometimes we failed to deliver goods ordered or to produce products required. There was no overall breakdown in management but we were facing a daily fight in many areas of the business; to put it bluntly, it was an "interesting time", Anand says with the expected emphasis on 'interesting'. 'We eventually decided we needed outside help and engaged McKinsey to help us set up our processes and our systems and the "whole nine yards". It was actually a collective family decision to bring them in. My father and Gyan made the final decision – they were the two guys who at that time were in charge – and I was cheering them on from the back.

'McKinsey was with us for almost two years and they helped us a lot with processes, reorganization, redoing certain things and, above all, looking at the way we did business. Many of our problems got sorted out just by putting in appropriate processes and systems. It was fabulous and people could see that the business had a lot of potential; by this time we were into oral care, skin care, hair care, and other personal care products. Just as they were finishing their role, the senior McKinsey executive on our account asked the family a simple question that frankly "stumped" us. He asked, "Just because your last name is Burman do you think you are the best people to manage this business?"

'This question set us thinking and we brought in Accenture to come up with recommendations on how to run the business. The outcome of this review was that we pulled the family out of the business, recruited the best managers to perform different roles. There have been a few "ups and downs" along the way but we did not give up and remained committed to the clear division of management and ownership. As a result we have some extremely competent colleagues working in the company and doing many things that I am not so sure that the family would have been able to do as well. Maybe we could have, but you know that families do things in a particular way. If you are not a family member and you are put into a senior position with the appropriate amount of responsibility, you tend to do things in a very different way from a family member. I think in general you look at issues more objectively and at a greater depth because, at the end of the day, your job depends on getting it right. It would be much more difficult to fire a family member from a job that he might or might not be doing well. To cut a long story short, over the period of the last twelve to fifteen years, we have slowly managed to move the family completely out of the day-to-day operations of the business.

'Of course we have family members on the Board and I am the current Chairman but we have nothing to do with the operations. The Board is more concerned with strategy and reviews. Our Family Council, constituted as set out in our family constitution, chooses the chairman. It is no longer about seniority in the family.

'Another important thing that has happened over the last fifteen years was the development of the pharmaceutical division; Dabur actually had two divisions at one time – a pharmaceutical division and a consumer products' division. Given my background I was the one who founded the pharmaceutical division some fifteen years ago. We concentrated on medicines for cancer. In 2003, we decided to focus more on the consumer products' division so we demerged the pharmaceutical division into a separate company, Dabur Pharma Limited with the same family shareholding. And as the years went by we could see that we did not have the expertise to maximise the opportunities for this sector and in 2008 we sold the company to a German group, Fresenius. The reason we sold the business was very simple. I honestly felt that the Fresenius could do a much better job in marketing the products than I ever could. In the Indian pharmaceutical scenario it is very easy – or, at least, relatively easy – to make the product. But to sell the product in different geographies, on the other hand, is a different story.

'We were a generic oncology company and one of only three companies that were dealing in generic oncology products. The difference and the value that we brought to the table was that we would do the entire shooting match: from making the raw material to marketing it ourselves we were offering it at the lowest cost in the world. We exported to 47 different geographies. In some we did exceedingly well. In Southeast Asia we were either the No. 1 or No.

2 oncology drugs' company. However, in some areas, like Europe, we were miserable. In Africa, we only supplied some products into Kenya, but that was it.

'As a result of this sale of one division, each of our families received a large amount at which point the Family Council took the next momentous decision, which was, from that time on, no family member should take a salary from any family company. Family members have the right to do any business they like alone or with other members of the family. The upshot is that Dabur India Limited is the only family business involving everyone in the family and the Family Council handles major decisions in relation to our shareholding.

'In fact, Dabur India became public in 1994 at which time we listed around 22 per cent of the shareholding. Since that time we have reduced our shareholding but still speak for around 68 per cent of the shareholding. As we demerged the pharmaceutical business after we went public, non-family shareholders also shared in the spoils when we sold to Fresenius. It is our philosophy – and that philosophy started off way back – when we have somebody to invest with us, we will always leave something on the table for our partner. There is no fun if I try to take all the "cream" myself. You will be unhappy and, if you are unhappy, you will make damn sure that I am also unhappy.'

For those of you who are used to reading my life stories you will see this chapter has followed a completely different format. Perhaps it is because Anand is a scientist, perhaps it is the way he approaches people, but once Anand pulled out the sheet of blank paper and progressively filled in the family tree through the generations on it, there was no way to stop him and find out more about his own life and the earlier family history. This seemed a good point to ask Anand about this.

'It is really hard to pinpoint what actual group we belong to – we are in a very "grey area". We actually migrated about 400 years ago from near Multan in today's Pakistan. We are Hindus – we are actually Aroras and this is part of the Khatri community – and there was a very large stronghold of Hindus around Multan. I believe the actual town we came from is Dera Ismail Khan. Families in our community started migrating eastwards into the state of Bengal and onto its capital, Calcutta. Almost all of the people we have talked about on the family tree, other than the generation below me, were born in Calcutta.

'We were in a typical joint family when I was born in 1950. It was amazing. I wish I could replicate that today. We all lived in a huge home and in this home all the parents had their own apartments with a drawing room and a bedroom and another bedroom for the kids. But there were also common areas for everyone including a large drawing room, kitchen and the dining area. If you felt like it you could eat and be by yourself but, more often than not, you would eat with everybody else. It was that much more fun eating with your siblings and cousins. Right next door to the house was another building which was the office. One did not even have to go down to the driveway to the street and back in to the office as there was a bridge made in between the two. It was a fabulous childhood.

'So there were,' – he says counting up from the family tree he had drawn – 'there were one, two, three, four, five, six, seven families all living in the one family home. Over time some of the family moved away to places like Delhi but for much of my childhood everyone lived there. But that was at that time and everybody had the same mindset and the whole of society was of a very similar mindset. But I accept times have changed, and you have to change with the times, and that this lifestyle is disappearing fast in India.

'Increasingly during the late '60s and on through the '70s the communist and extreme Left wing trade unions, plus the even more extreme Naxalites, caused massive labour unrest in Calcutta. As our home and the office were essentially on the same title the strikers would camp on our land and carry out what became known as a "gherao" (or "circle" in Hindi) and block anyone trying to come in or out of the property. As I was only about six or seven at the time they would make an exception and allow me to go to school. Usually there was no physical violence but the family would be trapped for days in the house and, of course, none of our employees could get to the office. Like many other business families and even multinational businesses, we decided to shift our business to Delhi. Since doing so we have not had any labour issues. The family compound and the office still exists in Kolkata, but we are now planning to tear down both and build a new office block.

'I was an only child and the oldest of my generation as my father was the oldest in his generation. When I was born I had a lot of trouble with my kidneys and was put on a saltless diet for the first nine years of my life. But, despite that, I was sent away to a boarding school, St Paul's in Darjeeling, when I was just seven. It was basically a Church of England school, but not strictly religious as we did not have any priests teaching us. For the first two years it was hell for me but after that I enjoyed it. All my uncles had gone to the same school but I was the last in the family to do so. Actually the school went downhill quite a bit due to the Gorkhaland[2] – separate state – problems.

'I have made lifelong friends from school and many are scattered all over the world. For example, from my class, one friend is a neurosurgeon in England and another is an investment banker in New York. The location of the school was absolutely fabulous. If you take a look at the pictures of our school – let me see if I can show you one,' and with this he pulled out a photo album. 'Here. See that. That is the Kanchenjunga Mountain range. Here. See this photo of the school grounds. It was gorgeous scenery all around and the temperature was fabulous all school year. All in all I received an excellent education there.

'When I finished school, I came back to Calcutta. I used to come back home once a year; we used to have a three-month holiday from school in the winter. I had nobody pushing me that I must become a doctor or I must become a lawyer or an engineer. There was no pressure of any sort – none at all. My father wanted me to do whatever I was comfortable with. So once I had finished my college, he suggested that it would be a good idea to join the family business. I had been to study in the US, but there was never any fear that I would not want to return to India. My uncles had all been to colleges in the US: Vivek went to the University of Miami, Gyan went to the Philadelphia College of Pharmacy and Science, Pradip went to MIT, and Siddharth to Berkeley. As for my generation, I went to the University of Wisconsin and got my PhD in pharmaceutical chemistry from the University of Kansas. Mohit and Gaurav went to University of Boston College, Amit was at Lehigh, and Chetan went to Boston University. All of us came home even though I am sure each of us could, at that time, have got our "green cards" and remained in the US.

'Actually I was all set to do my pharmacy studies in the UK but consulted my uncle Gyan who had also done pharmacy. He suggested I switch to the US, which I did. Gyan, along with my father, was my mentor throughout these years. Both were approachable and there were no boundaries between my father or my uncle and me. In fact, not long after I started my pharmacy degree I found myself enjoying the chemistry subjects more and switched to that major which I continued all the way through to my PhD where I specialized in pharmaceutical chemistry.

'There was some debate in the family as to whether I should do my doctorate or not but my father supported me to do it if I wanted to. I do not ever regret having earned the doctorate. It was rather a strange experience. I had come back to India for a holiday while I was doing my master's when I was about twenty-four or twenty-five years old. And in a typical Indian fashion, my father said that he was going to introduce me to some nice young ladies and there were introductions da, da, da,' Anand says mischievously, 'and it just so happened that there was one young lady with whom I got along very well with and so we got engaged before I went back to the US.

'The idea was that I would return in eight months after I had completed my master's and we would be married. One day when I was back in the US there was a very bad explosion in the lab that completely blinded me for about three months. Slowly, my sight started coming back, which was what the doctors had told us would happen. It took about eight months for my sight to come back completely and there were a lot of scars; it was bad news. I came back to India to recover and, by the time I was completely healed, I was ready to get married. But first of all I went back to the US, completed my master's degree and got admitted to the PhD. With this all in place I returned to India, got married to Minnie and went back to the US with her and completed my doctorate.

'Minnie studied architecture, but she never practiced. We have a son, Aditya who got a degree in Chemistry from my old university, the University of Kansas. He runs his own clinical diagnostics business. We also have a daughter, Anisha who is an artist and lives in England. She is our rebel, but that is fine with us.'

Given his comment about his daughter being a rebel and the fact that Anand and I were born in the same year and experienced late '60s and early '70s at university, I asked Anand about his US college days in that hippie 'flower power' era. 'I started off at the University of Wisconsin and Madison was a crazy place for this; it was a very liberal college. So I had the long hair and everything but there were no issues with my parents. My father was very relaxed in that way and my uncle Sidharth went to Berkeley, which was where it all started. When I went to the States in 1970, the musical "Hair" was still running on Broadway. Hopefully, I have been the same way with our daughter as my father was with me.'

Our time was drawing to an end and I looked at the family tree that Anand Burman had drawn. I suggested that there did not seem to be many girls around. 'In my generation, I will tell you,' he said drawing in female siblings on the family tree, 'Amit has a sister Gauri, Chetan has a sister, Devika, and Saket has a sister, Sumati. As I mentioned earlier we have a family constitution. We took advice from some specialists on such matters but found it quite theoretical. As a result the family got together and converted their advice into something more practical and applicable to our family. It is not that prescriptive and, as I mentioned, we are just coming to terms with the fact we need to appropriately deal with the women in the family. What the final solution will be I do not know at this point but I am sure we will come to a fair and equitable resolution.'

I thought this was an appropriate point to end our meeting and my 'takeaway' is that, not only had I met a remarkable man like all of the people in my books, but that he is the only one of the hundreds of business leaders who I have met, who seemed to think and express himself best by drawing and talking to a diagram on a blank sheet of paper. I wonder if it is the chemist in him.

---

[1]Dabur (www.dabur.com) is the fourth largest FMCG company in India with a market capitalization of over USD 5 billion. Its products are sold in over 60 countries and focus on hair care, oral care, health care, skin care, home care, and food.
[2]Gorkhaland – see Wikipedia (en.wikipedia.org/wiki/Gorkhaland) is a proposed state in India demanded by the majority people of the Darjeeling Hills area and the people of ethnic origin in Dooars in West Bengal. The movement for a separate state of Gorkhaland gained serious momentum during the 1980s, when the Gorkha National Liberation Front carried out a violent agitation. The agitation ultimately led to the establishment of a semi-autonomous body in 1988 called the Darjeeling Gorkha Hill Council to govern certain areas. However, in 2008, a new party called the Gorkha Janmukti Morcha, again sort a separate state of Gorkhaland. In 2011, they signed an agreement with the state and central government for the formation of the Gorkhaland Territorial Administration, a semi-autonomous body that replaced the Darjeeling Gorkha Hill Council.

❛ It is nice to read these theories in books but, you know, when it comes to it, I like people. I enjoy spending time with people and am in the fortunate position, I do not want or need anything from anybody. That makes life easy. If somebody wants something from me, I tell them, "Whatever you want to say, please say it simply; otherwise forget it." ❜

RAMESH CHAUHAN
Chairman and Managing Director, Bisleri[1]

I was early for my meeting with Ramesh Chauhan. As I was sitting in the reception I heard a voice coming up the stairs to the reception. And in walked a short man wearing sandals, long pants with braces over an open necked shirt and a French beret. It was none other than Ramesh. He had a friendly open face but I must admit his attire was certainly the most eccentric or unusual of all the Indians I had met for my two books.

He was arriving for work but immediately ushered me into his office with him before he even had a chance to speak to his secretary. His office was also a surprise. On the shelves behind his desk were rows and rows of bottles; many he said were of his competitors' products. Why were they there I asked him. He said whenever he has a packaging problem, rather than think about trying to 'reinvent the wheel' he looks to see what some of his competitors might have done to solve a similar situation. There was one other unusual thing about his office – there were lots of clocks everywhere. It cannot be that he is concerned about time because he told me that everyone is always late in India and that he could not work out why I was early. So, all in all, even before our discussion of his life story started, I felt I was meeting an interesting character.

Later during the interview, I asked Ramesh Chauhan about his beret. He explained: 'I have what is called a permanent cold. This goes back many, many years and I have never been able to figure out whether it is a summer or winter, rain or sunshine thing. All I know is that I have this cold that makes me sneeze, sneeze and sneeze. So I have tried everything you could think of. I went to see an ENT specialist; he sent me for an MRI scan and they could not find anything. One day a yogi told me that if I kept my head covered I would not catch cold. He went on to explain that in every part of India, in summer and in winter and in rain and in sunshine, there are many people who keep their heads covered. It could, for example, be a turban like the Sikhs or it could be a Gujarat fellow who would just wrap something around his head. In any event I started wearing a beret and so far it has worked. But in my club, the Cricket Club of India, there is this old stupid British rule that you cannot wear a hat when you come into the club. I told them, "Listen, this air conditioning bothers me and I end up catching a cold." The club secretary was very kind and suggested that I get a doctor's certificate that I needed to wear a hat. This worked and I can now wear my beret. However, I took it a little further and asked them if I could wear a wig instead. As I had suspected, wigs were allowed because they are, of course, not hats. So I decided to wear a wig from a place that sells and rents Bollywood costumes. The only issue was that it was a lady's wig – so what, I was not embarrassed and it only proved to show how silly the original rule is.

'I know it may not sound it but I am a very loyal member of the Cricket Club of India. I go there every day to play tennis. I finish my working day between one and one thirty. Then I go home, which is just around the corner, have lunch, sleep for one hour and then go to the club and play one hour of tennis with my friends. I have been doing this for the past ten years.'

I asked Ramesh about the derivation of his family name. 'I don't know exactly as there are *Chauhans* in Uttar Pradesh, Haryana, Punjab, Rajasthan, Gujarat and even in Maharashtra, where they are called *Chavan*. But you need to know that the spelling of many family names in India depended upon how British and other missionaries wrote them down. Even if you say *Chauhan* he may spell it with a "v" or "au". It also depends on where one puts the stress in pronouncing a word. But there are other issues. For example, most Bengalis cannot pronounce "w" as they pronounce it as "b" just like the Arabs would. But as for *Chauhan*, it is difficult to say where the name comes from. In fact I have concocted a story that our family is descendant of the great Prithviraj Chauhan who was the ruler of northern India in the twelfth century.'

I asked Ramesh Chauhan how far back he could go with his immediate family. 'My grandfather's family came from a very poor village, from Pardi in the district of Valsad, in southern Gujarat adjacent to the infamous Dang district, one of the most backward districts in India. My grandfather migrated to Bombay where he became a master tailor. This meant he would no longer do the stitching himself but that he would do the designing and then hand it over to other tailors. He had five sons and my father was the youngest. He was determined that all his children should be educated.

'The Parle Products Manufacturing Company was started in 1929 by my third uncle, Narottam. He was a mechanically-oriented person so he started a manufacturing business and made what were called "hard boiled" sweets. The factory was in a little shed in the Vile Parle district of Bombay. Somehow my grandfather had an enormous vision as, when my uncle was looking for a shed of a particular area to start the factory, my grandfather counseled that he acquire a much bigger plot than he needed. I suppose at that time the price of land was very low as Vile Parle was basically a jungle. I think Bombay at that time ended at Mahim and even Bandra did not exist. There were two plots in consideration and fortunately they bought the right piece as the other ended up being part of the current airport.

'Ours was a joint family business and my grandfather moved to live in the factory compound so he could keep an eye on his sons' business. It was there in 1939 that the family decided to expand into biscuits and we started a biscuit factory. That was the origin of the "Parle G", which is now the world's largest-selling biscuit. Although it is no longer owned by our side of the family, I understand it sells over 13 billion biscuits a month.' When I told him that this quantity staggered me, he replied, 'But it was not easy as apparently soon after establishing the biscuit factory, the family was in serious financial trouble. We had over-stretched our finances and there were serious thoughts that we might have to wind up the business.

'My grandfather's response to this situation was that he told each of his sons that they were responsible to take care of their family and make sure that there was food on the table but there was no room for any luxuries. As I am told, it was work 24/7 in order that the business survived.

'Indians at that time had very different ideas of biscuits. Surat had its biscuit. The Punjab had its biscuit. Bengal had some other kind of biscuit, so everybody had a different concept of biscuit or its equivalent. The upshot was that only few people were buying our biscuits. I am sorry to say this, but fortunately, for us Second World War broke out. All the ships that used to come to India with English biscuits had to stop because U-boats were knocking British ships out of the sea and the priority was to bring soldiers, guns and ammunition to India. The question of biscuits being imported was simply out. And that is how we got a huge jump in demand for our product. There was not only that boost, but we also secured a contract to make biscuits for the British Indian Army. The business did not look back after that. I think somewhere in most people's lives there is something lucky which comes in and this was it for us.

'We were at that time living as the classical Indian joint family sharing a single kitchen. All the kids used to line up on the verandah and sit there on the floor with a plate in front of us and the cook would come and serve all the children. But soon, there were too many kids around and it was a hell of a job to stop after all of us getting into fights and all the usual trouble. So, we were packed off to different boarding schools. In 1949, I was sent to a boarding school at nine years of age. All the boys except two, I think, went off. My elder brother and my younger brother both went, as well as my sister. I often tell my daughter that she has had a difficult life because she has to make decisions. I had to make no decisions. I was just told that I was going to a boarding school and off I went. I think the reason I was sent to this particular school was that some friend asked my father why his son was studying in the local school and why did he not send me to the Maharaja's school, the Scindia School in Gwalior, which is actually situated within the famous Gwalior Fort. The idea of a school meant for maharajas boosted my father's ego and so I was packed off there.

'The train trip took about 24 hours from Bombay to Gwalior. The school would organize special carriages for us because there were enough students going from Bombay and other places to Gwalior. It was lots of fun and I remember I used to get off at the station and admire the engine – this huge engine making so much noise with steam coming out – boom, boom, boom – and I think this is where I developed an interest in mechanical engineering.

'Looking back I suppose it was tough at school but we never thought of it in that way, because we had not seen anything better. We had cold showers and a bugle would blow early in the morning for us to get up and get dressed. There was also a bugle for lights off. But there was no corporal punishment – unlike St Peter's School I had been to in Panchgani near Pune which was founded and run by the Cowley Fathers. There,' he says with a laugh, 'I still remember what it felt like after a caning when you really could not sit down.

'I was not a bright student in terms of grades – B and C grades – but I was always interested in concepts and ideas. Once I had my Senior Cambridge, I returned home to Bombay. I was hanging around with my friends and enjoying myself but one of my older brothers told my parents he was worried as he thought I was going astray and they needed to bring me back in line. So it was suggested that I do what he had done and go to Chauncy Hall School, a prep school in Boston, and follow it with the bachelor's degree from MIT.'

Ramesh went off to Boston in 1957 when he was sixteen. 'It was a tough flight in those days with propeller Lockheed Constellations. You had to go through Cairo and Rome to London. Then at London we got to break and then take that flight from London to Boston which goes to Shannon island, where there was the duty free shopping, and then to Gander Airport in Newfoundland and from there to Boston. When I reached Boston, my cousin who had also gone to Chauncy and MIT met me at the airport. He took me to Copley Square where the school was located. He told me: "There's your school." Remember I had been to the Scindia School located in the impressive Gwalior Fort. I pointed at one large building and asked, "Is that the school?" "No," he said, "that is the Boston Library." I then pointed to another and he again replied that it was not my school as it was the Sheraton hotel. Then I saw a little sign for Chauncy Hall School. It was tiny, consisting of a cafeteria in basement and four floors. There were only seven classrooms. All the students lived in one building within walking distance of the school. The facilities were pretty good as each of us had our own room although we shared bathrooms.

'For some reason MIT had a very high respect for Chauncy and would always take its top two students. American high school standards at that time were very low and the Senior Cambridge standard I had taken was of a very high standard – it was actually equivalent to the first year in university. It was too simple and I did not know what to do with myself. I used to play table tennis and do photography. It was actually more of a prep school to prepare those who were not native English speakers and those who needed to be brought up to speed quickly in things like calculus.

'I must have arrived at Chauncy around January, and I was told that the college entrance examination had to be taken almost straight away, and that I could not wait until I had finished Chauncy, because by then MIT would have started. So I took the exam in March. A senior Cambridge student did not have to worry much about that. Then they said that I had to take the exam for a second time just before I went to MIT so that I could show what I had learned from Chauncy by getting better marks. Actually, I did worse in the second exam than I had in the first. By this time the Chauhans were pretty well known at MIT. The foreign student advisor there had a very efficient card index system. He would pull out a hand-written card and there was the whole history of all the Chauhans who had come to MIT, when they came and what happened to them at MIT.

'I was at MIT for five years, from 1957 to 1962. First year students at MIT did not know what subject they would specialize in because they would cull 200 of the 1100 students at the end of the year. We all took business management in the first year and in the second year we could start choosing our preferred subjects. By the time the fourth year came I had enough credits for a mechanical engineering degree and my advisor told that if I spent one extra year, I could get a second bachelor's degree in mechanical engineering. I had been attracted to mechanical engineering since my fascination in travelling in the train to and from Gwalior and

Bombay. I experienced back then the feeling of power that comes from a giant machine and had wanted to become an engine driver. Some people want to become a fireman but I wanted to drive trains. There was actually someone in my class at MIT who said he wanted to be a garbage collector. I asked him what bloody kind of a dream that was and he just laughed. This guy, who was a Canadian Jew, really taught me about Western classical music. I have kept in contact with him ever since and I saw him on my last trip to the US.

'When I finished at MIT, I knew that I had an excellent family business to return to in India. There is one thing that I regret in my business life and that is I did not stay and work in the US as an employee. This would have enabled me to better understand the work culture and how to work as a subordinate. I have got many people working here in India for me but I have never been in their shoes.

'In 1961, the year before I returned to Bombay from the US, the joint family business was divided. My grandfather had passed away in 1954 and my eldest uncle had predeceased him. It was my father who wanted to divide the business because his other brothers did not want to invest any money outside Bombay; they only wanted to invest in things that were right under their noses. This led to a conflict as the family had also invested in the soft drinks business that my father ran. We had our own brand of carbonated soft drinks like Gold Spot, Limca, Thums Up and so on. My father believed, just like Coca Cola, factories in different parts of the country were necessary, as one could not operate the whole of India from one factory, whereas you could do so with the biscuit business. It was this difference of philosophy that caused the split. However, all this was done amicably without any legal hassles and so, the other part of the family kept the biscuits and my father got the soft drinks division.

'When I came back to Bombay in 1962, my elder brother took me to a plot of empty land and said, "Build a soft drinks' factory here for our soft drink business". Unfortunately, he did not live long to see how I managed in those difficult days. He passed away in 1963 in an airplane crash in which he was piloting his own plane. Believe it or not but my sister also died in an airplane crash; she was in the Air India flight to Dubai that crashed after take off from Bombay on 1 January 1978.

'At the time I started in the family soft drinks business my father was still very much there in charge. My older brother was looking after the factory at Vile Parle and from which we had to move out. This was why I had to build a new factory. It was pretty complicated as many of the machines were bought from different companies. And, as it was still the period of the "licence raj" when approvals were necessary for all imports, it was a very slow and convoluted process and particularly as soft drinks machines were not seen as a high priority. Before we got the licences to import, we built our own machines under a tree by copying the Second World War machines. Even today when we are only in the water business I have kept one of these original soft drinks' machines for sentimental reasons.

'During the "licence raj" we were able to start 60 bottling plants for our Gold Spot, Limca, Thums Up, Maaza and other drinks' businesses. These were located all over India and primarily used locally-made machines. This was no mean feat. During those days the government also tried to control production levels of manufacturers and producers like us. But they were not very successful and there was plenty of ways to get around the restrictions. For instance, our licence would say we could produce x number of bottles per year. We would meet with the relevant official and request, "This is not enough for us and you know we have already crossed our limit." In many cases we could persuade them to assist us. They would say something like, "All right. Treat that limit as applying to the production from one shift." In other words some government officials would look for ways out. But it was terrible to get approval to import spare parts for the machines. I remember we had to provide 25 copies of the list of spare parts we wanted to import. As there were no photocopying machines we had actually to sit there and cyclostyle the list. It was so bureaucratic. Even today, I do not think we have improved much. The amount of paper work involved, even in preparing the Minutes of a Board meeting, seems excessive. I wonder who actually reads all this stuff and where do they file it all. I do not think the amount of red tape has decreased much – just think how many places you need to sign if you want to open a bank account in India.'

I asked Ramesh whether he had an arranged marriage. 'No, because my parents had both passed away by the time I got married in 1978 when I was thirty-eight. My wife, Zainab, was a very close friend of my sister. They worked together in the Bombay office. My sister was basically working to pass the time and when I needed someone from head office to move to Delhi to handle a new plant we were starting it was clearly not going to be my sister, so I asked Zainab to go. This meant I came more and more in contact with her and one thing led to another and we got married.

'Though I married very late, it was not because I was a playboy. I was just working very hard all day every day and never had time for anything else. These 60 plants we had around the country were all franchises so I would meet with the franchisee owners for lunch, dinner and tea to discuss how to grow the business. And we had some really good brand names such as Limca, Gold Spot, Maaza and Thums Up. The last we introduced in 1977 after Coca-Cola pulled out of India rather than make a forced sale of 60 per cent of their equity to an Indian company.'

I asked Ramesh how he had got the ideas for a brand. 'Take the case of Maaza, which is a mango drink. A lot of people ask me how my education has helped me with things like this and I always say that I do not know. But I do know that there is some kind of logical thinking that occurs. We had somebody who wanted a franchise from us for Dubai. So we asked ourselves what do we need to do to succeed in Dubai. I sat back and thought that we have to do something different. There were colas, lemon-flavoured, orange- and ginger-flavoured drinks in the market. What the hell could we introduce in which was not there already? One day when we were still building the Dubai factory I saw the chaos of the little shacks being erected for the workers. And outside the shacks I noticed lots of tall thin cans which I found out were mango juice coming from Japan and Taiwan. From that it seemed to me that mango flavour must be quite popular in Dubai and I thought we should make a mango soft drink and that is how Maaza was born.

'As Maaza was intended for Dubai and not for India I went to my Bombay competitor, Mr. Pundole from Duke and Sons that made the very popular mango soft drink, Mangola and asked him to help me on the assurance that I would not produce and sell mango-based drinks in India. I even offered to put my promise in a binding legal document. But he refused to share anything and so we had to do all from scratch. And of course, there were lots of teething problems. Firstly, we found there were lots of black specks floating around. So I went to our chemists and asked them to remove the black specks. They told me these were natural, as part of the fruit and could not be filtered or removed. Also, as these were part of the pulp, removing them could affect the flavour. But we had to do something. So we tried what is called a "colloidal mill", which is used for paints, but the colloidel mill took too long. Then we decided we would try and homogenize it. Thankfully, with homogenizing at 3,500 psi, the black specks disappeared. I was pleased we finally had an answer. It was more than an answer because we found that the viscosity of the product also went up and this allowed us to reduce the mango pulp. This meant the soft drink became more economical to produce. Solving a problem can lead to indirect benefits if you are prepared to face a problem head on, rather than say, no, no, no, nothing can be done, forget it. And that Maaza became a premium soft drink in Dubai; all the other soft drinks sold for one dirham whereas ours sold one and a half dirham.

'We sold our soft drinks' brands to Coca-Cola in 1993. Coca-Cola had come back to India after the liberalization and free trade introduced by Dr Manmohan Singh in 1991. So Pepsi came first with very tough conditions. However, when Coke came there were no restrictions at all and our bottlers, who were independent bottlers and who owned their own plant, told us that we could take on Pepsi but it would be really tough for us to take on both Pepsi and Coke together. At that time they did not know or realize what popular and money-making brands Thums Up and Limca were, because this was just after liberalization when the fancy and flair for anything foreign was huge. Coke had a good reputation and all the bottlers wanted to join Coke rather than remain independent. This meant I had practically no choice but to agree to go as a package to Coca-Cola. However, Coke insisted on a condition that each of the 60 bottling plants had to agree or there was no deal. I told the Coke executives, "Listen if there is one moron, a small guy somewhere who wants to be tough and does not want to go with Coke, what can I do?" I was not a director or shareholder of those 60 independent bottling plants. Thankfully, Coke understood and the final deal was that I needed to convince to sell bottlers accounting for 80 to 90 per cent of the existing business, including a few specified larger bottlers.

'The sale to Coke was a big deal, but it was heartbreaking. There goes the "baby" that you have nurtured and grown over so many years. I was literally crying at the final meeting to complete the deal. I was fifty-three years old and wondered what I would do next.

'Our two plants in Mumbai and Delhi became Coke franchises and we also kept the Thums Up and Limca brands. But within a few years we sold these businesses too but kept the real estate. One of the few brands we had left, lying around so to speak, was the Bisleri brand of mineral water that we had bought from its Italian owners in 1967.'

After the Coke sale in 1997, Ramesh and his younger brother also split. 'To put this quite simply, he has three daughters and I have one. In my brother's and my opinion there is the potential for these daughters to destroy the business. As soon as four sons-in-law come into the business, God knows what would happen. Fortunately, the business was easy to split. God has indeed been good to us. We have been very lucky but we have worked hard and got good results.' I asked him what benefits did he get from this final split. 'What I cherish most is the peace of mind, money after a while makes no difference.'

Since the split with his brother in 1997, Ramesh Chauhan has successfully concentrated on building up the Bisleri brand. 'We have made many mistakes and lots of people have let me down and I would say that a major weakness of mine is that I cannot gauge people. What they say or what they pretend often fools me; I consider this is a serious weakness of mine. The point is that if someone is working for me and I do not trust him, then what do I do. It is a matter of practicality; the moment you have to sit around judging your worker's motives and think about who may be trying to play a fast one on you I find this too much. I did four courses in psychology at university – I took one in abnormal psychology that covered the behaviour of rats where the Russian chap was training the rats to do good things to get a reward. It is nice to read these theories in books but, you know, when it comes to it, I like people. I enjoy spending time with people and am in the fortunate position, I do not want or need anything from anybody. That makes life easy. If somebody wants something from me, I tell them, "Whatever you want to say, please say it simply; otherwise forget it."'

All these experiences have led to Ramesh having certain philosophies. 'You know that I have a formula in India that the thickness of a company's files are inversely proportional to the sales of the company. The CEO who has the smallest sales usually has the thickest files and the CEO who has the largest sales may have no files at all. And another of my theories is that those CEOs with the biggest files will have the largest number of complaints – I tell these CEOs to stop spending time writing responses to the complaints and just concentrate on running their businesses.'

Meanwhile, the old Parle soft drinks brands, which were sold to Coke in 1993, survive and flourish at Coca-Cola India. No doubt Ramesh is proud as he looks as his 'babies' grow on the Coca-Cola India website – Limca has remained unchallenged as the No. 1 sparkling drink in its segment in the market; Maaza has gone from strength to strength and is in number one in the juice market. And as a further reminder, Thums Up is the largest-selling soft drink brand in India.

And whilst he might shed a tear or two, after all these years I can't see him doing any more than that. Ramesh loves what life throws up and his quirky view on it makes life interesting and fun for those around him.

---

[1] Bisleri (www.bisleri.com) is one of the leaders of branded bottled water in India. So well known is the brand that sometimes Indians incorrectly refer to 'bottled water' in general as Bisleri.

> I see that the younger generation in India, whether in my family or elsewhere, has tremendous ideas. They are entrepreneurial and passionate. I believe we will see them do a much better job than my generation.

ADI GODREJ
Chairman, Godrej Group[1]

I met Adi Godrej in his office in the sprawling Vikhroli complex that houses the head office of the Godrej Group. As the Chairman of one of India's oldest and largest groups some readers might expect Adi's office to be palatial. But that is certainly not the case; it is not the culture of the family or the company and as the interview progressed I could see it is certainly not in the character of the man himself.

I started the interview by remarking on my surprise at seeing the size of the Vikhroli complex given the cost of land in Mumbai. 'Yes, it is large. My grandfather is actually responsible for acquiring it. He bought 3500 acres in the middle of the Second World War. At that time Vikhroli was beyond the municipal limits of Bombay. But since then Bombay has expanded and now stretches far beyond, so we are fortunate to now have a large and valuable piece of land.'

I asked Adi to go back towards the beginning of the known history of his family. 'Much of this is recorded in two volumes on the family written by B.K. Karanjia, titled *A Hundred Years*.[2] Of course this is the modern history of my family as it starts with the life of my grandfather's elder brother, Ardeshir who founded what we know as Godrej Group today. But as a Parsi[3] family if we go back much further we will find our family's antecedents in modern-day Iran, or Persia as it was then. Ardeshir, who was born in 1868, like many Parsis up to today, trained as a lawyer. Fresh from law school he was given a brief in 1894 by a firm of Bombay solicitors to go to Zanzibar to argue a case for their client. The case was going well until Ardeshir discovered that he would need to lie or, more charitably, manipulate the truth to present his client's case. He refused to do this and no amount of persuasion by the solicitors or the client could convince him to change his principled stance. Perhaps if the solicitors had known that Ardeshir's principles were so high and inflexible that he had refused to share an inheritance, preferring it to be shared by his brothers and sisters, they would not have given him the brief in the first place. And so he returned to Bombay knowing he had probably destroyed his legal career before it had really started, but proud he had stood on principle.

'At the time Ardeshir was fighting his case, another young Indian lawyer, Mohandas Karamchand Gandhi, yes, the same Mahatma Gandhi, was fighting a case for the rights of Indians in South Africa. Gandhi and Ardeshir met when they were both back in Bombay. Both were principled young men but had different views on how India should gain independence from the British; Gandhi decided to wage a political campaign whereas Ardeshir's view was that India needed to first become economically self reliant.

'These discussions undoubtedly influenced Ardeshir to try his hand at commerce rather than continuing with his legal career. His first attempt was to try and make surgical instruments. He approached Merwanji Cama, a philanthropic Parsi businessman who happily advanced Ardeshir the necessary funds. Apparently, the instruments he designed and had made were of equal quality to the British imported instruments but Ardeshir quickly learnt that without a "Made in England" stamp on the instruments the medical fraternity would never trust his Indian-made instruments. He was obviously disappointed but it made him even more determined to prove that Indians could make most of what was needed in India. Old Mr. Cama was also not concerned and continued to back Ardeshir into his next venture which was lock making. Why he chose this we do not know but as we know he loved tinkering with mechanical things; it is quite likely he played with locks.

'And the business he built out of making locks was the real founding of Godrej Group. The official start date was 7 May 1897 in a tiny shed beside the Bombay Gas Works. Ardeshir believed, correctly as it turned out, that the market would be less fussy about Indian-made locks than medical instruments and particularly as he changed the design to make them more appropriate to Indian circumstances and, of course, they were much cheaper than the imported versions. Of Ardeshir's three brothers and two sisters, only my grandfather, Pirojsha joined him in the business as an employee. Pirojsha had studied engineering at the Victoria Jubilee Institute so it was probably most logical that he did so, whereas his two older brothers, Hormusji and Munchersha were not interested. The locks business became known as Godrej and Boyce (Boyce being a nephew of Mr Cama).

'From locks Ardeshir logically expanded into manufacturing safes and onto, less logically, soap which again proved to be a success. That business became known as Godrej Soaps. Ardeshir was never content with succeeding at one thing and constantly sought more challenges in diverse areas such as inks, toffees, perfume making, biscuits and even vineyards. Many of these ventures did not succeed during his lifetime but those that did made a mark.

'Actually despite his commercial success Ardeshir's private life was less successful. Not long after he married his young teenage wife, Bachubai in 1891, she died in tragic circumstances. She had gone with a cousin to climb to the top of Rajabai Tower for its view of the city. It is said that a thief approached and terrified them so much that the two jumped to their deaths. He never married again. Also, for all his own principled life he was a poor judge of men and many people took advantage of him.

'Despite the wealth he accumulated he continued to live a very simple life taking public transport to and from the office and only towards the end of his life my grandfather Pirojsha was able to convince him to use a car. And it fell to his son, being my uncle

Sohrab, to take care of him and ensure he was well cared for. My grandfather and Ardeshir's personalities complimented each other; Ardeshir was an introvert whereas my grandfather was much more of an extrovert. However, they had many disagreements and the story is that sometimes my grandfather did not come to the office until Ardeshir had left.

'Ardeshir died at the age of sixty-eight in 1936 by which time my grandfather was fifty-four. Ardeshir left his interest in the business to a charity – which Parsis often did. My grandfather, Pirojsha had made some money on the side in the stock market and used those funds to buy back the business from the charity. I think it is fair to say my grandfather was responsible for consolidating all of the successful businesses that Ardeshir had created and, in many cases, developing new lines or products within those businesses. Some have described him as "hard headed and practical" and there is general agreement that he continued the ethical practices of his brother, including making sure all taxes were paid. He was obsessive about quality and customer needs, which continues to be one of our group's values. My grandfather did not have the same inventive brilliance of Ardeshir but he did a superb job in creating and valuing teamwork and cohesiveness in the business. In fact, many of his labour policies were far ahead of their time in instituting policies such as providing for work place security in exchange for more leisure time for workers and greater productivity.

'My mother, Jai was very well educated and an intellectual and her own mother, my grandmother, was one of the first female graduates of a university in India. My mother had been a teacher when she married my father and continued to do it a little after she married and much later became involved in teaching at one of our schools. But she stopped while she was bringing up my younger brother and me. In fact she applied a lot of her ideas on my brother and me. For example, it was very typical in those days for reasonably affluent families to have a maid to take care of the children up to almost teenage years. She thought that would stunt my independence and learning process and so removed my maid when I was only four or five. Secondly, she encouraged me to go out into the streets on my own at a very young age; probably the age when she removed my maid. Of course the traffic was nowhere as bad as it is today but she taught me how to cross the road, how to walk on my own, and she delineated the parts of the streets near my house where I could go by myself. Of course she put very clear limits on where I could go but I remember there was a big garden near our home – it was maybe half a kilometer away – and that was within my range. Fortunately, in those days, there were no fears of kidnapping or anything of that sort.

'As I became older the responsibility she put on me increased. When I was only ten, I was entrusted with the responsibility of managing my own budget. I was given 75 rupees. From this I had to pay my school fee that was 11 rupees per month and manage all my other expenses such as my tuck shop lunches. And she certainly made sure we were not treated differently to other children at my primary school. I can remember our school uniforms came in two qualities; my mother made sure we only wore the cheaper one. She too always dressed very simply in a white khadder sari, which she even wore for her wedding. She strongly believed in excellence over elitism. I am a person today who is very self-dependent and self-sufficient in many ways, and I think I attribute that a little to learning these things from my mother.

'From my father I learnt about business and his interest in many different areas such as geography and history. Sunday lunches at home were always fascinating for me and particularly when the topic strayed into a discussion of such interesting subjects. My father was responsible for the soap business which I knew was going through a difficult time but he never showed it and I could sense the thoroughness with which he approached problems like this in seeking a solution. Other than my parents there were two more people who shaped me to be the person I am today. One is my uncle Naval and the other is my uncle Nari Dastur, who was my mother's younger brother.

'Naval was forty-six when I joined the family business but we worked closely together for many years. From him I learnt the importance of the group concept, the criticality of finance and the ability to take quick decisions. He taught me that I should try and become a reasonable expert in all areas of the business and to listen to professionals very carefully.

'My uncle Nari eventually retired as the Commercial Director of Air India but, early in his career, when I was only around ten, he was running Air India's office in Geneva. At that time my aunt and he were having their first child, so my maternal grandparents went to stay with them and took me along for almost two months. It was a wonderful experience for a ten-year-old Indian boy to be exposed to a completely different environment and it had a lasting impression on me. From Nari I learnt the importance of style and communication. He had a wonderful way with people and I learnt my lessons on leadership from him.

'I went to three different schools in India. First, I was in a nursery school. Then, I was in a girls' school where they took boys in the primary years. I must have been good at my schoolwork as I entered St. Xavier's High School at the age of seven and graduated at the age of fifteen. Most of the time I was in the top ten but in my last year I was first out of about two-hundred students. In our school we also had what is known as the Ripon Prize which was given to the student who they considered the best all rounder. I was awarded this and, given I was so much younger than everyone else, it was one of the proudest moments in my life. Despite the fact it was no doubt an unusual childhood it was one that was very happy and fulfilling.

'After school, I wanted to study in the United States. But, at fifteen, I was too young to get into a university there. So I went for two years to St. Xavier's College, which was part of Bombay University and was right next door to St. Xavier's School. There I embarked on a two-year course called 'inter science' at which point you are half way to gaining a Bachelor of Science degree. But after the two years, in 1959, I was old enough and had the grades to get into the Massachusetts Institute of Technology [MIT]. In fact, my father was a little disappointed that I decided to study in America as he would have liked me to follow in his footsteps and have studied in Germany, which he had done between the two world wars.

'I was very clear at that point that I wanted to study science and engineering so I registered as an undergraduate in mechanical engineering. But at MIT I got my first serious exposure to the humanities such as philosophy and economics, which were mandatory subjects. The only humanities I had studied in India were literature and history and I found this new learning fascinating. But, whilst I enjoyed these subjects tremendously, I knew in my heart I was of a scientific temper. And within six months of my being at MIT I saw an option, other than a straight mechanical engineering degree, which I thought might be more useful to me in my career and differentiate me from others. This option was to study management at the Sloan School of Management with a minor in engineering. At that time Sloan at MIT along with Wharton at the University of Pennsylvania were two of only a few leading US universities that had undergraduate courses in management. Otherwise management courses in most universities tendered to be postgraduate. In 1963, at the age of twenty-one, I graduated from Sloan with a bachelor's and master's of Science degree that combined a major in management and minor in engineering. It was the perfect combination for me as I realized that, when I came into the family business, I might not need to be involved with engineering matters in great detail. But if I could bring Western management thought processes, it could have a tremendously positive effect on the business as these were tried and true concepts in the developed economies and at least some of which might prove very useful in our businesses.'

I asked Adi whether he had lived in digs or dorms whilst at MIT. 'That is an interesting story. When I got to MIT, of course for the first few days, I spent them in a dorm. But I quickly discovered that a lot of undergraduates lived in fraternities. There was an Indian whom I had vaguely known back in India called Vijay Shah, who was one year senior to me at MIT, and he was already in this fraternity called Pi Lambda Phi. So, I met up with him and he invited me to his fraternity during what is called "rush" week. During this you meet all the different fraternities and then you and the fraternities decide which you would like to join and which would like you to join. As it happens his fraternity offered me a place and that is where I happily stayed during my time at MIT. It enabled me to develop a number of close friendships rather than having many less close relationships if I had stayed in a dorm where the people are constantly changing. In those days many fraternities were delineated, not legally, but on religious lines. Mine was mainly a Jewish fraternity and that also exposed me to a very new culture. Jewish Americans tended to be at the cutting edge of a lot of things that were happening in the US at that time so that helped me to better understand America. What was also interesting is that there were two African-Americans in my fraternity, one in my year and one in Vijay's year. In fact, the African-American in his year, Mike Evans, was ultimately elected the president of our fraternity. This impressed me. He was a very bright fellow.'

These comments led me to suggest from what Adi had already told me that he was quite a shy person. Adi replied, 'Well, different people might give you a different view on that. However, you are correct and I would generally assess myself as an introvert. But I am not shy of new things or new experiences. Whilst I may not be extremely gregarious – it is my wife, Parmeshwar who exactly fits that description. We are in many ways "polar opposites" but our differences compliment each other.'

I asked Adi whether he had felt any pressure to join the family business, 'No, I don't think there was any pressure of any sort. I had always envisaged a business career and I was always interested in the family business. When I was a child, in my spare time and in vacations, I would go with my father, in those days when the factory and the offices were alongside each other, as we have even now. And so I would visit the factories, I would visit the chemical laboratories, I would visit the offices, and hang around. So I was eager to come back to the family business and, looking back, have absolutely no regrets with that decision.

'As soon as I started in the family business I could see my idea to study management was the right one as the Group was really at a point where it needed to modernize its management processes. At that time my uncle Naval was running Godrej & Boyce, the locks and safes business, whereas my father was running Godrej Soaps that was much smaller. The total turnover of the whole group was only twenty million dollars of which 80 per cent would have been the locks, safe and allied business. At first I spent time in both companies but then moved full time into Godrej Soaps. I have to admit I really did not start off at the bottom but spent my time learning how the business was run. The business was actually losing money when I joined. My father, Burjor who had studied technology in Germany was almost totally focused on research and technology and developing more and better soaps but was disinterested in the business of selling the soaps. My eldest uncle Sohrab was responsible for sales and marketing and was more interested in ensuring all was in order with the government whose licence support was vital to the business. When I joined, I started using my management education to see how I could introduce financial and cost reporting systems, how I could control things, how I could expand sales and I went deeply into looking at how we were handling marketing. My grandfather Pirojsha who had built the soap business started to put huge pressure on my father and uncle to take steps to turn the business around. Having spent a few months looking at the business I was reasonably confident if I could implement significant financial, management and sales system changes we could make the business profitable again. But I knew if I proposed that I be given the mandate to do this there would be some resistance from the family. So, I approached my uncle Sohrab and persuaded him to let me make all these changes but in his name, so he would receive the kudos if it worked. Sohrab was really not interested in the day-to-day business, which he saw as boring and was delighted to delegate all the hard work over to me. To his credit he gave me a completely free hand. Within a year the company was back to making profits. My grandfather was happy, my father was happy, uncle Sohrab was happy and I was happy. From that point on I did not seek to take either my father or uncle's role and was happy to continue to play a role "behind the scenes" as it were. For example, if there was a directive to be made by my uncle, I drafted it for him and then implemented it on his behalf. As soon it was clear that the company was going to return to profitability I was invited in 1964 to join the Board of Godrej Soaps but not of Godrej & Boyce.

'Whilst I understood that formal management training made a lot of sense, within a couple of years many people in India recognized this too. It was the start of the creation of the Indian Institutes of Management [IIM]. Their graduates were some of the first people I recruited because I knew we needed top-notch professionals. Later, many of them ended up running our businesses.

'My uncle Naval, who was running Godrej & Boyce, ran things very differently to the way my father and uncle Sohrab had ran the soap business. He was open to new ideas and I developed a very good working relationship with him. I think he saw I could bring advantages and he sought my help in that company too. Initially it was politic that I had more of an advisory role. The family has a habit – in fact we still do and we will do it today – that, every Thursday, family members involved in the business meet for lunch and exchange notes and ideas, check what the progress is of different things and so on. That is where Naval and I would chat. Other times he would ring me up and ask me to pop over to meet him and discuss some issue or the other. As he was also on the Godrej Soaps

Board he was aware of the changes I had introduced under the name of his eldest brother. In 1972, when my grandfather Pirojsha passed away at the age of ninety, I was invited to join the Godrej & Boyce board. Up until he passed away, he had been the chairman of both the companies and responsible for their growth over many years and so his sons, being my uncles and father, had such enormous paternal and business respect for him, getting him to agree when he was in his 80s to make really significant changes to the way the businesses were run would have been extremely difficult.'

I asked Adi Godrej how he came to be married. 'When I came back to India I started dating girls, which was not very common in India at that time although it was of course a regular part of my life and that of my fellow students at MIT. But some girls from more modern families were allowed to date and especially in groups and this is how I met Parmeshwar. One of my school friends from St. Xavier's was a good friend of a boy who was at school with my wife's brother. My wife's parents, who were a little strict about where their two daughters could go, trusted this boy and he would invite them to parties or we would go out in a group. And this is how I met her. There was nothing between us for at least six months and then suddenly something blossomed and we started dating. We had to be careful because her parents did not want her to be obviously dating somebody. She was studying at the J.J. School of Arts at Bombay University. A neighbour of her parents was a commercial director of Air India and he suggested to Parmeshwar that she should join the airline as an air stewardess. Most of her friends whose opinion she sought, including some potential suitors, did not encourage her at all. But when she asked me, I told her that it would be a great learning experience to travel all over the world, and I encouraged her to join. So she did. Soon she was used as a model for Air India advertising and, being extremely attractive, became in demand for other modeling assignments. But after about ten months we decided to get married and she resigned. We were married in 1966. I was twenty-four and she was twenty-one.

'My parents didn't have a problem with me marrying a non-Parsi but I don't think my eldest uncle was very happy. I think he tried to create some problems because of my decision. He started telling some of the family members that they shouldn't go to the wedding but ultimately everybody came. I didn't pay much attention to it and eventually it resolved itself and I had no problems with my uncle regarding this. As you know the Parsis are such a small community there is a genuine fear that eventually we will disappear and it was this that would have been my uncle's main concern. There were potential problems also with my wife's parents. But I think once they got to know me they were comfortable. And her brother also by that time I knew quite well, so he was a good support. So there was some resistance, but not very substantial, and thus nothing I had to fight very hard against. My cousin Smita, the daughter of my uncle Naval who is nine years younger than me, also married a non-Parsi. As I had broken the path for her, there were even fewer issues for her.

'When we decided to get married I bought an apartment "off the plan" and which wasn't ready until a year after we were married. Until then we lived with my parents. The apartment was in the first tall building built in India. As a school friend of mine was developing it and I liked the idea, I felt safe buying it before it was ready. And that is where we lived when our eldest daughter, Tanya, was born in 1968, two years after we were married. After Tanya we had another daughter, Nisa, but she is nine years younger and then we had a son, Pirojsha, who is twelve years younger than Tanya. So, Tanya, like me, is by far the eldest in her generation. In my generation, it was nearly ten years before my cousin Jamshyd joined the business after me. He is seven years younger than me and he joined Godrej & Boyce, which was run by his father, Naval. My brother Nadir, who is nine years younger than me, joined Godrej Soaps some years later.

'The businesses have kept expanding quite well over the years, even during the socialist times when growth in India was low we were able to expand quite well. We were a private company throughout, so clearly we were expanding only through the generation of money in the business. Many other family groups like the Tatas and the Mahindras had already listed their businesses. We were a long way behind them and only took our first company public in 1993. Until 1991, India had been in the grips of the socialist "licence raj" and there had been price controls that seriously affected the real value of what we had built. There was also the Monopolies and Trade Practices Act which restricted expansion if the business turned over more than the Rs 200 million, which clearly affected our businesses. They would only give permission in these circumstances to build a factory in some backward area that was totally uneconomic. But after the economy opened in 1991 we wondered whether we would be competitive when international companies entered.

'As a result of these concerns, in 1992 I started meeting with Procter & Gamble and we formed a joint venture company around the end of 1992. Once we formed the joint venture we took Godrej Soaps public, as we believed we needed funding for growth. The joint venture with Procter & Gamble was mainly in the soap area and did reasonably well and we had common distribution. But they then decided soap was not to be a focus area for them long term, so they suggested we separate, which we did. As it happens we made good money both going into the joint venture and also coming out of it. With the money we made from their exit in 1994 we bought a very interesting business called Transelektra Domestic Products that was a leader in a fledgeling business for mosquito repellants. Having bought the business I went around the world looking for potential partners. I met people like S.C. Johnson, Clorox and Sara Lee Corporation. In the end in 1995 we did a deal with Sara Lee in which we sold them 51 per cent of Transelektra for around the price we had paid for the 100 per cent. A couple of years ago Sara Lee decided to withdraw and we bought their share and re-branded the company as Godrej Household Products.'

I asked Adi whether at the time of the Sara Lee joint venture he was already managing director of Godrej Soaps. 'For many, many years, my designation used to be director. I became a director in 1964 and I remained a director until my father passed away in 1994, which was around the time the Sara Lee joint venture was formed. As I mentioned earlier, titles have actually not meant much in our Group and my children often tease me about it. My response is to tell them not to mistake *de facto* with *de jure*.

'Although you probably do not know, but our drive to have an international presence began as far back as 1965 when Naval started a business manufacturing furniture in Malaysia for Godrej and Boyce and that made us the first Indian group to set up a manufacturing venture outside India. But there were also great limitations. We could not invest money because we were not allowed to take money out of India. The only equity we could provide for the company was machinery made in India. So it was a very complicated process. Forty-five plus years later, we now have manufacturing operations in over twenty countries. For instance, in Indonesia we have a very large operation in FMCG and that competes with international giants like Unilever, SC Johnson and Reckitt-Benckiser. In fact, our per capita sales of FMCG products in Indonesia are higher than in India. In the last couple of years we have also bought a company in Africa that manufactures in fourteen sub-Saharan countries. I expect in the coming years we will continue to acquire businesses internationally. Approximately 30 per cent of our global turnover now comes from outside India and which, of course, includes exports from India.'

Just as Adi Godrej has overseen the overall running of the Godrej Group for over twenty-five years, he has also been intimately involved in restructuring the family ownership in Godrej. 'We had confiscatory taxes in the 60s, 70s, and 80s in this country. At one stage we had a serious problem when the maximum marginal rate of income tax was in the order of 92 per cent and there was a wealth tax of 8 per cent on your net wealth. That's one of the reasons why we were better off remaining private, because if you were private, you paid your wealth tax on around 80 per cent of the net worth of the company. On the other hand, if you were listed, you paid the wealth tax on the listed value of the company that usually tended to be much higher. So remaining private helped us, but it meant that access to funds was more difficult. But, when the tax regime became so confiscatory and totally unreasonable, I came up with an idea. The family owned both Godrej Soaps and Godrej & Boyce. So I said let's gradually over three years sell the shares of Godrej Soaps to Godrej & Boyce, so that it became a subsidiary over a period of time. That way the corporate funds could go to the family to pay those confiscatory taxes and yet retain control. The family accepted this and it is how we were able to retain control. In addition, I also suggested to my elders that in order to minimize estate duty we should skip shareholdings between generations and thus avoid the duty payable if the shares passed generation to generation. This was also accepted and most of my grandfather's shares were transferred in exactly equal proportions to the five people in my generation. This principle continues until today, although in my case I have already transferred a lot of my shares to the next generation.

'Nowadays I don't get much into day-to-day management. In the first place, we usually have non-family professionals heading most of the businesses. From time to time, we make exceptions where a family member heads a business mainly to learn and acquire experience. Secondly, my children are now very much in the business. So, they take a lot of the responsibility that previously sat with me. I still am quite active at the board level and in strategy and major decision-making.' When I remarked that there did not seem to be the same tendency for generational separations in Parsi families that one finds in Marwari businesses, he responded, 'I think one of the reasons is that family numbers in Parsi families tend to be low and there is enough for them to do. And I think that, so long as the older generation is appreciative of the good ideas and passion of the younger generation, then it works well. If you start thinking only I am right and they are wrong, then that is likely to lead to a lot of tension. I see that the younger generation in India, whether in my family or elsewhere, has tremendous ideas. They are entrepreneurial and passionate. I believe we will see them do a much better job than my generation.'

With this it was time to bring the meeting to a close. Reflecting on my meeting I found Adi not only to be a gentleman and an upholder of the Parsi principles of 'good thoughts, good words and good deeds' but someone who has managed his career with practical humility within the complexity of a significant Indian family business.

---

[1] Godrej Group (www.godrej.com) was established in 1897. Its founder, Ardeshir Godrej, lawyer-turned-locksmith, was a persistent inventor and a strong visionary. His inventions, manufactured by his brother, Pirojsha Godrej, were the foundation of today's Godrej which has seven major companies with interests in real estate, FMCG, industrial engineering, appliances, furniture, security and agri care. The group's turnover was over USD 4 billion as in March 2013. 26 per cent of its business is done outside India in more than 60 countries.

[2] B.K. Karanjia, *Godrej A Hundred Years 1897-1997 Volume 1 'Life's flag is never furled' and Volume 2 'The Builder also grows'* Penguin 1997.

[3] The Parsis represent a very small minority of the Indian population, most likely less than 100,000 in a total population of over 1 billion. In fact, there are probably no more than 200,000 Parsis worldwide although it is extremely difficult to be precise. The Parsis fled religious persecution between the eighth and tenth century AD in modern-day Iran (or Persia as it then was) and settled mainly in the western Indian states of Maharashtra and Gujarat. The reason they fled was that the Parsis are by faith Zoroastrian and the Arabs who conquered Persia in the middle of the sixth century AD were Muslim and sought to convert everyone to Islam. At the time the Arabs conquered Persia the major religion was Zoroastrian.

The Zoroastrian religion was founded by the Prophet Zoroaster (or Zarathustra) in Iran approximately 3500 years ago. Zoroastrianism contains both monotheistic and dualistic features. Its concepts of one God, judgement, heaven and hell likely influenced the major Western religions of Judaism, Christianity, and Islam. If one were to sum up the principles of the Parsi way of life it would be 'good thoughts, good words and good deeds'.

In my experience the Parsis are extremely well respected by all throughout India and have excelled particularly in the arts, business, and the humanities. Examples would of course include Adi Godrej the subject of this chapter but also other industrialist families such as the Tatas and Wadias. Other prominent Parsis from different walks of life include the singer Freddie Mercury, the conductor Zubin Mehta, the author Rohinton Mistry and any number of famous lawyers and judges including Nani Palkhivala.

" I think Marwaris have a very good sense of commerce. We instinctively understand business as most of us grow up in a business family environment where it is talked about from an early age. You adapt to it much easier than to anything else. "

SANJIV GOENKA
Chairman, RP-Sanjiv Goenka Group[1]

I met Sanjiv Goenka in his office in Calcutta and started by asking him a little about his childhood. 'I was born in January 1961 into a Marwari joint family where the household consisted of my parents and my father's two younger brothers and their wives and children. There were eight cousins of my generation so we were a large joint family all living in one house.

'It was a very regimented upbringing for the eight children and our daily routine was pretty much set out and you did not have the liberty to deviate from it. Even a boarding school would have offered us more liberties than we actually had. There was the equivalent of a governess who would wake us up at 6 every morning. We had to get up immediately and brush our teeth before having our breakfast. At 6:30 sharp we reported to our study tables until 8 when we showered before leaving home at 8.30 for school, which started at 9.30. So we sat at the tables – whether we studied or not was a different matter – but we did have to sit at our tables and there was no getting away from that. All the boys studied in one room and all the girls studied in another room.

'It was pretty much the same schedule every day. School was over at 3:30 and we came home at about 4 and everyone was given afternoon tea and a snack. Actually it was milk, and our snack consisted of no more than two slices of bread. It was then free time. We had a large lawn at the back of our bungalow so we all went down and played. The boys and girls all played together, whether it was cricket, soccer, hockey, or badminton. But at 6 pm our tutor showed up and then we had to study until 7:30. At 7:30 we had a bath or showered so that we were ready to report for dinner at 8. Dinner was over by 8:30 and by 8:45 we were expected to be in bed. Lights out was at 9 – with all the boys in one room and all the girls in another room.'

I remarked that this seemed an amazing regimented existence and wondered looking back what Sanjiv thought. 'We were very happy because we did not know any better or different. It was actually even more regimented as we were not allowed to go out to the homes of friends from school and they were not encouraged to come to our home. There is absolutely no doubt we grew up very sheltered – sheltered from what I do not know but we were indeed sheltered.

'Our environment was one of routine without any discretion. My uncle Gouri, who was the youngest of the three brothers of my father's generation was in charge of us. He was the designated authority for the children so our academic monitoring was done by him; my parents had no idea how we were doing. So, it was a very unusual childhood. In our family if you spoke, if you spent time with your own child, it was considered selfish. We could spend time with our uncles, we could spend time with our aunts, but we could not spend time with our own parents – it was very weird, but that is the way it was.

'Our upbringing was not only regimented but very strict on discipline. The enforcer was the guardian – I do not know exactly how one should term him but he was the male equivalent of a governess – and he was harsh. So that part of childhood was not very joyous but, on the other hand, there was the fact we all grew up together in the same boat. The guardian lectured us that we had to share and that we had to make sacrifices. He lectured us that everything we wanted would not be achieved and that there were views other than our own. So we learnt to accept the differences among ourselves and others. So, I think there were some pluses – it would have been nice to have had the pluses without having the minuses; but that is the way it was. And the guardian was quite rough with us but it was something we had to put up with. I could not, for instance, go and complain to my mother. But she had to play cards every day with my uncle Jagdish, who is my father's second brother and with friends. They used to start around 3 every afternoon and continue until they went to bed. So, she never really had the time for her children and, sad to say, nor did I spend any quality time with my father while I was growing up.

'Whilst I could not spend time with my father, I could with my grandfather, Keshav Prasad Goenka [known by many as "KP"]. He spent a lot of time with all of the grandchildren and we sometimes used him to get liberties from our tutor and guardians. KP was much more than a grandfather, he was also a mentor and I became very close to him. He was the oldest of that generation and therefore technically the head of the family – if he said something, nobody questioned it. In terms of personality he was a very forthright, straight individual. I have to say he was not only firm but very loving – not with demonstrative affection – but was extremely concerned and considerate and was always there when you needed him.'

But, however close he was to Sanjiv, his grandfather still treated him and the other seven in his generation as sheltered and secluded children – not encouraged to mix with the outside world. 'We almost did not know how to greet somebody socially. However, my grandfather entertained a great deal – he either entertained in our garden or the courtyard or both depending upon the size of the crowd. But we were not allowed to mix with the guests so we knew few social graces.'

At school, none of Sanjiv's friends had as regimented a system as he did. But there were attempts to get around the system, little rebellions. 'We used to be given very little pocket money and so frankly what we would do was try to get a little more – it was not a very acceptable thing that we did, but we did it nevertheless. There was something called a poor box and we were given an amount every week to give to the poor. We would put 50 per cent of that amount into the box and keep the rest to have an ice cream or a snack at the school which, needless to say, we were not allowed to do. And then I think we started slowly taking initiatives on our own, which initially my uncle Gouri did not fully understand before it was too late. For example, we started saying that we had to stay on in school longer and that we were going to our friends' home for sports.'

Sanjiv went on to explain that the large joint family into which he was brought up could actually have been larger as, when he was two years old, his grandfather had separated his businesses from Sanjiv's great uncles' businesses. The joint family was again to split in 1979 when Sanjiv was eighteen as his grandfather divided the inherited and acquired family businesses between Sanjiv's father, Rama Prasad (but known by everybody as "RP") and his two uncles. And most recently in 2010, RP divided his businesses between Sanjiv and his older brother Harsh – Harsh retained the RPG Group name and Sanjiv formed the RP-Sanjiv Goenka Group.

The Goenka family business history goes back way before even Sanjiv's grandfather. The 'modern' part of the family history starts in 1820 with Sanjiv's great-grandfather's great-grandfather, Ramdutt Goenka, joining other Marwaris in the Burra Bazaar area of Calcutta, having made the long journey from the Marwari homeland in Rajasthan in the days before trains when it would take over a month to travel by road and then by river. Settled in Calcutta, Ramdutt managed to become a cashier at the British East India Company.

After working with the East India Company for some time he left and established himself as a trading broker forming the first Goenka firm, 'Ramdutt Ramkissendas' named after his son and himself. Ramdutt's grandson Ramchandra joined the family firm that, by the turn of the twentieth century, had expanded into jute and tea trading. By that time, Badridas, the second son of Ramchandra had been born. In 1905, Badridas became the first Marwari to graduate from Presidency College, Calcutta University – there had been a Marwari superstition that if you graduated you would die prematurely.

Each of Badridas and his elder brother was in due course knighted by the British for their services to business. In these pre-independence days Sir Badridas and his brother did not seek to establish their own group by owning business. Instead they continued in the grandfather's tradition of acting as 'banians' or agents of British firms and, later, associated with Duncan Brothers, one of the largest British managing agency firms with extensive interests in tea and jute. Sir Badridas was also very active in public life and became, amongst other roles, the first Indian chairman of the then Imperial Bank of India (now State Bank of India). Sir Badridas was still alive when Sanjiv was a small boy and, in fact, it was in his former room in the Alipore home where Sanjiv grew up.

It was the next generation, which included Sanjiv Goenka's grandfather, KP who founded a large business empire. This happened when he took over Duncan Brothers in 1963, having been its Chairman for a number of years. In the same year KP separated from his cousins in order to found his own dynasty – the first of the three Goenka family divisions. 'KP passed away in 1983 when I was twenty-two. He has been an extraordinarily important figure in my life; not only as a mentor as I mentioned earlier but as the 'passer-on' of family history. He also tried to explain the rationale of a joint family. In his own way I think he was trying to explain to us what he thought were the inconsistencies of joint family life and that he himself did not fully subscribe to it. However, he made it clear that, while he himself did not fully believe in it, it was the social norm of the day and he did not break away from it. He was very matter of fact about it. He said, "Here are the reasons that the joint family is the way it is. You must understand that you will not always gain from being in a joint family but you must also understand that, if it remains united, everyone in it will be much stronger – in the same way that a hand is stronger than the individual fingers."

'My grandmother died in an air crash in 1948 and, although my grandfather was only thirty-two at the time, he chose not to get married again. He used to tell us he did not get married for the sake of his children as he thought a stepmother would not have been a great idea. For me my grandfather was a very caring, and considerate man who sacrificed his own personal happiness and comfort for his family. There is absolutely no doubt I felt closest to him in the whole family.'

Sanjiv would have heard from his grandfather about his father's first day at work at Duncan Brothers on 1 May 1951. RP had joined the firm immediately on graduation from Presidency College – the same college from which Sir Badridas was the first Marwari to graduate. Sanjiv's father went to the dining room on his first day and found himself the only Indian. Apparently one of the Englishmen called out to a colleague, 'I say, old chap, do we allow people to have tiffin without a tie.' He replied, 'No, then should we not ask him to leave?' RP tendered his resignation on the spot and went home where he found his father was furious and in no uncertain terms told his son words to the effect 'Why did you try and go against the traditions of Duncan Brothers? They did not say anything to you. They were talking among themselves.' RP was obliged to retract his resignation. But his father was already in the process of taking over Duncan Brothers and so his pushing RP to go back may have been part of his plan to do so.

After the control of Duncan Brothers, for the first eighteen years of Sanjiv's life, his grandfather KP was busy with his father, RP and his other sons, Jagdish and Gouri making acquisitions, using the cash flow of Duncan Brothers to take over more companies. Phillips Carbon Black had already been set up by the family in 1960, and a stream of other acquisitions and greenfield enterprises followed – Asian Cables (1966), Swan Mills (1971), Oriental Carbon (1973), B.N. Elias Group (1973), Murphy India (1974), and Gujerat Carbon (1974).

However, RP was uncomfortable working with his two younger brothers. He wanted to be free of bickering and to be independent. Sanjiv's unhappy grandfather finally gave way in 1979 and split the family businesses amongst his three sons.

Sanjiv said of this: 'Frankly, at some stage joint family businesses are not competency driven because they are primarily age and hierarchy driven. This makes it extremely hard when an important decision needs to be made as, under the traditional model, whilst the eldest male member could theoretically make a decision without consulting the other male family members, for a decision to be effective it would need to have the support of all male family members. The separation was, I am told, amicable.' Sanjiv was still at school at the time, but understands the story is his grandfather drew up three lists of the family companies, each with an estimated combined asset base of Rs 1.45bn and roughly the same sales turnover of Rs 750m. He then called in his youngest son, Gouri and asked him to take his pick. He chose the list that contained what seemed at the time the first prize of the tea and cigarettes of the old Duncan Brothers plus Gujerat Carbon. Sanjiv's uncle Jagdish, was the next to choose and chose the cotton and jute businesses of the Duncan Brothers and the Swan Cotton Mills. That left Sanjiv's father, RP, with Phillips Carbon Black, the only family start-up, and Asian Cables, acquired in 1966 and Agarpara Jute Mills.

Exactly at the time the businesses were to be split in 1979, Sanjiv was finishing school at St. Xavier's and about to go to St. Xavier's College for a Bachelor's degree in Commerce. He was still living the restrictive family life at the Alipore mansion as the number four in the hierarchy of eight in his generation – including an older sister and brother Harsh. 'By this time I was certainly not completely compliant with what was asked of me and I frequently challenged the status quo. For example, when I finished my degree at St. Xavier's College my father wanted me to follow in Harsh's "footsteps" and, like him, do an MBA at the International Institute of Management Development in Switzerland. I rebelled at this as I said just because he had done it was not a good enough reason for me to do it too. My father relented and I joined the newly split family business of my father's.'

But Sanjiv was compliant in the case of his traditional arranged marriage just before he started work in the family business. When I asked whether he had any choice, Sanjiv replied, 'No, not really. I think I was told that I had to go and meet this particular girl for the purpose of marrying her. And so there were ten people from her side and my side and we all met together in the suite of a five-star hotel. We looked across at each other and then we were told that we could speak to each other for five minutes. Really, what can you say in five minutes so that you can make a decision? But that is what they wanted me to do and I said "ok". I was twenty and Preeti was eighteen. It was the same for my brother and my sister. It was the custom and so it was something that you expected and followed.

'Although it was an arranged marriage, my wife is not a Marwari – and so her systems and her customs and her traditions were very different from ours. She came from a very respected well-to-do family, but probably not as prominent as ours. It is often extremely difficult for a woman when she marries into a joint family and very often has to cope with a traditional Indian mother-in-law, like my mother. They can be very demanding telling their daughter-in-law how to dress and even how to smile. Believe it or not but my mother would tell Preeti that she was not supposed to ever give a full-throated laugh. It is almost like you were expected to become a clone of your mother-in-law and, if you complied, you were fine. If you did not comply, then they called you "fast". That was the terminology used in Marwari families for daughters-in-law who were not compliant. And if they called you that, then the aim was that you would not be popular. How my wife withstood is a miracle. But we were lucky to move out of the family home after only three months as I was sent to Hyderabad for work. I am sure this helped my wife cope with a joint family. And more importantly, it helped both of us to get to know each other much better. When we came back to Calcutta a few years later, we came back independent and a lot more confident. There was also a not so obvious advantage for me in being married as I could move out of the boys' dormitory into the house proper,' Sanjiv adds chuckling. 'We were provided with a very lavishly furnished room with an attached bathroom. Once you married, you were given every luxury – marriage was treated in my family as the ticket to adulthood.'

I asked if the tradition of arranged marriage had been passed on to the next generation. 'Well, my daughter Avarna had an arranged marriage but she and her husband met about thirty or forty times before they agreed. We arranged the introductions and then we waited for them to fall in love and that is what happened. You know arranged marriages will continue in India but not in the way we have known them. There are many cases where the children did not find the match for each other and there are many cases where they have come and told the parents, "Listen, we have not been able to find a match so please introduce us to someone who you think is appropriate and then we will take it on from there."' Sanjiv seemed relaxed about his son Shashwat, who was about to come back from his studies at Wharton, 'He may come back and say, "I have fallen in love with someone". If he has, he has.

'I started work with my father in 1981. There was a "sick" fibre company in Hyderabad making fiberglass and to which he sent me to sort out. It was the first time that I had been away from the family – on my own away from a sheltered and completely protected life into a completely unprotected and unsheltered life. That was wonderful, but so far as work went I had no formal training in management and no experience. This was the time of the 'licence raj' so there were controls on turnover with "sky high" interest rates of 20 per cent. It was a crazy situation and, even if I had been a genius, there was no way that the business was going to make money. However, it taught me how to face adversity and make difficult decisions. Looking back, it was a great learning experience for me.'

I asked Sanjiv whether he resented being parachuted in to run an impossible business. 'No, frankly, in India these things in those days were not resented. There is a lot of talk about it today but at that time it was pretty much accepted. What is done today is that you groom your child, he is given formal training and education for the needs of the business. For example, my son has completed undergraduate studies at Wharton. He will hopefully come into the business and "go through the grind" but, at the end of the day, it is pretty much a given that he will eventually takeover. When that will happen no one knows, but I do not think anybody within the company has any illusions that it will happen. However, I have to accept that his "going through the grind" is quite different to someone else doing the same in the company. That said, he will have to prove that he is worthy to take the role.

I have been fascinated with how many of the business leaders in India are from a Marwari background and asked Sanjiv if he had any thoughts about this. 'I think Marwaris have a very good sense of commerce. We instinctively understand business as most of us grow up in a business family environment where it is talked about from an early age. You adapt to it much easier than to anything else. But this is not exclusive to Marwaris. If you have common sense and you are basically intelligent, you will adapt to anything – how much time does it take? Whether it is power generation or whether it is CD manufacture or carbon black – as diverse as it gets – the principles, the guiding principles remain the same. You manufacture for the lowest you can – and sell for the highest price you can. It is fundamental and I think those instincts you are probably born with or you pick them up.'

The year Sanjiv was sent to Hyderabad was the same year his father started his decade of takeovers. RP became known as the 'takeover tycoon of India'. Freed from the constraints of the joint family business with his two brothers he started to build up the RPG

Group – he purchased Ceat Tyres of India in 1981, KEC International (power transmission) followed in 1982, Searle (pharmaceuticals and agro-chemicals) in 1983, HMV in 1988, and the retail Spencer's group in 1989.

It was in this decade that Sanjiv started to become close to his father who had ignored his children during their childhood. 'My father and I became very close over the twenty years before his death in 2013. At some point he started to spend time with me and guiding me. He was actually a very humble and caring person. He said when you are not in a position where you can assert yourself or you can exert influence you do not have a choice but to be humble. It is only when you get to a higher position that you can say that you are truly humble. He taught me that this should apply to all aspects of one's life from how you should greet a famous and important visitor as to how you would interact with one's staff at home. He was always a very warm person but, for whatever reason, he never spent time with us as children and, once he started spending time with us, the bond between us grew fast and strong.'

When his father acquired Dunlop India in 1984, Sanjiv was sent to manage it on his return from Hyderabad. This joint venture investment did not work out and the Goenka family gave up their interest in 1988. 1989 was an important year for Sanjiv and, as he tells it, the most important business year of his business life to date. The acquisition of Calcutta Electric Supply Corporation (CESC) was a decision that I took not only independently of my father, but against his view. In those days Calcutta used to have twelve hours of power cuts every day so it has been a very satisfying journey over the last twenty years to go from being the most inefficient utility in India to being the most efficient utility. At the same time, understandably we have gone from being hated to being loved. 'When I went and told my father I had closed the deal he did not eat dinner with me for two days in anger and disgust. Importantly, my mother supported my decision and whenever we brought the topic up he did not say, "I was wrong and you were right". Instead he said, "I bought it for you."'

Since then Sanjiv has been based in Calcutta whereas Harsh has been running the businesses in Mumbai. 'Then, in 2010, without consultation with either of us, my father split the group between Harsh and me. It was largely a simple matter of splitting the businesses geographically based on where we each had been living. There was no discussion among us beforehand but it was not a shock – I think it was pretty much expected that this was going to happen because both of us know our father's mindset. We knew his belief is that families must separate while relationships are positive. What we did not know was the timing and the timing surprised us. One day he came back from a visit to Mumbai and gave me a letter and walked away. The letter said I have decided to divide the businesses between Harsh and you in such and such a manner. So I went to him and asked why he had made this decision and he said, "Well I am going to be eighty next week and this is part of my unfinished agenda and, before I turn eighty, I want to finish it and I do not want any further discussion on this." That was it. Harsh and I subsequently discovered that he had actually already implemented the transfer of the businesses. In retrospect it showed great foresight on my father's part as almost certainly Harsh and I would have split the businesses but it would have been much more difficult if we had to negotiate the split ourselves. My father essentially went about the division the same way that my grandfather had done – he had done it with my father and his brothers in 1979 – whoever handles whichever business gets that.'

Sanjiv has found a change in his thinking since the separation, 'When you are together with a partner – and especially when, as in my case, the partner is a brother – you definitely have to think about his reaction before mooting your proposal. And sometimes you agree and sometimes you do not. But when you are on your own it is really your core team who sits with you and decides and then you make the call. So the responsibility and accountability is much more and the speed is that much faster.'

Sanjiv seems happy with his lot. 'If I was not sitting in this chair what would I be doing? I love my business, but is this my only interest in life? Certainly not. I would probably be a fashion or interior designer or something like that. For instance, when we are doing up our homes – and this office, for instance, a large part of the design is my decision. My wife is also a qualified interior decorator so that is something we share in common.'

Sanjiv fondly remembers and cherishes the closer relationship he had with his father until he passed away. 'When he was alive and I was in Calcutta we used to have breakfast together – it was a ritual that we followed strictly, my wife, my father and I. I do not know whether my mother regrets not having spent time with us as children but I know my father really did. He knows he did not spend enough time and he tried to make up for lost time and like, my grandfather did with us, he spent a lot of time with Harsh and my children, his grandchildren.'

There is little doubt that Sanjiv comes from one of the great Marwari business houses of India and the story that Sanjiv told of the separations of the family business over the generations is one which resonates with many of the life stories told to me by Indian business leaders. The trick seems to be to do the division while relations are good rather than when they have soured. In this the Goenka family seems to have been particularly successful and it would almost seem to now be in their DNA. One other positive message, which comes out of the story of Sanjiv's life, is the importance he places on having a close and positive relationship with his children. In this it is clear he has happily broken with his own childhood experience. Not only that, but he was very lucky to have had a second chance to build a close relationship with his father which he 'grabbed with both hands'.

---

[1] RP-Sanjiv Goenka Group (www.rp-sg.in) has an asset base of over USD 4.3 billion, over 50,000 employees, over 100,000 shareholders and annual revenues around USD 2.6 billion. The Group's businesses span across six sectors – Power & Natural Resources, Carbon Black, Retail, Media & Entertainment and IT & Education, include flagship companies such as CESC Ltd, Firstsource Solutions Ltd, Phillips Carbon Black Ltd, and Saregama India Ltd.

" In business, even if you are an average person, if you are honest, if you are willing to work hard and if you are sincere towards your objective, you will succeed. "

BHAVARLAL H. JAIN

Founder and Chairman, Jain Irrigation Systems[1]

My meeting with Bhavarlal Jain was the most complicated of all my meetings in India as we agreed to meet at his home in Jalgaon, which is located in western India in the far north of Maharashtra State. Whilst it has a small airport most visitors either travel by train or take a flight to Aurangabad, which is two and half hours to the south of Jalgaon. We had tried to arrange meetings in advance of several of my visits to India for this book, but as often happens for various reasons none of these eventuated. And then out of the blue on one visit to Mumbai there was the opportunity to meet, almost immediately, over the weekend that I willingly accepted. I arrived late on Friday night at Aurangabad and was driven to Jalgaon, where I spent a comfortable night at the Jain guesthouse.

Of course I arrived in the pitch black of evening and was a little surprised when I went outside the following morning to see that I was in the middle of what seemed an oasis with many trees and lots of other green vegetation whereas in the distance I could see the brown of the typical Deccan Plateau rocky terrain where temperatures range between 5 and 48° centigrade and average rainfall is only 650 mm.[2] I say I was only a little surprised, as I knew that Bhavarlal had made it his life's mission to bring rainwater harvesting and soil conservation techniques and thus a better livelihood to the poor farmers in arid regions of India.

After breakfast two of his executives, Dr. Bal Krishna and Kishore Rawale showed me around the vast complex comprising some 260 hectares including of course the key plant producing PVC and PE drip and sprinkler irrigation systems for India and export markets. What was particularly of interest was how Bhavarlal had managed to put so many of his ecological ideas into practice such as creating power from wind, solar and biogas and introducing close planting methods to conserve moisture. Other than this there were three other things I saw that morning and which made a lasting impression on me. The first was the huge Gandhi Museum he has recently created through an independent trust namely Gandhi Research Foundation. This has already become a major tourist attraction in the region with sprawling lawns and mammoth pink stone building as vast as 82,000 sq. ft. I saw many students happily playing on the interactive exhibits commerating Gandhi's life. The second is *Anubhuti*, the boarding school he has established and which seeks to educate its children of their Indian cultural heritage but with a global vision. But the third had the most profound effect on me and that was a billboard in the large exhibition hall which is primarily devoted to a pictorial description of all the different business activities of the company. This billboard had two main headings – 'Successes' and 'Failures' and listing examples of both. Certainly most of the people I have interviewed have openly talked about their successes and failures but this was, for me, an amazing public admission of failures. I sensed my meeting with Bhavarlal would be interesting.

Following a vegetarian lunch with Bhavarlal, two of his four sons, Anil and Ajit and some senior executives, I moved to Bhavarlal's office to chat about his life. We were joined by one of his grandsons, Athang who had arrived that day from the UK and sleepily listened to his grandfather's stories.

'My father, Hiralal Sagarmal Jain had hardly completed three classes in primary school when at the age of eleven he had to shoulder the responsibility of a huge family of fifteen people. As far as my mother Gauri Hiralal Jain was concerned, she could not write, read or count; she was 'so to say' illiterate. But, like many women in her position, she efficiently managed the household.

'My father and his three brothers operated a joint family business as petty traders and small farmers. They lived together in a small village of some 500 people called Vakod, which is about 50 kilometres from here (near the Ajanta Caves in Maharashtra). It was into this rural environment that I was born on 12 December 1937.

'When I was a child there was no electricity in our village. There used to be dacoits or armed robbers operating in the state at that time and every ten years or so they would raid our village and take everything of value. And all agriculture was done by bullocks instead of mechanical means. Basically the land was cultivated for subsistence rather than for creating a surplus or for commercial reasons. There was poverty, but I do not think that it was felt as much as it is today. Labour was cheap, grains were cheap and clothes were also cheap – cheap by a factor of about forty times less than the price today. I think it is fair to say I never felt poor as everyone was in the same position.

'The local school to which I went only had one classroom and two classes would be taught simultaneously by the same teacher using two different blackboards. The teachers were extremely strict and if you misbehaved even a little, they would beat you with a cane. Of course there was no talk about activity learning, learning through experience or experiential learning, nothing of that sort. It was a plain, simple teaching – with learning by rote – and, therefore, no real learning.

'There was no contract farming at that time; either the landlord or the farmers owned the land. But in my village at least, there was no landlord. Everyone was a small farmer with one hectare of land or maybe two. Over time they would either sell the land or they would improve it for their sons to inherit; if a farmer had two sons, the land would be divided in halves.

'In our village none of the homes had tiled floors. They were invariably mud floors and periodically they would be plastered with cow dung. In terms of sanitation, this was apparently good because cow dung is supposed to be antiseptic. And given that the summer is harsh getting up to around 47° centigrade, the fact that everything was made of mud – not only the floors and the walls but also the roof – would help keep the houses cool. I believe there are still some mud houses in my village. It is said the average life of these houses is fifty to seventy years whereas the life of cement, I am told, is only sixty years.

'As I would walk through the village to get to the local school, my mother would fetch a pail or a pot of water on foot. At the same time, she would take the family clothes to be washed at the river. I can vividly remember seeing her walking with a pot of water on the top of her head and with the washed clothes in her hands. This was a daily ritual she would perform at dawn.

'The people in my village tended to be very healthy but every five to ten years we would be hit by an epidemic of some sort. And when these epidemics occurred the death toll was often high. I have known one time when, in three days, 110 people died in my village out of the population of 500.

'But in spite of all that, the villagers were happy and there was a lot of love and affection. Everybody in the village knew everybody else and so there was a kind of empathy between them all, and, whatever they did, they did it together. I did not find them to be upset or blaming each other, or trying to kill each other, or trying to compete with each other. Envy and jealousy, and all of those things, used to be there; they are with all humanity from birth. But these were problems that the villagers could overcome and they would work hard at it.

'My father lost both his parents at the age of eleven and married my mother when she was only twelve and he was fifteen. Within a period of about nine and half years, my mother had seven kids, out of whom five died at birth or soon after, because of the lack of proper care, medicine and no hospitals at that time. So by the age of twenty-one and twenty-three respectively, the child bearing period was over. Only my younger brother and I survived.

'I was an average student at school. The remark that was given to me when I left the village primary school to join middle school in Jalgaon was "intelligence is moderate but behaviour is extremely good". Similar remarks about me were made by my teachers all the way through to my leaving the high school. Because my parents had not been educated, they wanted their sons to be educated at any cost. During my high school years they rented a small one-room or two-room apartment in Jalgaon where my mother and some joint family members stayed and looked after me. In time, they also sent for my younger brother.

'My parents were well off enough to finance our education. They were certainly above average but were not rich. Of course their financial resources were small. If, for instance, there was a marriage in the family, they would have to mortgage some gold that they had preserved; villagers, wherever possible saved in the form of gold jewellery as they did not trust cash against the mortgage of gold. This same philosophy continues to this day, which is why India is probably the largest holder of gold in the world. The moneylender would give them cash, which they would use to discharge their obligations. Once the harvest came, they would pay back the money with the interest and get their gold back.

'At high school I avoided science subjects like mathematics, physics, chemistry, biology and focused on the humanities such as Marathi, English, Sanskrit, history, geography, however, geometry was unavoidable. So my whole schooling was primarily focused on languages, which I liked and from a young age I had a flair for. I do not think anybody ever described me as naughty. I was a very disciplined and obedient student with an average IQ.

'I have come to believe that people with a very high IQ tend to create more "heat" than "light". And the IQ therefore becomes an impediment to their own success rather than helping them achieve their goal. To be successful in business, I would say it is more important that you have a flair and the ability to recruit and retain bright people with you. You need to cultivate them, and give them the opportunity and the scope to develop. You need to trust them and, if you trust them, they will give their best. You can hire brilliance, but you cannot hire compassion; you cannot hire integrity. You can hire the "hands" but not the "hearts"; you can hire probably partly the "mind", fully the "hand", but not the "heart". So far as I am concerned, I have always believed that it is the trust that I repose in people, which comes back to me in multiple measures.

'My parents had high moral values. Their honesty, their integrity and their common sense were unmatched. So, in short, I did not inherit intelligence and, secondly, nor did I inherit wealth. What I did inherit from my father was deep-rooted integrity and sense of fair dealing and from my mother I inherited compassion and strong common sense. She was a very outgoing person and she would go out of her way to help all the women in the village. Often she would help them without letting my father or grandfather know. So I believe I inherited a charitable disposition from my mother and upright dealing from my father.

'There is one particular memory from my childhood that sticks in my mind. In villages in those days there were weekly bazaars or markets, because villagers did not have their own vegetables and they did not have things like cotton or shirts to wear and so people would bring this sort of merchandise once a week to the market. When I was barely about eight years old, I went along with my uncle to one of these weekly markets. There I saw a huge heap of spinning tops. I was very attracted to them and thought that I must have one, and I do not know what made me do it, but I put one in my pocket and the seller did not notice. So I stole one spinning top and my uncle saw what I had done, but he did not say anything to me. When he came home, he told my mother what I had done. My mother, that day, beat me with a cane until the cane broke and I had bruises all over my body. Then I could not sleep but my mother massaged me and put some kind of ointment to sooth the pain.

'My mother could not sleep too and wept continuously. When my father got to know about the incident he too felt my mother had done the right thing and that I had to be taught integrity and honesty and for the rest of my life I would never forget that lesson. He told her not to worry, and that I would get over it in a couple of days. As the recipient of that beating, and as a father now, I feel that the "cane" works better than "words" in some situations. My mother was full of love as I was one of the two surviving sons. Even though she loved me more than life itself, this did not deter her from teaching me the lesson that in life integrity is important. For as long as I live I will never forget this experience. I believe it reinforced in me the importance of an honest approach to everything in life. Whether I have to deal with people or I have to make a deal, the importance of honesty is the paramount thought in my mind.

'My father became the agent for a cotton ginning pressing factory where the owners of that factory would never come to see what he was doing. They trusted him implicitly. I observed this and always felt that he was trusted so much because he was honest. I believe that it is putting two things together that forms a character. I believe for many people character is formed, firstly, through religion, and, secondly, at the home. Certainly as you have heard I had the right ethics taught to me at the home and perhaps I should explain a little about the impact and influence of the Jain religion on me.

'The Jain religion, in which I was brought up, is a very tough religion, and not one that everybody can adopt. Basically, for me it stands on three principles. One is *satya* meaning honesty or truth, which we have discussed. The second is conservation; Jains do not like to waste anything and they also do not like to invest everything that they have. They like to save. Of everything they make, Jains like to invest only 25 per cent and keep the rest for a "rainy day". This principle of conservation applies whether it concerns water, food or anything that they are doing in life. And the third principle, and also the most important, is *ahimsa*, which means non-violence. This is a disposition that Jains cultivate right from day one. For instance, if you see an ant walking on the floor, you put a piece of paper below her and take her and leave her outside your window. You do not walk on the ant and you do not trouble her. That is a trivial example I am giving, but non-killing and non-violence of that sort is built into our DNA. The vegetarianism comes out of that; you do not have to kill to eat.

'These are the principles that I learnt as I listened to the discourses of the sadhus[3] when they visited my village. They would come every year; Jain sadhus walk 20 kilometres a day barefooted. Jainism is the only religion in the world where there are close to twenty thousand sadhus and sadhvis, the female equivalent, belonging to this religion. We are a small community of about 1 per cent of the Indian population but the number of these sadhus and sadhivs, is quite large. However, Jainism does not believe in conversion; Jains do not like to convert anybody to anything. In addition to these key principles Jains also believe in other religions. Above all one should follow a number of other principles being *brahmacharya, asteya* and *aparigraha. Brahmacharya* refers to the importance of exercising control over one's senses such as not overindulging in sensual pleasures, *asteya* refers to the principle one should not take what is not offered and which in practice includes not exploiting the weak which is considered theft. Finally, *aparigraha* means non-accumulation, in so far as you should not accumulate anything more than what is needed for the bare necessities. That is the kind of teaching that has led me to say that 75 per cent of my family's total wealth should go into a trust. We are only the trustees of the wealth that we create and it must be given back to society. So this philosophy is similar to that followed by the Tatas.

'I believe that I was born not only for myself. If it pleases my mother that I should go to the religious teachers, I would go there to please her, whether I liked it or not. If something is to be done because my wife likes it, I would like to do it. If there is a friend who would like me to do something which is not violent or otherwise contrary to my faith or belief, I would do that. Because I believe that it is the difference you make to the lives of others that is a sole criterion for success. So, if I can please someone I care for, while not compromising on my basic values, there is no reason why I would not do so.

'After high school in Jalgaon, I went to college in Mumbai. For my first two years, I went to Sydenham College but it was too cumbersome to get off the train at Dadar Junction and then catch another train to go to Churchgate where the college was located. Therefore I switched over to Podar College for last two years because that was located closer to where I was staying in Dombivali. My life at college was not so different from village life. Although Dombivali was a distant suburb of Mumbai, it was much like a village in those days. I lived with my uncle who worked for an automobile company.

'As for Mumbai itself, I was never impressed or dazzled or lost as a villager would be coming to the city for the first time. Cities have never made a difference to me. I went to New York for the first time in December 1978 to sell what we were then manufacturing. My friends and family had all been worried about me going alone to New York, especially in the harsh winter with its minus temperature and snow, as well as a thousand other things about which they said I knew nothing. For instance, they said I would have a problem eating because I did not know about Western table manners. My answer was very simple. I said that one thing was certain: that there were no houses hanging in the air in New York. I also told them that I was certain that people there were not walking on their heads. So if these two things were certain I concluded that I was not going to find anything with which I could not cope. That the rest of humanity was the same as us, suffering from the same weaknesses and enjoying the same strengths. I knew, therefore, that I had nothing to be worried about. As for the table manners,' Bhavarlal smiled and said, 'I bought a small book called *Table Manners and Etiquette* and studied it before I left for the US.

'On my first day in New York I went to Penn Plaza in Manhattan where I had a cab waiting for me. I hired a cab not because I had money to burn, but because I calculated that hiring a taxi would save me two days. In those days, my country would not give me more than thirty-five dollars a day of foreign exchange. I worked out that if I saved two days from my trip, I would have saved seventy dollars, which I could spend on taxis. And I would be able to make at least four calls a day instead of two. The end result of all this robust common sense, which my parents had imbued in me, carried me in good stead and I was in no danger of being overly impressed either by big cities like Mumbai or New York.

'After I finished my commerce degree, I went to a law college at Mahim in western Mumbai. There was also a government law college in Mumbai but their graduation entry marks in law were higher than what I had achieved. Mahim was also more affordable and convenient, as there was a hostel where I could stay, so that I conserved all my energy for study rather than spending a good part of my life commuting! Commuting is a large part of anyone's life who lives in Mumbai.

'At the time, I did not give much thought to becoming a lawyer. Coming from a small village my sole focus was to study. I found the classes to be tough. I did not understand to English pronunciation and therefore had to concentrate all my energy to improve my English. I was very focused and spent most of my time in the library and there was little time for anything else. I had four close friends at college; one works with me as an associate and I am still in touch with another.

'I graduated from Mahim in 1961 at the age of twenty-four. I then had to decide what I was going to do with my life and career. While I was doing my second year law, I applied for two government jobs. The first was with the elite Indian Administrative Service (IAS) that provided a pathway to the important Federal/ State Government positions. The second was with my state's Maharashtra Public Service Commission, which would give me a career in State

Government service. Both were selective exams but I failed to make the mark with the IAS; my rank was 480 and they only took the first 350. However, I was successful with the Maharashtra exam and was gazetted. This meant I had a secure salary for life and the chance of a career to become a top state bureaucrat. Also during my legal studies I had worked in my holidays as an apprentice to U.N. Raisoni who was a top-ranking lawyer in Jalgaon. I also spent some time working with him after I finished. He told me that I seemed to have what is required for a successful career and invited me to join him. So that was the second choice available to me.

'I was unexpectedly faced with a third choice when I met a leader of our community, Mr. Bikamchand M. Jain who advised me against becoming either a lawyer or a bureaucrat. He told me that it was in my DNA as a Marwari or a Rajasthani to start my own business, howsoever small it might be. That this was what I was born to do. When I protested that I had no money to invest, he said that he would help me and that I could repay him later. People like B.M. Jain feel that Marwaris are designed by nature to be entrepreneurs or businessmen. Looking back, I would tend to agree with him because I believe that this is ingrained into us from an early age. For example, few Marwaris would think of a fixed-hour workday. Mostly they are in a joint family and experience the concept of business from their childhood. There is also the fact that the original Marwaris were refugees from abject poverty in Rajasthan and, having left with nothing, had to work tremendously hard to succeed. That made a huge difference. In business, even if you are an average person, if you are honest, if you are willing to work hard and if you are sincere towards your objective, you will succeed. Hard work and success together form a kind of byproduct of the Marwari upbringing. It just comes naturally.

'Whenever I was confused about what to do in my youth I went to my mother. Although I was by now a young adult, it was to my mother I went for guidance. You will remember she was illiterate with very little idea of the world for which they had educated me. Obviously I could also have gone to my father, but I was more attached to my mother whereas my younger brother was more attached to my father.

'So I sought advice from my mother and she told me that she did not understand anything of what I was talking about and that she could not make a choice for me. But I persisted and she gave me a wonderful piece of advice as a worldly-wise lady – not learned or educated, but wise. She said: "If you want to fill up your own belly and the bellies of four, five or ten people around you, you can go into business. If you are an advocate or a pleader in the court, you may probably be able to take care of ten more than that. But what I want you do and what I would love you to do, is that you do something which will not only fill up your belly and the bellies of the people around you, but also feed the mute animals and the birds and everything that exists on this earth. If you can do both of these things, I will be very happy." These words had a huge and a profound message which changed and settled my life.

'This did not happen immediately but the conflict in my mind was now capable of a resolution. I kept on thinking about it and I decided to see an astrologist. The astrologist I decided to meet was a pretty tough guy who had only one eye and charged 10 rupees for his advice, a large sum in those days. He looked into my eyes and then inspected my hand. He told me that I was going to deal in soil, that I was going to deal with iron, that I was going to deal with oil, and that I was going to be very rich. I replied that I had come to see him on a bicycle and that I did not see how I could become a very rich man when I did not have any capital to invest. I told him that I had little confidence in his advice or his opinion. He did not like my comment and said, "I would not accept the fee." However, if I succeeded to do what he said during my lifetime, I should come and tell him.

'From my mother's advice it was clear I was not going to be a lawyer or a bureaucrat. I started in 1962 as a small-time trader with a capital of about Rs. 7000 which at that time was the equivalent of USD 1000. Can you believe that those 7000 rupees were the savings of three generations of my joint family? Needless to say not everyone agreed I should be provided with these funds. My father had already retired so he took no part in the decision. On the other hand one of my uncles who was managing the household was understandably concerned that the family may need some of these funds for a "rainy day". But my mother stood by me and opposed my uncle, (who was like her own child, because she had brought up all my uncles like her own sons). She said that her son was for the first time asking for something after twenty-five years and that she knew that I would make a success out of it. However, if anyone thought it was too much, then it should be given as her share in the family and she would not ask for a single farthing after that. When she gave such an ultimatum, everybody was quiet. My uncle who was standing there, who was the *karta*, the head of our family, threw the keys to the cupboard in which the money was kept on the floor. My other uncle picked them up and brought the money. That is how I started business.

'One evening in 1964 I was sitting by a petrol pump which I owned, when a water-drilling rig came by. On the back of the rig there was a small but telling slogan, "Agriculture: a Profession with a Future". Ever since I came to love languages, I always loved quotations such as those of Winston Churchill and other prominent thinkers and leaders. And when I saw that slogan it somehow connected with my mother's advice to do something that would satisfy the birds and the mute animals. I realized that I was meant to do something like agriculture, where the birds would also come and they would have their food, the monkeys would also come and have their food and so would I. Everything about agriculture was compatible with Jainism and its compassionate approach towards life. So everything came together and my mind was firmed up that agriculture was going to be my profession.

'For the next fifteen years, I started one agency after another related to agriculture, whether it be seeds and fertilizers, pesticides, agricultural equipment etc. During this period I built up the business from my initial investment to an annual turnover of ten crores (Rupees hundred million). Most of the growth came from taking business away from other parties simply because they were incompetent or complacent. It was not because of any brilliance on my part. The foreign companies that were giving me agencies found it easier to deal with me since I spoke English. We came to be seen as an absolutely trustworthy firm for agricultural products.

'Not only did I start my business in 1962 but I also got married that year. Given the time, it was of course, an arranged marriage. However, the last word was mine. My family gave me the right to say "yes" or "no". I was given a choice of three shortlisted girls. The family of the girl I chose did not have anything to give by way of a dowry which my mother was expecting. Her expectations were in keeping with the tradition in those days and was also based on the fact that she had given a dowry for all my uncle's daughters. The girl I chose was educated and had a bachelor's degree. This in itself was good enough to cross her off the list. But as soon as she entered the room where we met in Mumbai, I was shocked. It was as if her silent charm and dignified poise hypnotized me. I lost all track of time and place and to this day cannot tell you who else was in the room. I was totally fascinated by her presence. Over the next hour or so we chatted and I learnt more about her. The fact she was educated I saw as a huge plus whereas many more traditionalists would have seen it as a negative. We were about to finish our meeting when she raised the fact she had been jilted. She told me she had been engaged earlier to this person, who left for the US the day after they were engaged. Subsequently, they exchanged a couple of letters in which he told her that he was not returning to India and that he wanted to call off the engagement. I will always feel guilty about this, but I asked her if she would let me read his letter calling off the engagement. She did not have a problem in showing me the letter. I was embarrassed by the trust she put in me and knew I should never have asked to read that letter in the first place. But there was absolutely no doubt this was the lady I wanted to marry. The most important consideration of course was that she was a Marwari and a Jain from Bijapur in Karnataka. This meant I was marrying within my own cast.

'The long and the short of it is that I managed to convince my mother, and Kantabai became my wife, in fact much more than my wife. Together we did not make just a pair – we were one person in two bodies – one soul in two bodies. Sadly, Kantabai passed away in 2005 at the age of sixty-seven with a neurological condition like Parkinson's. In fact I wrote a book about our life together called simply *She and Me*, and I will give you a copy of the draft in English. It has already been published in Marathi. She took care of this entire joint family which consisted of 110 people at any given time. This left me free to easily take care of the business. Together, we made a big business and a big family. Otherwise it would have been impossible.

'She never had any issues regarding her health till she was sixty-five. As for my health issues, I hardly ever had any. I have never suffered from any disease and all the elements of my body even today are absolutely intact, except for my heart, which has a major problem. I almost died when I suffered a severe heart attack in June 1982, when I was only forty-six years old. I was unconscious for three days. And I have since had another six heart attacks, two quadruple bypasses and an angioplasty. Doctors have sometimes said that I should take things a little easy, but I have never done that. I have kept myself busy and there is a tremendous pleasure that I get out of work. I do not know why I should be afraid of hard work or stress or strain as long as I enjoy what I am doing. And I have enjoyed every bit of it. Whether it was successes or failures, I enjoyed them equally, because I learned more from my failures than my successes. My work culture is: "Work is life; Life is work". I have never disturbed this balance. Kantabai knew and my family knows I am not crazy about business for the sake of money. Since my objectives in life are qualitative and not quantitative. Therefore, there are no limits to my work.

'Turning to my views on succeeding as an entrepreneur it is of course not necessary to have been top of my class. Such brilliant people are always available. But for success in business, what we need is people with robust common sense and a deep desire, a genuine desire to excel. It is necessary to be able to survive setbacks and learn from them. From the very beginning I have always liked to try new things and pursued innovation. If there was anybody who promised me that he had some new product or idea which I liked, and that he did not have money, I would be reminded that I also started without much money and that I should support him. I think it is this hankering for innovation that has kept me growing over the years.

'However, this approach has also brought me failures. For example, in the early days of 1965, three years after my business started, there was a guy who was laminating photographs which was a new technology at that time. I invested some money in it and lost it all. This was the first in a long list of my failures. Some day, I am going to write a book titled *The Failures of a Successful Man*. That would hopefully give an insight into the mind of an entrepreneur who thinks differently and who believes that making a difference to the lives of others is the real test of success. I am a simple man who thinks differently. I like to think differently about most things in life, except the tradition of my upbringing. I respect them as they are.'

I mentioned to Bhavarlal I was extremely impressed with his billboard in his exhibition room publicly recording his successes and failures. 'Yes, we diversified into too many areas where we had no expertise or experience. These failures nearly bankrupted the company back in 1997. At the time I took out a half page advertisement in the *Economic Times* where I apologized to our investors and other stakeholders. I stated: "I am sad that, for the first time since our inception, we have fared badly. We ventured into unknown areas like finance, information technology and granite at the cost of our core business. I feel it is my duty to account for, to own up, to admit my misjudgments and to apologize."

'I went on to say a number of things including "I'm confident that despite the hurdles, we have secured due recognition for this industry, and helped bring about the second green revolution in this country. Because our fundamentals are rock solid. Work. Hard work, continues to be an obsession with us. And hard work not only pays, but also brings honour and preserves character. With our voracious appetite for growth and a policy of plowing our profits back into the business, I believe there's a lot more we're capable of achieving. This is only the beginning."[4] And I believe in these words, even today.

'My sons and I always think on the same lines. I feel confident we shall never have family division. In my experience these tend to happen among families who have kept money as their motive for growth. Then everybody is ambitious and everybody wants to make more money, and then there arises a kind of conflict. That is why we believe that about 80 per cent of our wealth should go into a trust. So any one of the family cannot make a fortune but each of us work hard for success and create a huge reservoir of goodwill which is more valuable than capital. This can only happen if you do not value money beyond a good life. If you chase money, it runs away miles apart but, if you just do your job and let the money chase you, then it stays with you.' It was my turn to laugh as I told Bhavarlal he had just told a Burmese proverb that is quite similar. It says money has four legs whereas humans have only two. And four legs run faster than two.

'Many other families like ours have had business divisions. Our business currently has five divisions; so I could easily give one division to each of my sons. But it is they who have decided that during their lifetime they will not divide the business. I don't think they are saying this just while I am alive. They have told me that it is their considered decision. I did not enforce anything. Nor do I think that the size of the business matters. The size and the growth may be taken care of by the professionals; the family members are only leaders. It is no longer a family business; it is a business that is managed by the family.

'Nowadays I tend not to make any decisions unless they ask me. Similarly, I do not give advice unless they ask for it. But I do tell them what I feel and I do not remember any instance so far, where they have gone against my wishes. They will almost take every one of my wishes as a command. And I think that is appropriate since I am the one who has founded the enterprise which I know like the palm of my hand. Even today, when I am going around the plant and being photographed with people, I remember at least a few names of people who have worked with us for many years. And that gives me immense satisfaction.'

Whilst I am sure we could have happily chatted for many more hours, it was time to bring our meeting to a close so I could arrive in Aurangabad in time for my evening flight back to Mumbai. And as his driver sped along the country roads, I realised I had forgotten to ask Bhavarlal if he ever went back to the astrologer whose predictions he had so firmly rejected, to tell him that he was right after all!

---

[1] Jain Irrigation Systems Ltd (www.jains.com) derives its name from the pioneering work it did for the micro irrigation industry in India. However, the company has a multi-product industrial profile and manufactures drip and sprinkler irrigation systems and components; PVC, polyethylene (HDPE, MDPE) & polypropylene piping systems; plastic sheets (PVC & PC sheets); agro processed products includes dehydrated onions and vegetables; processed fruits (purees, concentrates & juices); tissue culture, hybrid & grafted plants; greenhouses, poly and shade houses; bio-fertilizers; green energy includes solar photovoltaic (solar lighting and appliances, solar pumping systems), solar water heating systems and bio-energy sources.
[2] Bhavarlal H. Jain, *A Telling Tale*, Jain Irrigation Systems, 2011 (2 ed.) p.7.
[3] In Hinduism, Sadhus are ascetic wandering monks. Sadhus are renunciates who have left behind all material attachments and live in caves, forests and temples all over India and Nepal. A Sadhu is usually referred to as 'Baba', which also means father, grandfather, or uncle in many Indian languages. There are 4 to 5 million Sadhus in India today and they are widely respected for their holiness and sometimes feared for their curses.
[4] A copy of this advertisement appears in *An Entrepreneur Deciphered* (edited by I.L. Dudhedia, Gimi Farhad and B. Krishnakumar, Jain Charities, 2009) pp. 166-67.

" Charity only destroys dignity and independence. We did not want to give them "fish", but to teach them how to "fish" – and also to teach them how to "market the fish". "

B.K. JHAWAR

Chairman Emeritus, Usha Martin[1]

I met B.K. Jhawar of Usha Martin at the Taj chambers in the Taj Bengal Hotel in Kolkata on a Saturday. I was immediately struck by the fact that he does not look his seventy-five plus years of age and, as with many of the people in this book, he radiates energy and an interest in life. He has an extremely open face and is quite fair in complexion; in fact I would have to say one might have difficulty in telling his nationality. I found him full of life, with passion and enjoyment, not only in what he is now doing, but also in looking back at what he has built during the course of his career.

BK talked first of the origins of his family and his family name, 'We are Marwaris and originally come from Bikaner, a city in Rajasthan. It is not a very common name, the original name might have been 'Jawahar' but then through passage of time and because maybe some people could not twist their tongue around it, the name changed slightly. Alternatively, in olden times, perhaps there was a deity in the family, you know, a family goddess. So, all those who pray to her become part of the clan. So, our goddess was also somewhere in Bikaner. We do not know now because all this is a long time ago.

'My grandfather, Har Gopal Jhawar came to Calcutta from Bikaner in the mid 1870s or thereabouts. He became a head clerk in a big – not a British company – an Indian family firm. He had three sons, my father and my two uncles and one daughter who stayed back in Bikaner. I know this sounds a small family for that time but, as you may know, many children passed away in their infancy and so it was for my grandparents who lost as many as eight other children. Sadly I never met my grandfather as he had passed away before I was born.

'My grandfather lived in the old part of Calcutta, called Bara Bazaar. It was at that point of time – I am talking about the early 1920s – where most of the Marwaris stayed because rents were very low. Like my grandfather, most of them left their families in Rajasthan where life was hard and opportunities few and came to Calcutta to make money to support their families. They used to stay in a sort of – I don't know what you would call it – they called it a 'basa', meaning a lodge. There they would each have a small room with a community kitchen. They would go back to their families in Rajasthan every two or three years for a couple of months before returning to Calcutta. Once the British built the railways it was simple to return but, before that, it was a long and difficult journey involving several means of transport. In fact due to the poverty in Rajasthan, Marwaris spread all over India and particularly to the major business cities of Bombay and Calcutta as they realized the opportunities would be greatest there.'

So that was the life of BK's grandfather. As his children grew up – and there was a gap of seventeen or eighteen years between the oldest son, Motilal, BK's father and the youngest son – they were brought to Calcutta by the grandfather to study and work. But until the death of his grandfather the family home was in Rajasthan and his grandmother never made the trip to Calcutta. By the time of his grandfather's death, his grandmother had died earlier, his father and his two brothers were all married. It was a joint family and, like in many other joint families, life for daughters-in-law could be hell if the mother-in-law was difficult. In the case of BK's family it was his father's aunt who created problems following the death of his grandparents. 'So, one fine morning, these three ladies, my mother and aunts, requested my father to move them out from Bara Bazaar. My father agreed, but there was a condition. He said, "We are very hard working, but we do not have too much wealth, so if you come you will have to do all house work as we cannot afford servants." They moved to South Calcutta, and with this change the family's fortune started changing too.'

BK's grandfather remained an employee and had a very good reputation for being strict, conservative, maintaining a high standard of business ethics and having prudent financial practices. 'In fact he had to suffer when sometimes he objected to dealings not passing through these criteria. He told his sons that "as an employee, many times I suffer due to my objecting to incorrect business ethics and I want you all to be entrepreneurs and not join in service." But of course there was no capital so the three sons became under-brokers of a company owned by another Marwari.' BK's father and his older uncle worked in the jute and hessian market, whereas his youngest uncle, who was almost seventeen years younger than his father, worked at the stock exchange. 'By 1932, the family had saved enough to build a home in Calcutta to house the whole family which eventually consisted of my parents and their three sons and two daughters, a childless older uncle and a younger uncle who was to have four sons and two daughters.'

BK went on to explain something that happened to him that, whilst relatively common in many Asian societies, is uncommon in the West. 'I was born in 1935. My parents felt sorry for my uncle and aunt who had no children so they gave my uncle the chance to choose one of their sons to raise as their own. I was the middle son and they picked me. I was maybe two years old and did not know of any of this until I was around twelve. We all lived in one house and there was no differentiation between any of the children of my generation. But I noticed one thing in my childhood that out of all the children, my adopted mother was overprotective of me. Nobody would dare to do anything to me. If some mischief took place in the family, for instance, and somebody was due for a thrashing, somebody else got it from the parents, but no one dared touch me. It was not that I was naughty but I did feel that I was a bit special. You could say I was the "apple" of my adoptive mother's "eyes". But I have to say that I did not feel any different once I found out I was adopted because we all lived together. My adopted mother died in 1957, just six months after I was married; it looked like she was just waiting for me, her "only child", to be married.

'During the Second World War, and especially between 1942 and 1944, whenever there was a danger due to the Japanese, we were all moved out of Calcutta to my maternal uncle's house in Uttar Pradesh. The war years disturbed our education not just because of moving, but because the school where I was supposed to attend was occupied by the army. This meant until I was in eighth standard I studied at home.'

After moving to South Calcutta, the joint family was reasonably well off, demonstrated, for example, by the fact they had a car. 'Even with few savings we had a good standard of living and one year when my father had had a particularly good year in the hessian market he took us all for a holiday to Kalimpong, a hill station near Darjeeling. He liked the place so much that he bought some land and built a summerhouse there. After that we used to go there by train every summer.'

I asked BK to explain a little more about his disrupted schooling. 'After the home schooling period was over my parents sent me to Hindi High School (now Birla High School) where I suspect many of the subjects of your book also went as it was the best school in the city and remains one of the top even today. On completion of my time at school I spent four years doing a bachelor's degree in Commerce at St. Xavier's College, which, at that time was affiliated, to Calcutta University. I passed in everything but was by no means an outstanding student. Worth noting as it may not be so usual for you is the fact that St. Xavier's College offered and still offers three shifts: a Morning Session (6am-9.50am), a Day Session (9am-4.30pm) and an Evening Session (3pm-8pm). After two years of college my father suggested me to move to the Morning Session so I could work with him during the days.'

BK told me the story of how he started work in the genesis of what became Usha Automobile and Engineering Ltd. 'During the independence struggle period my father became acquainted with G.D. Birla [1894-1983], the famous Indian industrialist.G.D. Birla moved to Calcutta during the 1930s and the family connection became even stronger in 1946 when my eldest sister married B.M.

Birla's son, G.P. Birla [1922-2010]. B.M. Birla [1904-1981] was G.D. Birla's younger brother. This family link was in due course to provide a huge opportunity for our family but first I have to go back to the war years when there were two British gentlemen working here in Calcutta – a Mr. Grant and a Mr. James. They had started a company, Grant James Limited that was involved in furniture making and were short of money. They approached my father who invested in the company. And it is here that "luck" played a part. My father used to visit B.M. Birla who, amongst other businesses, owned and ran Hindustan Motors – not for any particular reason but just to find out what the "great man" was thinking. On one such visit B.M. Birla asked my father what his sons and nephews were doing and he mentioned that my cousin MK and I had just started work in the office as apprentices. Now it just so happened that the supplier of spring seats for Hindustan Motors had just gone on strike. BM thought that if Grant James was making sofas it could probably produce car seats. I was only eighteen years old and my cousin MK was only a few months older.

'There was no time to waste because Hindustan Motors wanted the springs immediately as it was holding up their production. We went to Hindustan Motors on, I think it was a Thursday, to see what we had to produce and indicated we thought we could do it. They told us ok you need to start producing on Monday. It was that quick. But this was too good an opportunity and so on Monday we set up a tent under a tree and got started. Our family gave MK and me Rs 50,000 – at that point of time it was something like $10,000 – to set up Usha Automobile and Engineering Ltd for us to run. And Hindustan Motors provided us with one machine that was lying unused in their factory and with an engineer to provide as he knew what was required and, in any event, we could not afford one. I continued with my studies in the morning sessions from 6 to 10, rushed home for a quick lunch and then went to the stock exchange to work with my uncle for a couple of hours until it closed and then went to the factory until late at night.

'It was, as they say, a "baptism of fire". And we started to have success with the car seats, we started thinking about how the seats were installed in a car. So we started producing tubular frames that led us to producing tubes and silencer pipes and so on. Making these small advances we doubled our sales every year. Within five years we had expanded from a tent to two rented factories and on to a factory which we owned and from car seats to eight components for cars.

'I thought there was no stopping us and decided we should expand and produce components for other automobile manufacturers like Standard Motors and then other components for another large company, Telco. But of course there was something that could stop us in our tracks and that was a strike at Hindustan Motors itself. That was in 1958. Then, in 1959 my father died.

'The strike in Hindustan Motors had broken our back – I mean we really suffered – so I had gone to Delhi to see how we could diversify. This was the time of the "licence raj" when a permit was needed for almost everything. A licence was needed from Delhi to import even a bolt or nut and you had to go there to get the licence. I went to see this bureaucrat who, on seeing my head was shaven, realized there must have been a death in the family. He asked how I was, to which I replied I felt horrible and explained why. Not only had my father passed away, but we had all these troubles with our business in Calcutta with our major customer, Hindustan Motors being strike bound. I asked him: "Can you suggest an item we could manufacture where we do not have to depend on one customer?" Luckily for me this gentleman happened to be not only honest but wise and suggested the manufacture of wire ropes. He told me it would cost around fifty lakhs (now approximately USD 120,000) to set up a factory. At this point we did not even have five lakhs but I thought his idea made sense and went ahead and got the licence, which incidentally took nine months. But the real question was from where we would get the fifty lakhs needed to start the wire rope factory. I had one idea. When I used to go to the stock exchange each day, I frequently met H.B. Barat, a very old Bengali gentleman who had never married and thus did not have any children. He liked my family and said if I managed to get a foreign collaborator for the project, he would arrange the money for us.'

So BK suggested to his family that he should go abroad to look for collaboration. This was quite a big thing for the family as BK's elder brother was the only one who had ever been out of India and there were all sorts of doubts as to why anyone would want to collaborate with an unknown family in India. Eventually the family agreed and, in 1960, BK and his wife, who was only nineteen at the time, left on a three and a half month trip which took them all over Europe meeting with wire rope companies. He met with manufacturers in East Germany, West Germany, Italy, Holland and lastly in the UK.

'In the UK, I approached Martin Black through an introduction from their agent in India. Now, there happened another lucky break. A meeting was arranged and I went to their office. But, on that day, they had a robbery at their factory and all the directors except one were busy dealing with the police. This gentleman was W.S. Black who must have been even older than my father. He was the founder of the company and, as he was no longer involved in the day to day running of the business, I guess he had time to meet me. Before setting out on the trip I had wanted at least to know what wire rope looked like. To do this I smuggled myself into a factory in Calcutta making wire ropes posing as a scrap metal merchant to see what went on. Martin Black had received a number of invitations to collaborate with Indian companies but had not been interested in any. But W.S. Black sat in his chair and carefully read the paper I had written with my ideas of where the opportunity lay and the specification, sizes and quantities of the ropes that needed to be produced. Something in the paper triggered his interest and he started asking me details of this and that and after a discussion of four hours, he invited the other members of the Board to join us. Discussions continued over the next few days. The upshot was they indicated they would be interested in providing their technology but not in investing. I thought about this for a few days and checked out another option from a German company, which told me that I was too young for them to take the risk. I then rang Martin Black up as they had told me they would be having a Board meeting to discuss the opportunity. Whilst they had indicated they would be interested only in a technology agreement, I suggested an alternative structure where we would set up a company in which each of Martin Black and our family would take a 26 per cent share and the balance we would sell to the public. This seemed to interest them and, as a couple of their directors were about to visit the Far East, I suggested they come to Calcutta to explore this in detail. And so in August 1960 we met with the export director, George Black, W.S. Black's younger brother and John Goodlet (the Finance Director). Based on our projections with their royalties they would have recovered their investments in equity shares within five years. This was naturally attractive and so by early September the agreement was finalized with Martin Black and Usha Automobiles. Financing of the project was organized partly by long-term loan from ICICI Ltd and the raising of equity from stock exchange. As promised earlier, H.P. Bharat helped in organizing the successful placement of 48 per cent equity with the public. Thus Usha Martin Black (Wire Ropes) Limited was incorporated on 6 December and floated on the stock exchange in early January 1961.' The name was changed to Usha Martin Black Ltd in 1979 and further changed to Usha Martin Ltd.

With the company in place, BK still had to build the factory, which he had decided should definitely not be in Calcutta. This was the legacy of the strikes, first at Hindustan Motors and then at Usha Automobiles, which had prompted the move to diversification. 'The people who were working for us in Calcutta were excellent but communist unions from outside the factory controlled the workers. When we got wind there was going to be a strike at Usha Automobiles I went to Hindustan Motors and asked them which were the components that they were buying only from us. We immediately took out of our factory all of the dies and tools used to make these components and installed them in different parts of Calcutta including our home where we put up a tent. The upshot was we were able to honour our contracts with Hindustan Motors. But to avoid trouble with the unions we had to deliver the components at night. It was an absurd state of affairs and went on for many months. I decided that the new Usha Martin Black factory should be built in an area where there were no factories and where the locals would welcome the opportunity to work. I ended up choosing a completely tribal area outside Ranchi in what is now the state of Jharkhand (and was then Bihar).'

But, before the Ranchi wire rope factory could be built they had to obtain an import licence for the equipment. 'This took three months of visiting the relevant authorities in Delhi almost every day. The next issue to be solved was the lead-time to have the equipment made and shipped to India. It looked like it was going to take eighteen months but with the assistance of Martin Black we managed to install the equipment within record time of twelve months or so with the result the factory opened in 1962. This turned out to be three years ahead of our nearest competitor and by which time we were at full capacity producing 7,200 tonnes of wire rope per annum. That is another story because our licenced capacity was meant to be 3,600 tonnes but they made a mistake and indicated that was for one shift or something like that meaning we could double our production.'

BK was at pains to stress to me that the success of the company was also largely due to the excellent relationship with Martin Black. 'From the very beginning I was able to establish an excellent relationship with both the founders and operating directors. And even greater importance was my relationship with their production director, Alec Johnston who became my counterpart. His contribution to Usha Martin Black was immense; he was a selfless man.' Another reason for the success was the involvement of BK's younger brother, Brij who had gained a mechanical engineering degree from Jadavpur University in Calcutta. Brij moved to the UK for intensive training at Martin Black until the factory was ready and then moved to Ranchi to run it. John Goodlet helped us to establish a prudent technical system.'

When I asked BK to what he attributed the rapid success of the joint venture, including turning a profit in its first year, BK responded that there were two things in particular. Firstly, their emphasis on the importance of developing export markets and secondly, the emphasis on vertical integration.

He expanded by explaining: 'As this was the time of the licence/permit raj domestic growth was around 2.5 per cent per annum. We wanted to grow at a rate of 50 per cent so that we had to globalize. By 1965, we were exporting to Bangkok, Singapore, Kuala Lumpur and Hong Kong. There was also a Rupee payment arrangement with Russia and the Eastern Block that led to huge counter trade orders.

'And vertical integration was also critical as it allowed us to control our costs of production. I could see we needed our own steel plant to have timely supply of wire rods to fulfil export orders requiring short deliveries. The event that made this abundantly clear was when, following a lunch with Mukand Iron & Steel executives who were our sole supplier during the licence raj of steel rods, they informed us they were raising their prices by 25 per cent and reducing supplies to us. After much lobbying, we finally got a licence in 1971 for a steel billet factory that we put into Usha Alloys & Steels Limited (UASL). To show you how fed up people were with the licence raj our offer to the public of shares in Usha Alloys was oversubscribed by 71 times. The plant for the manufacture of steel billets in Jamshedpur was ready in 1973. But due to government policies it was not until 1979 that Usha Alloys was able to set up in Jamshedpur a steel plant with a wire rod rolling mill, so that our Ranchi wire rope plant could be fully supplied. But the formation of Usha Alloys in 1971 was the start of backward integration.'

The expansion and growth of Usha Martin was not only into vertical integration but also by horizontal diversification into other products like rope accessories and splicing equipment and in the manufacture of wire drawing and allied machines and, as mentioned above into developing strong export markets where eventually Usha Martin established local entities to make product locally such as in Thailand.

'In the 1980s many UK manufacturing businesses declined both for economic and shareholder issues. The first reason is obvious but the second is more subtle as the owners and builders of British manufacturing businesses were getting very old or the businesses had moved into the ownership of third and lower generations. Many of the descendants were either not interested in working hard or had no interest in the business built by their forebears. Sadly, this was the case with Martin Black and by the time we were producing 2000 tonnes per month they had dropped to producing 200 tonnes. Ultimately they were not able to survive in the wire rope business and we bought their shares in our ventures.'

The end of the license raj provided new challenges and opportunities. 'We were in a better position than many of our competitors as we were already exporting 65 per cent of our production. But we needed to improve our equipment. Between 1993 and 1995 we invested more money than we had invested in all the previous thirty-five years. And the expansion has continued until today such that Usha Martin is now the largest steel rope producer in India and the second largest globally.'

I asked BK what else was happening on the family front during all these years. I learnt that the link with the Birla family that started when BK's sister married G.P. Birla [son of B.M. Birla] became even closer. His younger sister married another Birla and BK himself married Uma, the daughter of Mr & Mrs B.D. Daga who was the granddaughter of G.D. Birla.

'Despite the initial success of Usha Automobile & Engineering and its relationship with Hindustan Motors I felt long term it may not have been viable and suggested my cousin MK to diversify/ look for additional "string to the bow". We decided on a company making tipping gears – hydraulic tipping gears for trucks.' This led to a joint venture with Telehoist of the UK based very much on the joint venture with Usha Martin who obviously spoke in glowing terms of their experiences with the Jhawar family.

By this time BK was totally focused on the Usha Martin wire rope business and following family discussions, as with many Indian joint family businesses which have grown large or unmanageable due to the number of family members, they agreed in 1969 to separate their various businesses. As part of the separation, Usha Automobile went to his cousin MK along with the joint venture with Telehoist that was the origin of UT Limited. MK was founder chairman until his death in 2002. Usha Martin went to BK and his brother Brij.

Over time, BK and his brother Brij introduced their respective sons into the business, BK's son Prashant and his nephew Rajeev. At the age of sixty-two in 1998, B.K. Jhawar told Prashant and Rajeev that he would in the not too distant future retire from day-to-day operations 'to become non-executive chairman'. 'They did not believe it but in 2001, I really did retire and become non-executive. They thought that I would be controlling, breathing down their necks, but I said, "Now you are on your own. If you want any advice or any help come to me but I will not volunteer it and I will not interfere." Now we share the same office building, but I have a separate entrance and a separate lobby. My office is totally separate from the working of the company. Prashant is the chairman and my nephew Rajeev is managing director. My brother Brij has also moved to become a non-executive director.'

Having dealt with the family generation succession within Usha Martin, BK became interested, like many others interviewed for my books on India, in the idea of a family constitution. 'Rajeev and I went to a course on family business at Indian School of Business, ISB Hyderabad – of course I was the oldest person there at seventy-years of age. Then Rajeev and Prashant went to another course at IMD and worked together in the family and encouraged them to look at the issues. By then, we had met Prof. John L. Ward (Kellogg

School of Management) who is one of the finest family business experts in the world. He helped Prashant and Rajeev to draw up a family constitution. We also got the grandchildren involved in making the vision and purpose of the family institution for the future. All of this was put together and we signed the family constitution in late 2010.'

When B.K. Jhawar retired, his intention was to devote most of his time to the corporate social responsibility arm of Usha Martin, Krishi Gram Vikas Kendra[2] (KGVK), which was set up in 1972. The politicized labour unrest of Calcutta, which had initiated the development of the new wire rope plant well outside Calcutta at Ranchi in the tribal belt of Jharkhand, was to be replaced by a different kind of unrest. As B.K. Jhawar explained, 'Within a few years of starting the factory we suddenly found discontent in the outside community. Analyzing this, we understood that for those people working inside our factory their standard of living started improving; their wives started wearing sandals instead of going barefoot, wearing nylon sarees and putting on lipstick. But those outside in the local tribal community were left behind. They were not left behind because of us but they thought that we were the reason for the difference in affluence and the social divide between those who were our employees and those who were not. So outsiders came and started creating trouble in the plant. Inside the factory, everything was all right, but outside there were so many disturbances that the factory also was affected by stoppages. Faced with people who seemed to be creating trouble for no good reason, we tried really to work with the community. Since the factory could take only limited people, we decided to engage with the community to generate goodwill. We started the Usha Martin Workers, Welfare Department in an attempt to do this, but very quickly realized it was not a job for a welfare department.

'Soon we realized that the size of the problem in the community was so large that the solution lay not in any single initiative. We realized that this was a dangerous minefield. But one thing was very clear – you could not live on an "island of prosperity surrounded by sea of poverty". And we also knew we could not be a 24/7 Santa Claus, just writing cheques. Charity only destroys dignity and independence. We did not want to give them "fish", but to teach them how to "fish" – and also to teach them how to "market the fish".

So, we decided to create an independent institution, but financially supported by Usha Martin. So KGVK was created in 1974 to engage in the sustainable and integrated development of rural Jharkhand. Two of the fundamental principles underlying all the activities of KGVK have been those of entrepreneurship and partnership. We developed a P4 (Public-Private-People's Partnership) approach, designed to involve the community in every activity to create a wider sense of ownership, because if you are not going to make people into partners, then you end up being a donor and there will be nothing sustainable created without the direct involvement of the local people and their link to the market.'

BK and I had by now spent many hours chatting and darkness was falling over Kolkata on a Saturday night and I knew he had to get home for a dinner party so we called it a day with his open offer to come and see what Usha Martin and KGVK are doing. As I leave these interviews I always try and reflect on what has made the person I have met successful and, by that, I do not mean in money terms. Not only does one usually need clear thinking and passion to succeed and which BK has in abundance but, one can also see in BK's life story, the importance of honouring what one has agreed with one's partners or customers, whether or not you need to move 'heaven and earth' to do so.

---

[1] www.ushamartin.com started in 1961 in Ranchi, Jharkhand as a wire rope manufacturing company, today the Usha Martin Group is a USD 1 billion conglomerate with a global presence. The group manufactures wire rods, bright bars, steel wires, speciality wires, wire ropes, strand, conveyor cord, wire drawing and cable machinery. With continuous growth in both the domestic and international markets, Usha Martin, the group's flagship company has emerged as India's largest and the world's second largest steel wire rope manufacturer.
[2] See www.kgvk.org for more details of KGVK.

> The national flag is the most solemn symbol of our country, and when our citizens gather around the flag it is absolutely non-controversial and allows them to rise above their religious affiliations, their political affiliations and, above all to demonstrate that they are proud to be Indian.

NAVEEN JINDAL
Chairman, Jindal Steel and Power[1]

I met Naveen Jindal in an airy room full of natural light, located at Jindal Steel and Power's head office in Delhi. He was friendly and open in describing his life and that of his family.

The Jindal family, shared Naveen, so far as they can trace back, hailed from the village of Nalwa in the state of Haryana in north-western India, about 170 kilometres to the west of Delhi. Nalwa is close to Hisar, the administrative capital that has become known as 'The City of Steel' and which, as you will read, closely ties in with the Jindal family.

'My grandfather, Net Ram inherited around 200 acres. Net Ram was a farmer but somehow his sons became involved in the creation and running of several completely distinct business empires. My uncle, Bhavichand Jindal ran the B.C. Jindal Group,[2] my uncle Sitaram Jindal ran Jindal Aluminium[3] and, my father, Om Prakash Jindal ran the O.P. Jindal Group.'[4]

It is the O.P. Jindal Group which is now split up between Naveen and his brothers. The eldest brother, Prithvi runs Jindal Saw Limited,[5] the next oldest, Sajjan runs JSW Group,[6] Ratan runs Jindal Stainless Limited[7] and Naveen, the youngest of the four, runs Jindal Steel and Power.

To understand Naveen's life we need to go back to the life of his father, Om Prakash (or OP Jindal as he became known). This is best described in Anil Dharker's book, *The Man Who Talked to Machines*.[8] One of OP's teachers complained to his father, Net Ram: 'Your son is more interested in machines than books.'[9] Apparently he loved taking apart machines and putting them back together – all based on instinct rather than training. There was another characteristic in OP and that was physical prowess and an interest in sport that has come down through the generations. One of the family legends OP would have heard as a child was that one of his great uncles was a giant of over seven feet, and was considered the strongest and bravest person in Nalwa. He is said to have taken on dacoits (bands of robbers) and frequently separated fighting bullocks by himself. This is specifically linked to a story about OP, who loved bodybuilding and in fact told his parents he wanted to be a professional wrestler. The story goes that once when one of two bullocks used to till the fields fell ill, OP told his father, 'No problem. You have a bull right here.'[10]

His mother is said to have told her friends, 'Om Prakash hasn't got feet. He's got wheels.'[11] She could tell her middle son would never stand still. Combined with this, we have Net Ram becoming increasingly despondent about the future of farming in Nalwa for two main reasons – the dependence on the monsoons and the constant disputes over land ownership. He advised each of this three sons to leave Nalwa and 'go east' to Assam and Bengal rather than west to Delhi which, although the political capital, was far behind Calcutta in terms of commerce. By 1946, OP's elder brothers DS and BC had moved to Calcutta and were working as trainees in the wholesale and retail cloth trade and OP, being the next eldest boy, was in line to move there and join them. But, before allowing him to leave, OP was married off at the age of sixteen to Vidya Devi, a sister of his elder brother DS's wife, who was thirteen at the time.

Four years later OP, left his pregnant wife behind in Nalwa and moved to Calcutta. And it was not long after he arrived that he experienced his 'Eureka' moment; a life-changing event which I have noted is experienced by many of the entrepreneurs covered in my books. His moment came while he was walking in a field outside Calcutta, where he came across a pile of pipes all marked with 'Made in England'. It immediately came to him that India must make pipes rather than import them. He started by trading steel pipes and tubes, many of which had been left behind by the Americans after the Second World War. Within a couple of years, OP was able to put his dream into practice, as in 1952, at the age of twenty-two, he was able to establish a factory in the Howrah district across the Hooghly river, not far to the west of Calcutta. The factory was to make pipe bends and sockets and half of the 40,000 rupee investment was borrowed. The inputs primarily came from waste pipe products from Tata. OP was in charge of production, and his elder brothers looked after marketing, finance, and administration. It was at this point that OP's skill with machines started to make a competitive difference. Threading for the pipes was initially done manually, but OP found a discarded threading machine, renovated it and installed it into the existing machinery so that it bacame an automatic process. His product was different and superior to those in the market and, for the first time, the Jindal brand became known.

However, OP did not want to make Calcutta his permanent base and decided to set up a new plant in Hisar near the family home in Nalwa. As Calcutta was the major business city of India at that time, many mocked OP for even thinking of doing this. But he was right and fast forward a decade or so – Hisar became known as 'The City of Steel'.

When Net Ram asked OP how long it would take to build the pipe plant in Hisar, OP told his father that it would take six months and that it would earn 40,000 rupees per day. Net Ram is said to have responded that one year and Rs 500 per day would be enough. But, of course OP succeeded exactly as he had believed. When Net Ram first saw the quality of the product produced by OP's plant, he told his son: 'If you go on working like this, your name will one day be like Tata and Birla.'[12]

By this point, India was well into the 'licence raj' regime, and it became increasingly difficult to obtain steel strips, which were the raw material for the pipe plant. OP was forced to do what many other manufacturers were forced to do – backward integrate – which meant in his case making steel strips, largely using machinery he had himself designed and built. Jindal Strips came into existence in 1970.

OP's strategy by now was clear – focus on steel and aim for import substitution. And where the inputs to make the products were not available, then to produce the inputs as well. By 1975, OP had expanded into producing stainless steel, and later steel slabs, hot-rolled plates, and large diameter pipes (submerged arc welded) for the oil and natural gas sector.

Naveen was born in 1970 in Hisar; his three elder brothers having been born earlier; Prithvi Raj in 1951 not long after his father moved to Calcutta, Sajjan in 1959, and Ratan in 1962. There is a reason for the almost twenty year difference between Prithvi and Naveen, and that is due to the fact that they had different mothers. Tragically, Vidya Devi, the mother of his three older brothers and four sisters, fell desperately ill with cancer and passed away in 1964 when Prithvi Raj was only thirteen. OP was himself only thirty-four and had six children and the answer was clear – he needed to marry again. The seventh daughter, Asha was a baby when Vidya Devi passed away and was adopted by OP's younger brother Sitaram and his wife. And who did OP marry and who was in due course Naveen's mother? He married his late wife's sister, Savitri Devi at the suggestion of his in-laws as she would be bringing up her sister's children. Savitri Devi was fifteen at the time; only two years older than Prithvi Raj. In due time, Savitri Devi and OP had three children – Sarika, Seema, and Naveen. Naveen says, 'In fact till I was thirteen, I did not know our elder siblings had a different mother. But there is absolutely no doubt that Savitri Devi became the mother to all of my father's children and the respect in which she is held continues to this day.'

The year 1970 was an important one for the family business. It was in that year over a family dinner that OP and his brothers carved out the existing businesses between them. Some family members may have felt it was a little unfair, but then nobody complained about it. They stuck to the decision they made. Three of the brothers have continued the Jindal businesses from 1970 to the present day. As mentioned earlier, Bhavichand kept Jindal (India) Ltd, the original 1952 family business; Sitaram had been involved in Jindal Aluminium since its founding in 1968 and so kept that business. OP kept the strip mills, the pipe business for the oil and gas industry and the stainless steel plant.

I asked Naveen to go back to his childhood: 'I am the tenth child my father had. So after they had me, they finally got what they were looking for and he stopped – no I am just joking,' he chuckles. I am the youngest in my generation. I was not really the last spoiled child in the family as my father was always so busy with his work and anyway, I do not think he ever believed in spoiling anyone. His principles were very, very clear: you must not "spare the rod and spoil the child".

'When I was a young boy, I did not know what I wanted to be. At times I wanted to join the Indian Army and at others, I wanted to be a pilot, but most of the time I wanted to look after my pets. I had a whole menagerie of pets in my house. There were rabbits, guinea pigs, and hamsters. There were dogs, white pigeons, parrots, fish – whatever I could lay my hands on. I used to spend lots of time by myself "hanging out" with my pets and roaming about our large garden where I would climb trees to find birds' nests. Of course, this was at a time when there was no television or computers in Hisar, so we did not have much else to do.

'I think my interest in joining the army came from my love of shooting and riding horses. My father used to ride, so seeing him ride I also wanted to ride, whereas this was of little interest to my siblings. My father used to go on long rides along the canal near our home. Sadly, I never went with him but used to wait for him to return and then sit on his horse and take it for rides around our garden. As for my interest in shooting, this was probably sparked by the fact my father kept guns for protection and there were armed guards in the Hisar factories. Although my father almost certainly did not know, some of the guards let me play with their guns and shoot drums for target practice. As you will hear, this became more than just a passing fad.

'When I was about fifteen, the family moved to Delhi. I am not sure what the reason was for the move as my father still used to spend a lot of time in Hisar. I think it was probably just following a trend that once businesses got to a certain size, it was necessary to spend time in the administrative capital of Delhi and particularly during the "licence raj" era. But my father's business activities were expanding beyond Calcutta and Hisar. There was a small factory in Delhi, but Maharashtra became important too and our first steel plant was set up at Vasind in 1982. And it was at this point my brother Sajjan moved to Mumbai to run that plant.

'Whilst I had gone to government schools in Hisar, once we moved to Delhi, I was sent to a private boarding school. First I went to Sawan Public School and then, for my last two years of eleventh and twelfth, I went to Delhi Public School on Mathura Road. So far as my academic studies go I guess I was an average student but,' Naveen says smiling, 'certainly no genius.

'It was while in Delhi that I started to take rifle shooting seriously. I joined the Delhi Rifle Club and started to take part in competitions. I found myself wining medals and in fact that is how I got into Hans Raj College in Delhi University – it was on the basis of the sports quota. I also joined a riding school and from there I graduated to the polo club and started playing polo. I asked my father to buy me a polo pony which he did, but when I asked him to buy me another, he asked me why I would need more than one horse as he said horses never get tired. I had to make him understand polo. Whenever I needed something from him, would I go and massage his feet. Then he would ask me what I wanted and I would tell him. He would say that I was not going to listen to him anyway, so that I might as well go and buy it. Then one day – this was many years later – he told me he had heard from other people that I now had forty polo ponies and asked if it was true. I told him it was and I think he was genuinely shocked. It is difficult to say which is more of a passion: shooting or polo but, as my son also became more interested in riding and polo, I started to do this with him. In recent years, I injured my back so have had to take a break from polo. Incidentally, the Jindal Steel & Power polo team has become an integral part of the Indian polo circuit, with multiple tournament wins over the last fifteen years.

'In 1990, I went to the University of Texas in Dallas to do my MBA.[13] While I was in the US, I continued my interest in shooting and learnt skeet shooting at which I became quite proficient. In fact, I created the national record in 2003 in Skeet Shooting at the Hyderabad National Championships by shooting 122 out of 125. Since then, I have represented India many times internationally but nothing much to write home about. I cannot say I am a naturally talented shooter. I have found I have to work very hard at it. So, the more time I spent, the better I got and of course that is true with most things. But it is difficult competing against people who shoot as a full-time job.

'It was while I was in Dallas that my political career started as I was elected president of its student government. In fact, it was the same time that my father entered Haryana State politics when he was sixty-one. Everyone tried to persuade him not to do so but he felt it was his duty. He was fed up with corruption and bureaucracy and hoped he could change the situation by being on the inside. He was also not interested in retirement and I can remember him telling me that one of our relatives had fallen ill because he was retired. He moved from State to Federal politics in 1996 when he became a member of Lok Sabha, the federal parliament. It was remarkable for an industrialist to join active politics. My father contested six elections, and for anyone, let alone an industrialist, to contest any election is not easy in India. Given the kind of malpractices that happen and the kind of atmosphere in which the election take place, we do actually need electoral reforms. I decided to enter politics primarily because my father has been a role model for me. He has always been an inspiration and I helped in his political affairs when I returned from the US. I was proud to be elected to the same constituency as him, Kurukshetra in Haryana in 2004 and was re-elected for a second term in 2009. I also felt that one can accomplish a lot through politics, because most people who join politics are in for the wrong reasons. My father always used to say that God has been so kind to us that we in turn must also do something for others.

'I returned to India in September 1992 and immediately joined the family business at its new steel plant at Raigarh in Chhattisgarh. On the following 26 January, which is our Republic Day, it is customary for all factories, schools, and government buildings everywhere in India to hoist the national flag. We did the same. The next day when I came to work, the flag was gone. So I wondered why the flag, which had been looking so good, had been removed. While I was in the US, an American friend of mine had gifted me an Indian flag that I had put up on the wall in my office when I was president of the student government. No one ever objected to it – in fact I used to very proudly tell people about it. So when I was told that we could not fly the flag, I was surprised that I could do it in the US, but I was not allowed to display the national flag in India.

'I decided there must be something wrong with the law and decided to find out more. I found the rule was that the flag could only be displayed on government buildings, except on the national days when other citizens were permitted to fly it. I felt this was nonsensical and so I asked our people to continue flying the flag at the Raigarh factory. Some time later, the police came and removed the flag. My immediate instinct was to commence an action against the government. Our employees were not happy with my plan as they felt that this was likely to cause us grief with the government and that we would lose the case anyway. But I drew inspiration from my father who always used to say that that we should stand up for what we believe in. One of his sayings, and he had many,' Naveen smiles, 'was that "the brave die only once but that a coward dies many times". So I challenged the government and after ten long years, on 23 January 2004, the Supreme Court of India declared it is a fundamental right under freedom of speech and expression for any citizen to fly the national flag in a respectful manner. The national flag is the most solemn symbol of our country, and when our citizens gather around the flag it is absolutely non-controversial and allows them to rise above their religious affiliations, their political affiliations and, above all to demonstrate that they are proud to be Indian. It is my dream that more and more people display the national flag and draw inspiration from it and do their own job well. If we all did this, there is no power on earth that can stop India from becoming a very prosperous country.'

I asked Naveen why he decided to go into the family business. 'Well, actually there was not much of a choice. By the time I came back from the US, I was smart enough to realize that it was much better to join my father and get a head start in life rather than start any other career – as I have told you I knew I was never academic enough to be a doctor or an engineer. And childish ideas of joining the army had vanished once I had started shooting and riding for myself. Actually, I was "thrown into the deep end" as the Raigarh plant had only been opened the year before and it was not doing so well; it faced many challenges. It was making losses, the production was not right, and there were a lot of pollution issues. But my father was always very optimistic about its prospects. He used to say that this plant would make a lot of money one day. I used to think that he was just saying this to encourage me so that I did not lose heart. But he was right and slowly but surely, all the issues were sorted and the plant began to make money.' This plant was the start of Jindal Steel & Power Ltd, of which Naveen Jindal is now the chairman.

I asked Naveen whether at that time the four brothers were working together with their father. 'No, not really, because my father had a lot of foresight. He realized that his children could live together and that they could eat together, but that it would be better if they worked separately. So he arranged for us to work in different companies and in different parts of India. The remarkable thing is that, given all of the problems with the Raigarh steel plant, one would have thought he would have involved one of my older brothers who already had experience with many of the issues. But apparently he told them that this plant was being set up for me to run and he felt if any of them got emotionally involved in sorting out its issues, it would be difficult to move them elsewhere. So when I returned from the US, it was just my father who was involved in the running of the plant in Raigarh.

'My brothers were already well-settled into other businesses. As mentioned, Sajjan Bhaiya had moved to Mumbai for the Vasind steel plant, and which was the start of JSW Steel Ltd Group. My oldest brother, Prithvi Bhaiya, managed the Jindal Saw Ltd group, whose first steel plant was commissioned in 1986 at Kosi Kalan, in Uttar Pradesh. Ratan Bhaiya managed the inheritance of the original O.P. Jindal Group company, Jindal Strips in Hisar which over the years has expanded into stainless steel production. The JSW Group has its corporate headquarters in Mumbai whereas the other three groups share the corporate headquarters of the overarching O.P. Jindal Group in Delhi.

'We were all are very happy with what my father decided for us. He established a clever owning and operating structure for the five of us (his four sons and him) that continues to this day. It worked like this – obviously I am describing this in brief – each of the five of us should own 20 per cent with my father providing the voting power of his 20 per cent to the son running the business. So if I am looking after a particular company, I get 20 per cent plus my father's 20 per cent share. Whilst my father theoretically gave up everything, in practice he still had everything because, whatever shares we had as his sons, we knew and felt they were really his. With the passing of my father, my mother has the same feeling of still owning it all. And indeed whatever she wants, we will do it for her. So we do not really have a concept of exclusive ownership. The 20 per cent remains true in principle to this day for all our promoter shareholdings. Obviously, there is flexibility if any of us want to swap shareholdings or realize some capital or whatever, but the basic principle remains. It is a simple principle and it has worked well for us.

'It was indeed fortunate that my father had instituted this system many years before he passed away, because as you may know he died at the age of seventy-five in a helicopter crash on 31 March 2005, en route from Chandigarh to Delhi. In India, the death of the founder so often leads to inheritance issues but in our family, the principles he had instituted many years before meant that there were absolutely no issues in this regard. Incidentally, not only did my mother take over his position as chairman in the OP Jindal Group, but she became the Congress candidate for the Hisar State Assembly in the by-election after my father's death.'

I asked Naveen to reflect a little on his father's life and particular stories which stick to his mind. 'My father never valued academic study as he believed everything can be learnt practically and, in the case of our businesses, on the factory floor. He relented a little as he grew older but, and this was another of his characteristics, he was a man of few words and when he made a decision it was extremely difficult to get him to change it. The best strategy in such a situation, Naveen says laughing, was for them to seek their mother's aid and this is what Sajjan successfully did when his father refused to allow him to study engineering at university.

Anil Darker also deals in his book with several stories of OP's 'black and white' view of life and business.[14] One involves OP's general disdain for unions, having seen the damage they caused to Calcutta business. Back in the 1980s, one of most feared union leaders in the country was Datta Samant. The two of them first 'met' on a flight from Ahmedabad to Bombay when by chance they were seated together. On learning that the gentlemen sitting beside him was O.P. Jindal, there was clearly tension between the two. Samant's view was undoubtedly due to the fact that all of OP's plants were operated without any unions. Later, Samant and OP directly came up against each other when OP bought Khemanchand Agarwal's plant in Tarapur on the condition that there would be no unions. Samant called the workers out on a strike that went on for six months. On a critical day at the end of that period, OP was to have a meeting with the workers and, as Anil Darker puts it, 'Samant's men were determined to wreck it and OP found his car being stoned and people being beaten up. With the courage for which he was justly famous, OP waded through the crowd and clambered up on a platform. "I have no problem with a union," he declared. "But there can only be one leader. I do have a problem if you owe your allegiance elsewhere. I have a simple solution, if you do not accept me as your leader...." Here OP paused dramatically, took out a matchbox from his pocket, lit a match and pointed it at the factory building. "If you don't accept me as your sole leader, then *mein isko jala doonga* (I'll burn it down)".[15] The strike ended and Samant's union was thrown out; the first time Samant had not got his way. Whilst he may have been anti-union, OP was clearly pro-worker and it was one of OP's cardinal policies that workers should be provided with housing and essential needs for their families such as education.'

Naveen continued with other stories of his father, 'As you have heard, he was a brilliant and instinctive engineer. I remember there was a very large boulder on a property where we were erecting a plant. It was far too heavy to be moved without substantial earth moving equipment that the civil engineers were planning to contract. My father asked them whether they had thought about just digging a hole beside the boulder and pushing it into that. Simple, isn't it?' says Naveen smiling, 'He was very practical.

'I was once with him on a trip to the US where we were looking to buy some second-hand equipment. My father could just look at a machine and know it inside-out in seconds. Two engineers were showing us around the plant and we stopped in front of a machine my father was not interested in buying. He looked at it for a few seconds and then asked them, "Does it work like this?", and proceeded to explain his thoughts. They were absolutely shocked as it was a complex piece of machinery they knew he could never have seen something similar before.

'Despite his wealth, my father remained a simple man all his life and did not like to put on airs. There are countless stories on this. I am told that one day some important visitors came to meet my father at home. The guard pointed out that my father was the man sitting in the chair on our lawn. These guests told the guard this could not possibly be my father as he was wearing a simple vest and pajamas. On another occasion, my father was inspecting some land in Bombay where he thought they might build a factory. It was a huge piece of land and as the road was not driveable for a car, my father and his colleague, Khemanchand Agarwal needed to walk a considerable distance to meet the agent selling the land. Mr Agarwal was walking well ahead of my father when my father spied a boy on a bicycle and borrowed it from him putting the boy on the back. When my father cycled up to the agent, Mr. Agarwal was already talking him and explained to the agent that this was my father arriving on the bicycle. He is said to have asked, "That's him? Your OP Jindal seth is the man riding the cycle. Mr Agarwal, do you take me for a fool?"[16]

'His frugality was legendary. He hated leaving tips and when we were adults and when the family went out to dinner with him, one of my brothers or I tried to get the bill before him and, on those rare occasions when he did and we knew he would leave little, one of us would hang around until he left and add some more. Whilst he never denied us spending money, as I have explained with my horses, but he would purchase bales of off-white material to be made into our everyday wear. And in the days before mobile phones, every senior executive knew never to call my father from a hotel phone and that it was much wiser to wait for him to call.'

But it seems that according to Anil Darker, OP's concern for economy came not from being a miser but from his roots in a small Haryana village 'roots, which he neither tried, nor was ever able to shake off. He spoke in Haryanvi, a language some would consider crude, but most consider earthy...Those roots showed up in the beedis he smoked rather than cigarettes, the roasted grams he preferred to canapés, and the cards he played in the evenings with close friends as a form of relaxation rather than going to parties or watching television.'[17]

This traditional conservatism extended to OP's attitude towards women, although he became much more liberal over the years. As children the daughters were not allowed to bring boys home to play and in fact they were not allowed to go and play at their friends' homes. Friends had to come to the Jindal home. However, OP did believe in his daughters being educated. 'Educate a girl, he used to say, and you educate two families. Educate a boy and you only educate him.'[18]

I asked Naveen whether it was true that his wife, Shallu also broke down some of his father's conservative attitude to women. 'Yes, my father was very displeased when my sister, Seema danced at our sister, Sarika's wedding. However, some years later he seemed happy to accept that Shallu, not only learnt the dance form Kuchipudi, but gave stage performances.'

His mention of Shallu turned Naveen's mind to his own family. 'I married Shallu in 1994 when I was twenty-four years old. It was an arranged marriage just like all my siblings. Times have however changed and I cannot say whether my children will also have arranged marriages. In fact I never thought that I would have one, but then I did. I have an eighteen-year-old son, Venkatesh, and a fifteen-year-old daughter, Yashasvini. I encourage them to do whatever they want and do not see them entering the family business unless they really want to. This does not mean that I have not done what I wanted. In fact, the challenge for me is that I want to do too many things and there are only so many things you can do well. What I am trying to do now is to find the right balance and do fewer things better.' As we had already spent a considerable time together, I took this as my cue to bring our meeting to a close and enable him to get back to balancing what is an extremely full life.

---

[1] Naveen Jindal is the Chairman and the member of the Jindal family responsible for running Jindal Steel and Power (www.jindalsteelandpower.com). Jindal Steel and Power Limited (JSPL) is one of India's major steel producers with a significant presence in sectors like mining, power generation and infrastructure. With an annual turnover of over US$ 3.6 billion, JSPL is a part of the USD 18 billion diversified O.P. Jindal Group (http://www.opjindal.com).
[2] B.C. Jindal Group (www.jindalgroup.com)
[3] Jindal Aluminium Ltd (www.jindalaluminium.com)
[4] O.P. Jindal Group (www.jindalsteel.com)
[5] Jindal Saw Ltd (www.jindalsaw.com)
[6] JSW Group (www.jsw.in)
[7] Jindal Stainless Ltd (www.jslstainless.com)
[8] Anil Dharker, *The Man who talked to Machines-the story of Om Prakash Jindal*, Eminence Designs Pvt Ltd, 2005
[9] ibid., p.21
[10] ibid., p.24
[11] ibid., p.30
[12] ibid., p.47
[13] *A few years ago the Management School at University of Texas in Dallas was renamed the "Naveen Jindal School of Management.*
[14] ibid., pp.108-110
[15] ibid., pp.109-110
[16] ibid., p.76
[17] ibid., p.81
[18] ibid., p.88

> I would not be giving you the correct impression if I were to claim that I was all the time on the "up". I have had "down" periods too, but even in the worst of times, I never changed my value systems of kindness, honesty, and integrity – I would not allow anything to affect that. Even more so in the tough periods you have to rely on your honesty and integrity.

B.M. KHAITAN

Chairman, Williamson Magor[1]

The first thing I felt upon setting foot in 4 Mangoe Lane in Kolkata, where Williamson Magor has its office, is the enormous respect in which its chairman, Brij Mohan Khaitan, is held. You can feel this respect from the security guards at the gate all the way through to the receptionist, lift operator, his secretary, and on into Mr. Khaitan's office where we met.

B.M. Khaitan has a corner office on the top floor, which is where he has sat for many years. On meeting him, I was struck by the peace that he seems to exude. I guess I should not have been surprised, as it is not uncommon to find this peace in elderly people who have accepted their lot in life, whether it has been full of success, failure, or a mixed bag. And, boy oh boy, what a wonderfully interesting and satisfying life I learnt he has led.

B.M. Khaitan looks more like someone in his seventies rather than a gentleman of eighty-five. He seemed a bit careful and slow on his feet but still manages to play golf a few times a week. While it is clearly a working office, as he pointed out to me, he has a near clear desk as he no longer shoulders day-to-day responsibilities and spends his time in the office meeting old friends, talking to staff, updating on his philanthropic initiatives, and giving advice to anyone who seeks it.

After we settled down with a cup of tea, we started our meeting with him telling me: 'I belong to an era where old traditions were respected and given more prominence in business than they are today. I think that one of the reasons for any success that I may have had is because I stuck by these old traditions in this ever-changing world of today. Maybe, because of this, I stick out like a sore thumb. Today, you can see these completely different ideas and traditions being followed in the same business. But, in our case, I believe we have tried to stick to these old traditions.

'I have been associated with Williamson Magor since I was in my late teens and it has been a great honour and satisfaction for me as it was a highly respected company when I joined, as I hope people still see it today. It was simply my own intuition that I came into contact with the company. There was maybe some good fortune that a working relationship developed into friendship and then into partnership, but this was also the result of honesty and sincerity being tested.'

I asked Mr Khaitan to tell me a little of the story of Williamson Magor before we turned to his life and how he came into contact with the company. It all started back in 1852 when three Williamsons – two Georges, and a Captain James Hay Williamson – leased land and established tea gardens, whilst the younger George worked for the Assam Company's tea plantations in Assam. The North Eastern Assam Valley, about 450 miles long running east to west and 50 miles wide, was the location chosen by the East India Company in the 1840s to produce tea in competition with China tea. And Calcutta was the centre from which Assam tea production would be controlled and through which it would be shipped throughout the world.

The link between the Williamson and the Magor families began a decade later in 1866 when James Williamson met R.B. Magor who was at that time an assistant at the Great Eastern Hotel in Calcutta. In 1869, they formed the Williamson Magor partnership that grew steadily and by 1894, moved into offices in 4 Mangoe Lane.[2]

R.B. Magor and J.H. Williamson, while pursuing their partnership interests acting as agent and secretary for many tea estates, also took share holdings in them and served on their Boards of Directors. Williamson Magor & Co. worked closely with the London partnership of George Williamson & Co., who became the overseas partners and selling agents of Williamson Magor until 2001. R.B. Magor died in 1933. Thereafter, Pat Williamson, the grandson of J.H. Williamson, was eventually to introduce Mr. Khaitan to Williamson Magor in 1947.

I asked Mr. Khaitan to turn to the story of his own life. 'I was born into a very fine family where my four uncles were all lawyers. The family law firm, Khaitan & Company, was founded in 1911 in Calcutta by my uncles. As you may know, the firm exists to this day and is now one of the largest law firms in India.

'My uncles realized that my father, who studied up to college level, was not capable or interested in becoming a lawyer so he was given their shares in a small commission agency business they also owned. The uncles were far too busy with their legal business. Whereas it could be said my uncles became rich from the law, this was not the case with my father's business. My father initially struggled to make ends meet and eventually you would say we were comfortably off. But, being part of a family that was rich, he got marked as also one of the rich, but actually he was not. My father had five children; three daughters and two sons. I was born in 1927.

'I always knew that I wanted to be successful. I think that there was maybe a psychological factor because I was surrounded by my wealthy and successful uncles and their children. I was very aware of the success of my uncle, Debi Prasad Khaitan, who was the founder of Khaitan & Co, and who went on to become a member of the Constituent Assembly. Another uncle, Bhagwati Prasad Khaitan, studied at Presidency College, Calcutta, completed law from Calcutta University, and went on to England for further studies, before joining Khaitan & Co. All of this, I have to say, gave me a bit of a complex. I don't think it worried my father at all because he was quite a sporting type and, being a sporting type, he used to treat everything in a very light manner, whereas I did not.

'Until I was five or six, my parents and my uncles and their families all lived together in the joint family home. I think the time we moved out was when the legal business and the commission agency business were split between my uncles and father.

'I went to St. Xavier's Collegiate School in 1936 at the age of nine. It was a Jesuit school and is still located in Park Street, just as it was back then. The family followed the traditional Marwari community belief in the importance of education, and hence, all of us went to good schools and colleges. I know my father found it a financial strain, but I stayed at St Xavier's until I had completed my education.' I was pleased to hear Mr. Khaitan tell me that he was a very mediocre student, as I am sure it will give hope to many young people reading this book that to be successful in life does not mean you have to be a top student. Mr. Khaitan went on to say, 'I have never settled down in my mind that I must do anything at great depth, because I always got bored very quickly. If I want to do something then I want to get on with it rather than procrastinate. In this respect, I am similar to my father. My mind is very like my father's but, on the other hand, I am very soft hearted like my mother. In most of my decisions, my heart rules over my head. I consider that to be one of my biggest weaknesses. I always think that I had better be kind and that I had better do the decent thing.

'From day one at St Xavier's, I was exposed to the western way of thinking, because all the Jesuit fathers who taught there were mainly Belgian, Italian, or English. As a result of that, my thinking was oriented – if I may use the word – towards the West and I became more and more western, not only in my thinking but also in my friendships. By the time I finished my matriculation, I did not have very many friends from our own Marwari community. My uncles travelled overseas frequently and had "seen the world" as it were; meaning they were far more westernized than the traditional Marwaris in Calcutta. This was often a sore point in the local Marwari community, in that they thought all the Khaitans were westernised and ostracized them. Actually, the opposite was true, and it was the local Marwari community at that time who thought that they were better than we Khaitans. However, I do not mind admitting today that I owe quite a lot to the way of thinking taught to me by the Jesuit fathers as it undoubtedly helped me in my personal development and in my career.

'I also learnt the discipline that the Jesuits imposed, and this has led to me being very disciplined in my life. As to following a formal religion, it does not worry me if I am to go to a cathedral, church or a temple, but I am nevertheless very religious minded. The Jesuits never tried to persuade me to change my thinking, but in a very subtle way they pushed me towards the western way of looking at things.

'My working life really started in 1946 when I was working in my father's commission agency business and came into contact with Pat Williamson of Williamson Magor. I wanted to sell him fertilizer and plywood. I think I must have impressed him with my straightforward approach and he soon came to trust my honesty and commitment to service. This led to a close friendship between Pat and me.

'In 1948, I started playing golf with him and other expatriates at the Royal Calcutta Golf Club. Pat and I also became regular racegoers. My lifestyle became completely westernized, from friendships to the western way of doing business. I do not mind accepting the fact that, even today, I would still take decisions that are more westernized in approach than Indian.

'When India became independent in 1947, the attitude of the expatriates underwent a significant change. Earlier it was more a colonial attitude. This was not the case after independence, when westerners would accept you as a friend, if they liked you. And if you were accepted as a friend, you were treated as a friend. This is not how some Indian businessmen behaved at that time who, in my opinion, treated the friendship purely for the business opportunity it offered. This I would not do; I would go for tradition. If I make a friend, I make a friend and I am not going to change that, if he is "down and out". When I first encountered Williamson Magor, there were still the original British families involved. They invited me to come and join; it was not an aggressive encounter or anything like that. When they asked me to come, they said: "We would like you to come and help us and also become our partner".

'I was welcomed into Williamson Magor, which was not the case in that period with some other English companies, where Indians were slightly aggressive in plotting to take them over. But I naturally did not take that route. I took the friendly route. I knew that Williamson Magor was a good company and that I would be working with them as an equal partner. Pat Williamson and I were friends first, and became partners, not only in business, but also in racing horses.

'I don't mind saying my whole attitude to the social side of things was completely westernized and, until my son got married to Sanjiv Goenka's sister, I don't think I had a single Marwari friend. When my son married, the whole thing changed as the Goenka's were eastern oriented. So I have adjusted myself in and moved on. Today I have learnt a lot that I was not observing in the past. I have become a lot more religious and might be seen, one might say, as an orthodox Hindu. However, even today, I like going to a church service. It is very nice to have a feel for all religions and there is no sense of compulsion that I should do this or that.

'My son's marriage was an arranged marriage. I knew the family head K.P. Goenka and his son Rama Prasad Goenka, and he asked if my elder son, Deepak would like to be engaged to his daughter, Yashodhara. I told him it was up to my son. The two met and must have liked each other as they ended up marrying and it has worked out very well. They were far richer than me and I was hesitant to make the connection in case the gap was too great. But, to be honest about it, whilst I think I was widely respected in the western business community, the connection with the Goenka family did give me a lot of prestige in the Indian community.

'Respect is something I learnt from my father. He was an excellent sports person and, given his easy manner, he made friends easily and particularly with westerners of that time who loved the sports he loved, like golf. He was in fact the fourth Indian to become a member of the Royal Calcutta Golf Club in 1947. As a child and as a young man, I could see his friends respected him and, to my knowledge, he never had an enemy. I think he saw sport as a way of making life-long friendships. And I have carried on that sporting tradition. Even today, at eighty-five, I still play golf with my friends although I do not play a full eighteen holes. I play three to four holes walking, and then I take the buggy. When I look back, I say "thank God" I got into this sport. Even at this age, I can get out on the greens in the open air with the trees and nature and enjoy myself.' I told Mr. Khaitan that as a golfer myself, I could relate to this sentiment, as I am sure any golfer reading this chapter can and hope that we too can also be doing it at that age!

I asked B.M. Khaitan to go back to how he became involved with Williamson Magor. 'When I left school, I had no idea of what I was going to do. That said, I did not have many alternatives either.

My father did not have the resources to start another business for me, so I joined him as a commission agent in his business while studying for a B.Com at morning college.

'Amongst my father's customers were two small businesses; one involved with fertilizer and one with plywood. I took responsibility for them and they were to change my life. Williamson Magor became my customer and I looked after their annual requirements for fertilizers and plywood. They trusted me and I did not let them down. It was after ten years of this association that they asked me to join the partnership.'

I asked Mr. Khaitan if his friendship with Pat Williamson went beyond business and golf to racing. 'Yes, from 1949 onwards I was racing with them. It was Pat Williamson who got me into owning race horses, which I stress was, at that time, not such an expensive pastime as it is today. We used to buy four horses a year and own a quarter of each; meaning we each effectively owned just one horse. Having obtained an income channel from Williamson Magor as a steady supplier of the company and which was completely clear of any ambiguity or conflict, I earned enough to enjoy myself and to keep racing and golfing, and from that point on was never short of money in that way.'

Pat Williamson, with whom B.M. Khaitan shared ownership of his first horse, Red Rival, was the grandson of the original J.H. Williamson and number two at that time at Williamson Magor. Number one was Cren Sandys-Lumsdaine, who had married Richard Magor's sister and who found peacetime Calcutta a little dull after the Second World War. He did his best to cope by indulging in a passion for fast cars. He drove a beautiful Bentley to the office in Calcutta each day and it is said his mongrel dog followed him later in a rickshaw. The mongrel had lost both ears – bitten off by the cats that lived in the drains.

Around the time B.M. Khaitan started working with his father in 1947, despite his western viewpoint, he followed the custom and had a traditional arranged marriage. 'My father started to slow down after I joined him, and he retired in 1950. When he passed away some time later, he left all his money to my sisters and I was happy not to take anything because I was doing quite well. My brother then joined me in the commission agency business and together on our own we built it up. When I joined Williamson Magor as a partner in 1962, I gave my brother my share in this and in all the other investments I had made. One might say I was not under any obligation to do so but, as I was his younger brother, I did not want any dispute or unpleasantness. I was also happy to do this as I felt in my mind that Williamson Magor was my future. My brother continued in the commission agency business which is today run by his only son.'

Not long after becoming a partner in the business, Mr. Khaitan was appointed its managing director in 1964. 'I kept Williamson Magor going through the difficult years in Calcutta after 1965 with its Marxist government and the many union problems we experienced. I kept it very steady. I did not allow anything adverse to happen. We did not get the same devaluation shock as others did. Many British executives running British businesses in Calcutta during this period left en masse. It did not matter to them what happened to the company as they still got their salaries, which were not tied to the success of the company. My situation was different; I was disheartened but I did not give up, and in fact, grew the business during those difficult times.

'Even the fact that other Indian businessmen were leaving Calcutta for places like Delhi, Bombay, and Madras did not influence me. I used to have problems with the unions but, as I said earlier, my heart is a bit on the softer side; and so I made large concessions to keep the unions happy even though it meant our profit margins suffered. Even in those difficult times when there was large anti-foreign feeling, I managed every bit of the foreigners' commitment in India. And with that came loyalty. Even today, I do not mind admitting, that I have sixty to seventy expatriates on the pensioners' list. After they retired, I have continued to pay their pensions to them and, where relevant, to their widows. I have never regretted doing this and don't know of any other company of that period that has continued to honour its obligations in this regard. That is part of my life, because these were my friends.'

It was during this period that 4 Mangoe Lane was redeveloped into the ten-storey building, which houses Williamson Magor to this day. The new offices were opened in 1968.

In 1974, B.M. Khaitan merged Williamson Magor & Co Limited with Lord Inchcape's Macneill & Barry Limited to form Macneil & Magor Limited. Although Macneill & Barry Limited had only been incorporated in 1949, it was the consolidation of traditional old Inchcape family interests stretching back even earlier than the origins of Williamson Magor. The third Earl Inchcape had come to India in 1946 to work in the Indian family businesses, and on his return to London, he separated the shipping businesses, which included Mackinnon Mackenzie and Company (see below) from the other business interests, which included the manufacture of tea, jute, and engineering as well as agency and trading divisions. Thus in 1949, Barry & Co, Macneill & Co, and Kilburn & Co were amalgamated to form Macneill & Barry. These companies were the inheritors of family businesses set up by the third Earl's grandfather, the first Earl Inchcape, before 1915. The first Earl had come out to Calcutta in 1874 as plain James Lyle Mackay to work for Mackinnon Mackenzie & Company, which he took over on the death of William Mackinnon in 1893.

'After the merger with Inchcape, the circle of business grew but the tea business of Magor and Williamson was carried on under my leadership. In 1982, when Lord Inchcape retired, I met with the new chairman of Inchcape and suggested we demerge the businesses given that there seemed to be little interest of Inchcape in India at that time. He agreed, and the result was they sold their shares to Richard Magor and he became a partner of Macneill & Magor. It was not a very happy parting from Inchcapes, but one that left me with a lot of assets including jute mills and tea gardens. In one go, we became a very large company.'

In 1985, the Guthrie family in England wanted to sell their shareholding in the McLeod Russel group with its extensive Assam tea plantations. The managing director thought that the Williamson Magor group would be the obvious buyer. He knew, however, that he had to tread carefully and telephoned B.M. Khaitan and gave him the following coded message: 'There are two trainers in Yorkshire with three good horses which they are prepared to sell, they are going to race fairly soon and they are probably worth 25 Bob each way, but there are two jockeys who should be looked after.' Mr. Khaitan understood exactly what all that meant and flew to London. He had known the Guthrie family for twenty years, and agreed to buy the Guthrie Group shares in McLeod Russel. By the time the name of the group was changed back to Williamson Magor in 1992, it had become the single largest producer of Assam tea, a position which it still holds today.

'In business, as with everything in life, there are "ups and downs". I would not be giving you the correct impression if I were to claim that I was all the time on the "up". I have had "down" periods too, but even in the worst of times, I never changed my value systems of kindness, honesty, and integrity – I would not allow anything to affect that. Even more so in the tough periods you have to rely on your honesty and integrity. One of those tough periods was from 1998 to 2004. I had bought too many big companies when the down cycle came. But the one thing that was always on my mind was that I would not let the bankers down – even today, I would not allow a person whose money was with the company to be let down. Through the worst period, I kept on saying that we would give them their due and we honoured it to the letter. Of course, I had innumerable sleepless nights and at times I used to feel that we were coming to the end of the world. But I would say to myself "never mind, things will change, they have to change". And then in 2004, things started falling into place. Even today, I can proudly say that you will not find any banker or financial institution that will say a bad word about our company's honouring of its financial obligations. Integrity and honesty do count for something in the banking world and in the government circles.'

Williamson Magor has today become purely an investment and group shareholding company for the group's interest in, not only tea, but in engineering and Eveready batteries. The connections with the Williamson and Magor families have also ended. In 2001, George Williamson & Company in London ceased to be the overseas partner and selling agent for Williamson Magor as it had developed its own network. And in 2005, the Magor family sold their stake in Borelli Tea Holdings and, as a result, Williamson Magor thereby acquired another seventeen tea estates.

I suggested to Mr. Khaitan that he gave the impression of being proud and satisfied with the life he had lived. 'There is no doubt that I am really happy to have come from being a young person walking the streets of Calcutta to sitting up here today. God has been very kind to me. He has given me everything and has shown me the world. I have lived the best life and I am still living it. I have been able to keep my own style of things and I cannot for a moment even think that from 1947 onwards I would have been able to come so far. God gave me Mangoe Lane and, at the end of the day, I think that is a great achievement by itself.' And with that thought, we brought our meeting to an end. The lasting impression of my meeting which has stuck with me ever since is how few people in the twilight of the lives can be as content as B.M. Khaitan is. Honesty and integrity seem to have a lot going for them.

---

[1] Williamson Magor (www.wmtea.com) is one of the world's largest tea producers with plantations and operations in India (Assam and West Bengal) as well as Vietnam and Uganda.

[2] As an aside, it is understood that 4 Mangoe Lane was where in 1778 Sir Philip Francis seduced Catherine Grand, later Princesse de Talleyrand, who was married at that time to a British civil servant George Grand. What made the affair worse was that Sir Philip was the deputy to Warren Hastings, the governor general of Bengal (of which Calcutta was the capital). This led to the famous Grand vs Francis court case and which scandalized Calcutta society in 1778. The court case did not end the issue and Sir Philip subsequently fought a duel with his boss, the governor general – in which Sir Philip was injured and returned to London where he maintained an implacable enmity to Hastings and which culminated in the celebrated corruption trial of Hastings. Hastings' seven-year trial was largely the work of Sir Philip, who used his connections in Parliament to turn the trial into a Whigs vs. Tory showdown. At the end of the trial Hastings was acquitted but not before he had spent all his money in defending himself.

> I think that in family businesses, ownership and management have to be segregated. You may inherit wealth or shares or a controlling interest in a company, but you do not, per se, just go and manage a business unless you are capable. All of our businesses are professionally managed.

SANJAY LALBHAI

Chairman and Managing Director,
Arvind[1]

The more I get to know Indian business houses, the more I see similarities between Indian and US or European equivalents. When foreigners think of Indian business, I think it is fair to say we tend to firstly think of Mumbai and Delhi, and then for IT we might add Bangalore and Hyderabad. But, this is not the complete story because, as in the US and Europe, there are some very large businesses established in smaller Indian towns and cities. The presence of large businesses in smaller cities is exemplified by meeting in Ahmedabad with Sanjay Lalbhai of Arvind, which is the largest producer of denim in India; in fact Ahmedabad is known as the denim worldwide hub.

My meeting started with Sanjay explaining – 'My great grandfather's father's name was Lalbhai Dalpatbhai, and in his memory my grandfather adopted his name as our surname and changed the family surname from Sheth to Lalbhai. We are from the

Jain community,[2] originally from Osia in the adjoining state of Rajasthan, but we have now been in Gujarat for over 400 years. It was, however, my grandfather Kasturbhai Lalbhai who started this group, albeit the family traces its initial business success back to Shantidas Sheth in the 1600s.[3] Kasturbhai was born in 1894 and died in 1980. He lost his father in 1912 when he was just seventeen years old and had to discontinue his education and get into the family business. His father had founded our first textile mill, and it was into this business that my grandfather entered.

'My grandfather prospered during the 1920s and 30s and it did not take him long to expand from one mill to four between the brothers, and three for his sisters and so there were seven independent composite textile mills which did everything from spinning all the way to finishing. Not only that but each of the mills was separately listed on the stock exchange. We were a joint family but, as you may know, the fact my grandfather involved his sisters in the business is most unusual as typically daughters would leave the family business when they married. This was not for him and he kept everyone together. These businesses were collectively known as the Lalbhai group.

'In 1941, my grandfather started Anil Starch Products Limited, a starch factory with his cousin Chinubhai Manibhai Sheth. This company continues to this day and became the eighth listed company in the overall family group. Then in 1947, my grandfather founded what is now known as Atul Limited producing dyes and dye intermediaries. It has become a very large chemical business and over time entered into joint ventures with global players such as with American Cyanamid to make the formulations in pharmaceuticals; with ICI of London to make vat dyes; and with Ciba-Geigy to make resins. This became the ninth publicly quoted company.

'The physical complex of our group was much ahead of its time as it was built on 500 hectares. The different joint ventures each reflected their origins in the factories and buildings they erected. It is, if I might say, a beautiful campus and is much like a factory in a forest because of the almost 40,000 trees, which were planted in the complex. On one side there is a river, on another there is a small hillock, the third side has the national highway joining Mumbai and Ahmedabad, and on the fourth side there is the sea where the river ends. This enabled the factories to have not only water, but to take care of effluent appropriately. This was all due to my grandfather's vision. Over the years Atul bought out its joint venture partners so that the whole campus is now owned by Indians.

'This was the world into which I was born in 1954. As my grandfather lived until 1980, I came to know him well. For many years, he lived in the same house as his two brothers and their families. But eventually, by the 1930s, this became impractical due to the number of family members and everyone moved into their own houses, although the business continued to be run along joint family lines.

'My grandfather was not just a great industrialist, his contribution in the field of education in Ahmedabad is immense. He, with a close relative, Vikram Sarabhai, who was one of the most prominent scientists in India, built some of the finest institutions. These included PRL (Physical Research Laboratory), ATIRA (Ahmedabad Textile Industry's Research Association) and IIM (Indian Institute of Management) Ahmedabad. He also founded the Ahmedabad Education Society in 1936 which established several colleges of repute in the city, like LD College of Engineering, HL College of Commerce, MG College of Science, School of Architecture, and many more. Currently, I am the president of the Society and my father is the chairman.

'To build the IIMA campus, my grandfather brought some of the best-known architects in the world – like the American Louis I. Kahn – so that the campus would be architecturally of a very high standard. IIMA has just celebrated its 50th year – IIMA had an affiliation with Harvard Business School. Although he could not finish his education because of the early death of his father, my grandfather knew the importance of education, and sent my father to MIT for his undergraduate studies and to Harvard Business School for his MBA.

'He was a very religious person, and at the age of thirty, was elected chairman of a very large Jain trust – the Anandji Kalyanji Trust. This Trust manages a large number of our Jain temples all over India – and they are some of the most beautiful and famous temples. He continued in this role for fifty years. My father then headed the trust for another thirty years and now my cousin Samveg Lalbhai is the current chairman.

'Despite his lack of higher education, my grandfather was very well-informed and articulate. He read extensively on varied subjects, and you could say that he educated himself in this manner. He picked up English and could talk on any subject. He rubbed shoulders with the political leaders and business leaders of that time. He was very close to the prominent business families of his time – the Birlas, the Singhanias, and the Bharat Rams. Many of these businessmen visiting Ahmedabad stayed at our house, and so we knew all of them personally.

'He was also very close to Sardar Vallabhbhai Patel. It was Sardar Patel who lobbied for the merging of all the princely states after independence and the political landscape of India today is thus partly due to his role. Sardar Patel always stayed with us and the signing of three of the treaties with the rajahs took place at our house. As a little kid, I could appreciate the importance of my family because I realized not every family would have Prime Minister Nehru visit and bother to spend a few minutes talking to you. Though our family was very well connected, we grew up in a very simple manner. For instance, I walked or went to school on a bicycle.

'My grandfather was very particular about maintaining discipline at home. So every morning, we all had breakfast together. He was very particular about punctuality; you could not be a minute late. He used to say that it was the biggest arrogance to keep anyone waiting because it showed that you did not value their time. You learned his values because of the way he lived, which was simple. He may have donated millions of rupees for charity, education, and religion, but he himself lived a very simple life. He had seven sets of clothes that he marked with numbers from one to seven, and wore them in sequence so that each set would get used equally and thus would undergo the same number of washes – he was that meticulous.[4] [If you read the end-note it might explain a little more about why Kasturbhai was the way he was.]

'He conducted meetings that were to the point and brief. He did not allow people to ramble on and stretch meetings into hours. Knowing this trait, people came well prepared and rarely extended meeting beyond 15-20 minutes. Despite being such a disciplinarian, he was very tolerant – he allowed us all our own space. For instance, I liked dogs and birds and all kind of pets, and though he did not like them, he allowed me to keep them. As a teenager, I loved listening to rock music and I sported long hair but he did not wield the whip, he allowed me to outgrow my rebellious phase. Though he was a devout Jain, he did not insist we follow all the usual rituals but allowed us to develop our own understanding towards religion. So you can see that he did not impose his views on us, rather he allowed us to realize matters of discipline ourselves.

'I was the eldest grandchild in the family. My grandfather had two sons; my uncle Siddhartha was older than my father. However, he married later than him and so my cousin, Sunil is younger than me. We were five grandchildren in all: my sister and me, and my cousin, Sunil and his two sisters. I was as mischievous a boy as any one could be and found it hard to settle in any school and so had to change three schools before I finally did settle down. By that time, my mother had started a school and I finally finished my schooling through her school, Rachana.

'I went to college in Ahmedabad and then to an engineering school because my father had gone to MIT and done his engineering. But I did not like engineering, so I went back to Science and graduated in statistics and maths. Then I went to the US to do my MBA. However, I did not enjoy my time in the US and came back to India. Later I went to Jamnalal Bajaj Institute of Management Studies in Mumbai, which was one of the premier institutes at that time, where I got my MMS (Master in Management Studies).

'I do not think being rebellious is necessarily a negative trait. On the contrary, that phase allows you to experience the negative side of life and change through personal experience. When I came back from the US without a degree, some people felt that I had failed. But, in my opinion, it was completely different. I had the courage to say that the course I was enrolled in did not make sense to me because it was for people who had some experience in business. I had gone straight from my graduation, so I did not have the requisite kind of background or grounding in a business environment. Instead I joined a course here in India that gave me a wonderful grounding. To this day, what I learnt at Bajaj has stood me in good stead.

'Looking back, I have no idea why I was rebellious. Possibly, I did not like that kind of structured education. It did not make a lot of sense to me and I wanted to play, whereas the teachers wanted me to study. This was, of course, the 60s; the era of hippies, free love, long hair, and rebellion. I used to play in a rock band and we loved playing Beatles' music. It was really amazing that my parents gave me the latitude to do whatever I wanted.

'After my MMS in 1979, I wanted to join the family business because I never fancied myself as working for a large multinational or Indian company. On the other hand, I did not think that I would fit into normal corporate life and that I would be more involved in start-ups. For the first four years of my time with the family company up to 1983, I was involved with materials management at Arvind. I found it boring and so at that time, I started a number of businesses with my friends outside the family business. Quite a few of these new businesses did not work, but some of them did. I started a finance company, a fasteners company, a company making gum tapes with a Taiwanese machine, a texturing business (that is a textiles' process but with manmade fibers versus cotton with which my family was involved), an air-conditioning business, and a recruitment business. I think I started something like fifteen businesses.

'I was funding all of these, I was stargazing and I always had a working partner. So I never ran any of those companies; I was like a venture capitalist. I no longer have an involvement in any of them; I sold the last one a year or so ago. The finance company grew large and I sold it for a good sum. I joined hands with Hitachi in air-conditioning, and eventually sold the company to them. I also bought into Trikaya, an advertising company started by my friend Ravi Gupta. Eventually we sold that to Grey. It was Ravi who introduced me to the importance of brands and, as you will hear, that has had a major impact on the direction of Arvind. My involvement in so many different businesses is because I love doing something new. It gives me lot of pleasure to conceive a new idea and make it work. I am still doing this today, but now it is all within Arvind and nothing on my own.

'When I joined Arvind in 1979, there were seven mills and seven companies, all quoted, and my grandfather and his two brothers each had a one-third shareholding in each of the brothers' companies. And in the sisters' companies the brothers had a little less. The three sisters did not have any kind of shareholding in the companies owned by the three brothers.

'I started working for Arvind, which at that time was not run by my father but by my uncle. My generation was not necessarily put to work with another branch of the family as most did work with their fathers. But at that time my father was running Anil Starch and, as there were already two other family members of my generation in the business, he felt it was best I work elsewhere. So when I joined Arvind, I worked with two of my uncles.

'During those days, Ahmedabad was still rightly called the "Manchester of India", because it was the centre of the textile industry. This textile industry was part of the "organized sector". However, at that time the "unorganized sector", operating power looms, were starting to make inroads. This was the time of the "licence raj" so the organized sector was heavily controlled by licences. We could not add to our size. There was a licence on the number of looms we could have. And we had organized labour unions as well, so that altogether we had a lot of restrictions on how we could perform. Meanwhile for the unregulated power looms, there was no licence for them to start, so each new business could start with 20 looms, 30 looms, 40 looms or more. They had no unions and were evading taxes – and the taxes were very high at that time. So the unorganized sector very quickly grew and that threatened the existence of the composite organized textile mills.

'To my horror I found that I was going to inherit something which was not going to be very valuable and we were all jointly – meaning my uncles and everyone in the family – simply managing a hitherto successful business. The family did not know how to react to this threat which was coming from outside. They had never experienced something like this. We had to think of a strategy to counter this threat.

'So I started looking at what we needed to do to survive this onslaught. At that time, 98 per cent of our goods were made for the domestic market and we were mainly making fabrics like saris and all kinds of dress materials for Indian women. We needed to make something that was different; we needed also to produce something that was globally in demand and not to be solely dependent on the Indian market. We needed to get into a technology that was difficult for the power looms to get into. At this time, my brother-in-law had started a jeans brand called "Flying Machine". It was amongst the first Indian brands of jeans in India. He told me that there was no denim available in India, and that he had problems importing denim because the import duties were very high.

'We came up with a unique technology using the printing machines we owned. I suggested we should use indigo dye on a twill; twill is a weave three up, one down which is usually used for denim. Denim is typically made with indigo in the threads forming the warp and white threads forming the weft. As the indigo bleeds, it reveals the white in stages. That's what gives denim the much-admired faded look. We did not adopt the actual technology, but printed the twill and produced denim. "Flying Machine" in turn became quite a successful brand. As Indians started buying denim jeans, we realized that young Indians wanted to dress differently; they were looking to dress in a western fashion.

'At the same time, the media too was starting to open up. Television was coming in and Bollywood movies started showing our actors in jeans and T-shirts, and khakis and denim-style dresses. So, slowly but surely the Indian youth started to dress differently; even I wore jeans and we imported jeans in those times. So I could relate to this and with a little bit of success with the "Flying Machine" brand, we decided that we would manufacture genuine denim. Arvind was the first company to make denim in this country. There was no local denim machinery available and we imported the machinery. We started a very small 3-million-metres-a-year plant, which was indeed a very small denim plant, and then we built the business into one of the largest in the world.

'While Arvind not only survived, but flourished, the other six mills did not change from producing their traditional products for the Indian market and, as a result, they all eventually did not survive. In fact Arvind, took over most of them. You may be surprised to hear that there are only two traditional composite mills operating today. There used to be 75 composite mills in the city. If you look at the skyline of Ahmedabad today, there are still many beautiful chimneys but the mills that used to exist beneath them are gone. More than 150,000 organized workers lost their jobs.

'Arvind has remained predominantly a textiles company, but its turnover has grown from some USD 15 million per year to USD one billion per year. And now we are in the entire value chain of textiles. We start from contract farming with cotton farmers in Vidarbha, Maharashtra, and Gujarat. We work with almost 4000 marginal cotton farmers who grow organic cotton and initiative cotton. Then we convert the cotton into four or five kinds of fabrics. Globally, we are the largest denim producer with an installed capacity of over 110 million metres per annum. Then we are the third or fourth largest in the world for yarn-dyed woven fabrics with only the Chinese ahead of us. We also make khakis, gabardine, dockers, and knits. And then for women, we make voiles; voiles are very thin fabrics for blouses. These are the five types of fabrics we make.

'We convert these fabrics into garments and supply to almost all the major global brands. Name any brand you can think of in Europe or US, we are supplying either fabrics or garments to them. We also have one of the largest portfolios of brands in India (and which takes me back to what I learnt from Ravi Gupta) and we are also into textile and apparel retailing; that is, the whole chain from cotton to the shop.'

I told Sanjay that I had been surprised to read in *DNA*, a leading daily newspaper, a quote of his about Indian denim now being cheaper than Chinese denim, and how he was looking at markets like China rather than Europe or America. 'It is true that now we are supplying into the Chinese market; earlier China was always a threat to us. But it is not true markets like this will be taking over from America and Europe, which is where most of our denim goes. What I was trying to tell the paper was that we were looking beyond our three predominant markets, which are America, Europe, and India. Now I want to service the domestic market of BRIC countries; so I want to sell into China and I want to sell into Russia for their domestic growth and that is what I was saying – and into Indonesia also, but they are very competitive in denim and they also have a large tariff for imports, so we have to work at it. We are building a very aggressive and large sales force to look at these markets – people in many of those markets are used to synthetic fabrics. Now, Arvind will also offer them natural cotton fabrics and apparels.'

I asked Sanjay about the Arvind brands. 'In the premium segment we are licensed for Gant, Tommy Hilfiger, Energie, and Miss Sixty in perpetuity for India and the adjoining neighbouring countries. Then we have Arrow, US Polo, and Izod in the mid range. Arrow is a complete lifestyle now – including suits, shirts, socks, and cufflinks – it is an entire wardrobe for men. In the value, segment we have Cherokee, and we have Mossimo. And we are in the process of buying or licencing many more. [Not long after we met, Arvind announced the signing of the Debenhams, Nautica, and Next brands for India.]

'Not only this, but we have our own value retailing chain called Megamart, started in 2007, where all our value garments can be purchased for the whole family. Finally, in 2010 we opened Arvind Stores, which sell fabrics and tailored clothing. So we tailor as per your measurements and chosen fabrics. We can make a suit, we can make a shirt, and we can make trousers for you. We have also customized jeans with twenty different washing characteristics. You can design your own individualized jeans with your buttons and trims and with the wash you like. The jeans can be sent to you in ten days wherever you are. This is the first time in India that anyone is doing it. Levi's is doing some customized jeans but it is much more expensive. We know teenagers love to do their own thing with their jeans.' Sanjay then adds laughing, 'We also do jeans for the over 40s as we know Indian men tend to have very different physiques by then, a bit generous around the waist, and cannot fit into "ready-to-wear" jeans.

'We have also expanded into technical textiles, which means new areas involving advanced materials. There are currently three: one is protective textiles, like fire-retardant high visibility fabrics; the second is industrial fabrics, which includes filtration fabrics for all the chemical units and backing fabrics and belting fabrics; and the third is we make glass fabrics which go into automobiles and aircrafts and are used for the blades of windmills on wind farms. We have just signed a collaboration with PD Fibre Glass, a German company which has been in the business for thirty years.

'Out of the nine companies which my grandfather had started, there are three left. In the textile business, the brothers' companies have merged into Arvind; we bought them over from my cousins. As for the textile companies that we did not buy, they were closed down, as there was no alternative. The chemical company, Atul, is now run by my cousin Sunil and we have a small cross-shareholding. The starch company, Anil, is no longer a family company and is now owned and run by Amol Sheth from my grandfather's cousin's family. There was no acrimony between anyone when we parted.

'There are now around 120 people in the Lalbhai family. We are still quite close; for instance, I am going on vacation with my cousins. There are six male cousins in my generation and we are all going together on a vacation with our wives and children. Last year also we had a joint holiday. So we are very close but our businesses are separate. There is financial separation. Apart from the small cross-holding I mentioned between Atul and Arvind, all the other family members have opted out and cashed in their shares and run their own independent businesses. I think that in family businesses, ownership and management have to be segregated. You may inherit wealth or shares or a controlling interest in a company, but you do not, per se, just go and manage a business unless you are capable. All of our businesses are professionally managed. My sons have joined the business and are independently managing different units within the Arvind group.'

I asked Sanjay about his own family. 'I got married in 1979. It was an arranged marriage. I was compliant about that, but my parents did not impose it on me; they had never even seen the girl. I went and selected her and after I decided, I introduced her to my parents. This was contrary to the normal arranged marriage. It was arranged to the extent that I decided that I wanted to get married, so we had lined up a number of girls for me to meet and the first girl I met, I liked her very much and I got married to her. It was my aunt – my mother's sister – who put her on the list and arranged the meeting. I was twenty-five and I wanted to get married; so I got married. There was no compulsion from the family. The family was pretty liberal on things like that; there have been girls from our family who have married out of our caste and there have been lots of love marriages. I would say it was quite a liberal family where we have each pursued our own lives. My mother worked – she ran the school I mentioned earlier – my father worked and my grandfather always worked.

'I have two sons. The elder, Punit, is thirty-one. He is working in Arvind's new projects including our water treatment business and fabrication engineering unit. He started there because he went into environmental science. He did his master's in Environment Science and Forestry at Yale and then an MBA from INSEAD, Paris. He also played the lead role in establishing glass fabrics joint venture with Preiss-Daimler Group of Germany, and will continue to oversee it.

'The younger son, Kulin, has recently graduated from Harvard Business School. He first did his undergrad in Electrical Engineering at Stanford and then joined McKinsey for two years. Then he joined me for a year, which was when he started the Arvind showrooms and Arvind Shops, before going to Harvard. Punit was never clear whether he actually wanted to join family business; he used to say that he wanted to teach or pursue research. He finally took the decision to join the business and feels that from this platform, he will be able to make a significant difference to society. Currently he is on the board of the Sustainable Apparel Coalition, which is working towards bringing sustainability to the value chain of the textile and footwear sector.'

And what does the future hold for Sanjay, I asked. I knew that we are both baby boomers with the future getting shorter every day. 'As for myself, I am not really a workaholic. I love my life outside work and because I have very good professionals – very capable professionals run each business – I am now more into education. For example, I am the chairman of the Ahmedabad Textile Industry's Research Association. We have also founded a new university, a private university called Ahmedabad University through Ahmedabad Education Society, the Lalbhai family charitable trust. I am still the chairman and managing director of Arvind but my role is more of reviewing.'

I asked whether they had created a family constitution. 'We haven't, but I agree that it is something we need to do now to ensure that Arvind will survive irrespective of who is managing it. We need to be clear about the governance issues, and what the rules will be, and how to ensure that they are followed. At this point, it is loosely understood but we need to set down in "black and white". It is now a large business and a lot of lives depend on it. We are also a publicly listed company so one cannot treat it as one's own family business any more.

'Looking back, I am also a little concerned that I have not consistently created shareholders' value. We almost "died" in 1996 because denim sales collapsed and Arvind went into a debt restructuring. It was one of the largest debt restructurings successfully handled in India. From then to 2002 were some of the most difficult years of my life. Arvind had 68 lenders from all over the world, and I had to sit across the table with the creditors and negotiate our financial restructuring plan. In hindsight, I hope and believe that one of the main reasons we were successful is because we were open, we were candid, we admitted our mistakes, we admitted that we had messed up, and then explained how we were going to recreate value. I borrowed, begged, and sold every asset I had and put it into Arvind, and slowly, we have rebuilt the company.

'During the difficult years, we could have folded up; it was that bad. We had borrowed too much and our cash flow dried up. At that time, we felt that we could not go wrong because the rupee was depreciating and we were exporting; India was one of the most competitive countries in the world. Then the rupee started appreciating and everything went wrong. Cotton started to become expensive; Indian cotton prices got in sync with world cotton prices, whereas previously we had a huge advantage on cotton because Indian cotton could not be exported. With liberalization, a lot of things changed which we had not predicted. We made some fundamental mistakes, and I can blame myself and no one else.'

Although this may seem a rather pessimistic note on which to end our meeting, it reflects something enormously positive about Sanjay and, for that matter, many successful entrepreneurs the world over – not just the ability to admit you messed up – but the drive, passion, and belief that you can work through the mistakes and take the business on to greater heights in the future, as indeed Sanjay has done.

---

[1] Arvind Limited (www.arvindmills.com) is the largest integrated textiles and apparel player in India with leadership position in several global markets.

[2] See James Tod's classic work, *Annals and Antiquities of Rajasthan* published in Delhi in 1971. Tod's work is based on his survey between 1818 and 1822 when he was the political agent of Western Rajputana. According to Jain traditions, the Oswals were originally Kshajtriyas who got converted to Jainism in ancient times. The Jains divided into two major groups: the original converts are known as Visa Oswals and all other called Dasa Oswals. The Lalbhais were Visa Oswals. Oswal Jainism derives from the place of its birth, Osian where the original convergence believed to be taken place around 500 BC, although this cannot be proven. The Ksajtriyas connection with the Oswals has never been in doubt and, according to Tod, they were Rajputs with the origin being about the middle of the second century BC almost certainly from that of the White Huns who destroyed the Gupta empire about 500 A.D. Jainism was, amongst other things, a protest movement against the supremacy of the Brahmins which prevented the Jains from upward mobility in the Hindu Varnashrama hierarchy. This led to them being more involved in agriculture and mercantile businesses, which they eventually dominated like others from Rajasthan. As you read elsewhere in this book, the Marwari left Rajasthan due to the harsh conditions and so it was with the Oswal Jains.

[3] See Dwijendra Tripathi, *The Dynamics of a Tradition: Kasturbhai Lalbhai and his entrepreneurship* published by Lalbhai Dalpatbhai charity trust in 2010. The following is extracted and edited from that book. Shantidas' main interest was

certainly jewellery where he was a broker and banker and in a document of East India company in 1636 he was referred to as 'Governor's broker'. Through his wealth Shanti Das built a gigantic Jain Temple known as Chintamani which was made of marble. It was largely due to Shanti Das' influence with the imperial court of Shah Jahan that the rights of Jains were confirmed in 1630 over ancient shrines on the Shatrunjaya hills near Bhavnagar at Sankeshwar near Palanpur and the celebrated Kesariyaji temple near Udaipur in Rajasthan. Shanti Das' religious efforts received a major setback when Shah Aurangzeb came to Ahmedabad as its governor. Being a bigot, Shah Aurangzeb could not tolerate that the most imposing building in the city should be a Jain Temple; namely Chintamani. So, he converted it into a Muslim mosque. Shantidas appealed directly to Shah Jahan who ordered the property be returned to the Jains, along with restitution of any damage done to it. However, this order could not undo the consequences of Aurangzeb as orthodox Jain monks would not permit the use of the building as a Jain shrine as it had been defiled, but the message of Shah Jahan's gesture was unmistakable. It showed he had sufficient leverage with the emperor to have the prince overruled. Shah Jahan's order was almost unprecedented in the history of Islam. Whilst it may seem that this decision is corrected legally in so far as Aurangzeb had seized someone else's property, it is almost certain that Shantidas used the leverage he had with respect of the large loans he had made to the emperor in financing his invasion of Qandahar. When Aurangzeb became emperor, Shantidas must have been extremely worried given his run in with him over the Chintamani temple. However, Aurangzeb and his family owed significant money to Shantidas and it seems that Shantidas did not have any further problems with Aurangzeb and indeed seems to have developed a positive relationship with him.

[4] See Dwijendra Tripathi, *The Dynamics of a Tradition: Kasturbhai Lalbhai and his entrepreneurship*. Following extracted and edited from that book. Lalbhai created tremendous fear amongst his children, including Kasturbhai, Sanjay's grandfather. Apparently the sound of his horse-drawn carriage arriving was a signal to the children to hide themselves or start doing their lessons. They did not seek his permission for going to the circus, drama, or on a picnic. As a stern disciplinarian, Lalbhai demanded complete submission to his orders and none could ever take liberties with him. He was also extremely punctual using the old adage of 'time is money'. Legend has it that to make sure he used every second, his horse-drawn carriage had to start moving as soon as he stepped into it. The general atmosphere of the household in which Kasturbhai spent his childhood was one of Jain ethics. His father insisted on strict observance of religious rituals and every member of the family spent time each day in the prayer room of the house. Lalbhai was also extremely frugal. The family ate simple food and, only on special occasions, were the children to find any change in the menu. Tea was even forbidden, as it was present in most Indian homes, and milk was served at supper.

❛ My father and uncle had a sort of vision, a dream; they were not interested in really doing anything which did not add to value creation of India's economic role. They were not interested in a "quick buck" and they were not interested in retail. So they concentrated on basic industries, which they thought would supplement India's effort and that is the history of this company. ❜

KESHUB MAHINDRA

Emeritus Chairman, Mahindra & Mahindra[1]

I have found that every meeting has a surprise in store, something unexpected that happens, or something new that I learn and, in the case of the meeting with Keshub Mahindra, it occurred before the meeting even started! The interview had been set up by Mrs Mehta, his ever-efficient secretary, who greeted my colleague Matt Gorman and me with a question, 'Do you know how long I have worked with Mr Mahindra?' Of course I had no idea. 'Fifty years,' she told us. I asked her how that was possible and she explained how working for Mr Mahindra was her first job, and she has worked for him ever since.

She led us along the wide corridor of the executive floor of the Mahindra & Mahindra head office in Mumbai to Keshub Mahindra's office. The executive floor is unusual as it only has four main offices – the board room, the office of Anand Mahindra, the Group's CEO, the office of Keshub Mahindra, its chairman (and Anand's uncle) and one other office. There is a feeling of peace and quiet, which certainly cannot be said for many Mumbai offices.

Forewarned by Mrs Mehta as to how long she had worked with Mr Mahindra, I was not surprised to find that I was meeting an elderly man, but certainly not one who did not look anywhere near his eighty-eight years or act it. He was dressed in a suit and tie, which I imagine is how he feels most comfortable.

We started the meeting with him talking about his childhood. 'I was born in 1924, in Shimla, the hill station in Himachal Pradesh and I spent most of my young life in the north of India. That is where we come from, as we are Punjabis. My father, K.C. Mahindra [1894-1963] and his elder brother were both born in Ludhiana in Punjab.'

On completion of his secondary education in India, his father went to Cambridge University. 'It was rare in those days to go abroad and I think that indicates part of our family characteristic: our tremendous belief in education. Most families in the north like ours were at that time largely involved in farming, and so it is perhaps even more surprising to find this emphasis on education. And out of my family comes this extraordinary event where my father goes to Cambridge. Not only that, but two of my uncles went to Oxford and I think another went to Imperial College in London. Clearly, my grandparents must have been well to do in order to be able to afford this. But for me, the question is how did they end up there? And it was, I think, a conviction of my grandmother, who spoke no English, to educate her children. My grandparents had five children: four sons and a daughter. My father was the second oldest boy, and was very close to his older brother J.C. Mahindra [c. 1892-1950] who started Mahindra & Mahindra. JC was Anand's grandfather.

'My father came back from Cambridge and joined an English company called Martin & Co. This company had an office in Calcutta. Sadly, my mother passed away when I was only a couple of years old and this led to a huge change as I was sent to Lahore to live for the next five years with my maternal grandfather. This was pre-partition so I went to a local school in Lahore and spent the summers at the family home in Shimla. Before partition, Punjab was Punjab. There was just the one state, but after partition the state was split into two with a west Punjab and an east Punjab. The assets of my family were all in Lahore, which, of course, ended up in west Punjab. So they were all lost. Well, that's life.

'I was not brought up in a very regimented family. And the family was not influenced by any religious drive, so that we were really let free and, as long as you behaved yourself, nobody bothered you. Although we obviously had staff, we were, unusually for the time, brought up by parents rather than by staff. As my mother had passed away, an aunt looked after me.'

I said to Mr Mahindra that it did not seem he was brought up in a strict joint family structure. 'Certainly that is true. Ours was not a joint family as such – it was perhaps a mixture of following the values of a traditional Hindu joint family and those followed by the British. Although we were brought up by our parents rather than staff, it was not as close a relationship as you see today. It was a much more formal arrangement. For instance, on Sundays at home we had to put on a tie to have lunch – and, of course, we had to be there. We all lived together in a huge house, which had different parts. Nobody thought of living any other way – we took it for what it was.

'Even though there were lots of people living together, we had no major conflicts and our cousins were treated as brothers – we saw no difference.' When I asked Mr Mahindra whether the joint family had managed to stay together, he responded, 'Yes, except the current generation is probably not as close as my generation is. The current generation is spread out in India and abroad, there are many more of them, and they have their own ideas.

'I do not think that Partition had any great effect on us because, as I said, my father was living and working in Calcutta. Once I completed primary school in Lahore, I moved to the well-known St. Xavier's in Calcutta [which many of the Calcutta subjects of this book also attended]. At school, I was into sports; I played hockey, football, cricket, athletics for the school, and I played tennis and squash for the college. My father too was a keen sportsman and won a blue at Cambridge for rowing. If you ask me whether I was much into studies, I think that I was not; whereas my father was gifted academically. But there is no doubt I was provided with the finest education in the world.

'After St Xavier's, I was meant to have gone on to Cambridge, to keep up the tradition with my father having been there, but I had a very strong grandmother who said: "My grandchild is much too precious, he is not going to England during the war". So I was to go to the United States.

'There is an interesting story behind it. I think it was early in 1941 when three of my friends and I boarded a ship in Calcutta bound for the US. We were heading to the west coast because we were admitted to study at Stanford. When we got to Batavia, now Jakarta, the capital of the Dutch East Indies, the captain came and told us he had received a message that we were to disembark and return to India immediately. This was our first trip outside India and we were young and enjoying the freedom and the excitement. So I sent my father a telegram to say we would continue on the ship to the US. What I did not count on was that the next morning, a number of soldiers came onto the boat and ordered us off. We refused and said, "Who the hell are you to tell us to get off the boat?" They did not listen and the long and short of it is that we were physically hauled off the boat and put on a plane and sent back to Calcutta.'

As I chortled at this story, Keshub Mahindra went on, 'Then we learnt what had happened. My father was apparently a great friend of the then prime minister of the Dutch East Indies and rang him up and asked him to get us off the boat and send us back home. We had no idea of the war and were just young men off on an adventure.

'But Calcutta was also thought not to be safe as there were fears the Japanese would start bombing there too. And so I was sent to an agricultural college in Lyallpur, that is now in Pakistan. But I did not spend too much time there as my father was invited to go to Washington as the head of the Indian Purchasing Mission – part of the Lend-Lease concept at that time – and he asked me to join him. The British flew us to the US in December 1942. Certainly, this was seen as much safer than going by ship.

'Instead of going to Stanford on the west coast, I went to Wharton on the east coast and Anand's father, my cousin Harish, went to Harvard which is, as you know, also on the east coast. We were there for four years right through to the end of the war. I must say it was an easy life – I do not think that I really felt the war in the sense of what one reads about and what actually happened in Europe and in England. I do not believe many Americans living in America really felt it. After graduating in business from Wharton, I worked in the US for a year at a steel mill in Pittsburg. I came back to India in 1947, just after the partition.

'My father was not particularly close to the British government, but they obviously had respect for him or they would not have invited him to go to Washington. On his return to India in 1945, he was appointed the Chairman of the Indian Coal Mission. His role was to develop strategic coal policies and apply the latest methods of coal mining in India. His Coal Commission Report became a seminal document.'

All through his schooling, Keshub's father, K.C. Mahindra was still at Martin & Company in Calcutta, where his mentor was the senior partner, Sir R.N. Mookerjee [1854-1936]. The founder partner, Sir Thomas Acquin Martin (1850-1906) was also still in the firm. Martin & Co was engaged in construction, as well as iron and steel production and the firm had a substantial presence in Calcutta. The Victoria Memorial Hall in Calcutta, which was completed in 1921 at about the time Keshub's father joined the firm, was one of the firm's most famous contracts. Keshub's father later wrote a biography of his mentor, who was knighted in 1922.

'In 1945, before I returned from the US, my father and my uncle – that is Anand's grandfather – founded Mahindra & Mohammed. In the case of my father, his steel experience came from Martin and Co and particularly from his involvement in setting up a steel plant, the Steel Corporation of Bengal that was floated by Martin and Co on the stock exchange. On the other hand, my uncle had significant experience running steel plants from his time with Tata Steel from 1929 to 1940. And during the Second World War, my uncle had been appointed the Steel Controller of India.

'The original name of the company is another interesting story. There was a gentleman called Ghulam Mohammed who was a great friend of my father's. In fact, they grew up together in Lahore and before the Partition they were great believers in Hindu-Muslim unity. So when my father and my uncle started this company, they invited him to come in as a small shareholder. This he did and his name was put in the company name to show this unity. Then in 1947, he left to return to Lahore, which was by then in Pakistan and became the country's first finance minister. He was later appointed governor general of Pakistan. Following his return to Pakistan, the company's name was changed to Mahindra & Mahindra.

'My father and uncle had a sort of vision, a dream; they were not interested in really doing anything which did not add to value creation of India's economic role. They were not interested in a "quick buck" and they were not interested in retail. So they concentrated on basic industries, which they thought would supplement India's effort and that is the history of this company. We are now into all kinds of things, but fundamentally we are still devoting ourselves to basic industries.

'I have been with the company since 1947, which is almost from the beginning. But since 1979, I have not had much to do with actually running the company. My role has been as Non-Executive Chairman, until last year when I became Emeritus Chairman, just keeping an eye and leaving the execution of the company in professional hands. This is not always family. There were two non-family managing directors before Anand came in. That does not mean that I have been absolutely silent here since I became Non Executive Chairman. No, far from it, but the fact is that I am not involved in the execution and implementation, although I used to be involved in strategy, development, what was happening, of course, but not on a day-to-day basis.

'In fact there has never been that much family involvement in the company. In this whole company with over 140,000 people, there are two family members and that is it. This has always been true right from the beginning. There was never any automatic right for family entry into the business according to the rules laid down by the founders – that is my father and uncle – that we would hire no relatives unless they were qualified. So we have had family members but never, I would imagine, more than ten. This made us highly unpopular in the family. There was resistance because everybody thought it was his or her right to have a job. But we said "no". It did not take more that fifteen or twenty years for everyone to agree that you can have a job, but you have to first get qualified and if you did and wanted it, you could get a job. But, in fact, not many have joined; but then again we are a relatively small family. I have three daughters, and not one of them is interested in business. Their husbands have their own businesses. Now I have two grandsons who are in their twenties and they also have their own businesses and are not interested in joining a big company. I have nine grandchildren in all, with a couple of them living in the US, and the rest in India. I also have one granddaughter who has just graduated from Wharton and the last thing she wants to do is business. I asked her, "Why then did you go to Wharton?" She said, "Because I wanted to prove to everybody that I could graduate from Wharton." Then I asked "What then do you want to do?" Her answer was "Charitable work". Good for her.'

I asked Keshub to comment on whether they have looked at having a family constitution to handle ownership and management of the company. 'As far as our family ownership of Mahindra & Mahindra is concerned, that is a very difficult question to answer. It varies over the constituent parts of the group. We certainly do not need a detailed family constitution or anything like that for what is to happen in the years to come, because our family is small and the rules are already clear. In this regard, we are probably not a typical Indian family firm. But I think those typical joint family firms have to change, as they cannot go on being entirely run by the family. Look at what happened to the Mafatlals, a big textile family. In the 1960s they were the third largest family in India after the Tatas and Birlas. Today, after family infighting, they are nowhere.'

With his mention of his children and grandchildren, I asked him about his wife. 'We were married in 1956 and, interestingly for that time, it was not an arranged marriage. We were a little fortunate, because we were not a traditional Hindu family so we were not besotted with any rituals or religion; fairly liberal attitudes prevailed. I met my wife in London through friends. She was from Bombay and had finished her college studies and came to London to study to become a chartered secretary. As a result of our marriage, she never completed her studies; in these days likely she would have insisted, but not in those days.

'We got married in Bombay and lived in the same house in South Bombay for many decades until apartment blocks encircled us. At that point, my wife and I gave up and moved to an apartment. It was a very sad day when we did, as it was a lovely house with an acre of garden.'

Keshub then turned to philanthropy, which is clearly close to his heart. 'We have a number of large philanthropic foundations which concentrate on education, because we fundamentally believe the key to development is education; particularly in a country like India. And you may be interested to know that we are concentrating on educating young girls. At the moment we are educating about 80,000 girls a year all over the country. We have other foundations too such as talent scholarships and we run a number of schools and colleges. I have been chairing these foundations.

'I particularly like the American approach to philanthropy. For instance, their concept of "earn and return" is something that I admire a lot. They earn their money and then they give it back to society in very big bountiful terms. It is not just Bill Gates, it is everywhere in the US. Europe has the same concept to some extent, England has it to some extent and India has it too. But in India it is often done differently. Most Indian philanthropists prefer not to give their monies to a third party to manage, but like to manage it themselves. This is an important difference between Indians and Americans. I think there is a degree of Indian egotism that says that they can do it better when, in actual fact, they do not have the faintest idea.

'By the way, even though I have been in a non-executive capacity for many years I still come to the office every day – but not necessarily for the whole day. I come mostly in the mornings but once or twice a week, I stay the whole day. Apart from the office, I enjoy myself. I read a lot. I used to play a lot of golf. I was not a very good golfer – I think I may have got my handicap down to 5 at some stage.' I interjected to tell him if I could get my handicap down to 5, I would consider myself a good golfer. He laughed and continued, 'I used to play until I hurt my back a few years ago and then sadly I had to give up the game. I used to play at the Willingdon Golf Club in Mumbai, but most of my tournament golf was in England and the US. I am a member of St. Andrews and often played there. I also played a lot at Sunningdale when I was in London. Although I have not spent a lot of time there, I love England and I love London. I do not have a house there, because the thought of putting up a home is too much trouble. It is easier to rent a hotel room when you visit a place; even for a month or so. Unless you visit a place very often, I can see no point in owning properties.

'I still travel, I go to the UK and I go to the US and sometimes there is a trip to Europe.' I told Keshub in ending our meeting, it was inspiring to hear how active and interested in everything he remains and joked with him that I could see Mrs Mehta and him easily adding another decade or more of working together. And for those of you who know me or have read my earlier books on life stories, you would have noticed that I very much enjoy talking to those who have had long and interesting lives. There is so much we can learn from them. Not only that, but one is constantly reminded of the history they have lived through and which, in Keshub's case, covers a large slab of the whole of the twentieth century.

---

[1] Mahindra & Mahindra (www.mahindra.com) has a leadership position in many sectors, including utility vehicles, information technology, tractors, and vacation ownership. It also has a growing presence in the automotive industry, aerospace, consulting services, defence, energy, financial services, logistics, real estate, and retail. The group turns over more than USD 16 billion with its headquarters in Mumbai and a work force of more than 180,000 people across 100 countries.

“ I think that the biggest victory we have had is the one in Delhi on compressed natural gas (CNG). We pushed very hard from the 1990s saying that the pollution levels in Delhi had reached such high levels that we needed to do something about it to prevent it affecting our health. ”

SUNITA NARAIN
Director General, Centre for Science and the Environment[1]

As is sometimes the case, one ends up in the wrong place for a meeting. I went for my meeting with Sunita Narain to India Habitat Centre in central New Delhi, where the Centre for Science and Environment (CSE) has an office. It was only 5 minutes from my hotel and I thought how wonderful to start the day with a meeting so close. But I found this was not to be, as my meeting was at CSE's main office some 45 minutes away. Fortunately, Sunita could wait for me because to reschedule the meeting would have been difficult as I was leaving Delhi that evening.

On my way across town, I reflected on why I was meeting Sunita. I have found there are relatively few leading women business entrepreneurs in India, although there are many women in leadership executive roles in big companies. However, I wanted to stick to those with an entrepreneurial flair and this led me to decide to expand my coverage to social entrepreneurs where there are a number such as Sunita.

CSE has its own building set in a garden which has clearly been architecturally designed to make maximum use of light and space; as one would expect from the leading Indian NGO in environmental issues. I could see Sunita waiting for me on the balcony of her second-floor office. As it was a beautiful December morning it would have been wonderful to have sat on that balcony for the meeting, but the ever-present street noise, as in most Indian cities, made it impossible.

On meeting Sunita, I found that she was a smallish woman with a lively face. We sat down in her office and our meeting was proceeding smoothly, if not a little too formally for me, when into the room burst Paranjoy Guha Thakurta, a well-known investigative journalist. He also anchors a current affairs TV programme where a panel would discuss different topical issues. He was desperate for Sunita to come on a panel in the immediate future to discuss climate change and the outcome from the United Nations Climate Change Conference in Durban from where she had just returned. Immediately Sunita's whole demeanour changed, and I could see from the banter between Paranjoy and her that she was actually a very humorous person. Much of the discussion centered around who would be on the panel with Sunita. Clearly, she likes lively debates, and thus they spent most of the time trying to find somebody who had the completely opposite view to her own to make the discussion more interesting. She was absolutely not interested to go on the show if it was to be a tepid discussion. Evidently, she was very practical, because Paranjoy was trying to set up a lunch with her for one day and then do the TV panel another day. Sunita told him this was too complicated and she eventually persuaded Paranjoy she would come on the show and that they could catch up over a coffee afterwards.

Once Paranjoy left, we started to chat about "robber barons". 'I think there has never been a time in India like now when we have had such an intense period of quick growth matched by weak regulatory institutions, weak laws, and weak governance. There are a lot of people getting rich very fast and making use of the natural resources of this country in a way that benefits themselves as individuals but is doing damage to the country. I personally hope and believe it will start tempering down as some of the biggest of the big have already been caught "in the net" as far as law enforcement is concerned. I am sure this will make more people to think carefully about the environment rather than just think that they can get away with whatever they want to do.'

I mentioned the current 2G-telecom spectrum case where many of the accused such as Andimuthu Raja, the telecom minister at the time were denied bail. 'This was very unusual and I think that is the mood of the nation right now. I think the courts were responding to the mood of the nation; the fact of the matter is that never before have people at this level been denied bail. Earlier you were caught, but then you went home and you lived in comfort and then some day you might get called to court and by then it was already too late and the public memory was dead and gone and it was over and forgotten. But this time, the general mood has changed. I think that this is part of the cacophony that you are seeing in India right now. Whether it is Anna Hazare and the Jan Lokpal Bill or whatever, there is generally a mood in the country saying that "enough is enough" and you are now beginning to see that reflected in the courts as well. There is a feeling that people cannot just get away with this, and we need to have people who step up and say "sorry".

'And I think that is what has happened when people have not gone to jail in the past. I know there are a lot of cynics in India who say that they know they will soon be out but that does not matter; the fact is that they have gone to jail. It is an extremely important occasion and I would imagine it as a turning point in this country.

'As you know CSE is focused on the environment, so we spend a lot of time looking at abuses of power and looking at how companies are trying to get away with the rape of our resources. We have constantly made it clear that this cannot go on. But in the past, there has been a general tendency either to ignore the issues or to hope that they will just go away. That is changing and I think that now it is going to come home to those who ignore this. I believe it is very good for India's democracy because we need industrialization and we need development on the one hand but, on the other hand, we do not need the rape of our resources and the impoverishment of our people. However, to find the right balance between these two dynamics is not easy.'

I asked Sunita whether she thought that there would actually be effective enforcement of the laws. 'That is difficult to say. For that to happen, the institutions of legal enforcement need to be very independent and the investigations need to be good. But right now, interesting things are happening in this country. There is a "fear factor" of the law among business people. In the field we work in, there is an increasing fear of environmental regulations. We have just had this massive case. As with all such high-profile cases, there are always two sides to the story, but the fact is that environmental laws were effectively enforced. There is a famous hill station near Pune called Lavasa that is being developed by a real estate baron called Ajit Gulabchand. Ajit has been marketing this development as "India's first hill station since independence" – it would be the Switzerland of India – and the target market is "rich and famous". Suddenly, the Ministry of Environment slapped him with a notice noting that he had not even bothered to get permission and ordered construction to cease. Now there is no doubt in my mind that the ministry needs a lot of its procedures cleaned up and it needs better regulation, but there is also no doubt in my mind that, if you have been caught doing something wrong, you cannot cry as he did and say "why didn't you catch me before" or "why did you not catch the five other people who are doing the same thing, rather than me". The fact is that he did not get away with it. Construction was halted for over a year, and then conditional permission was given for certain parts of it to go ahead but only after a criminal case had been filed against him. So it was no small matter.

'It is, however, interesting that opposition is developing to unregulated development and particularly where the developers ignore existing laws and regulations. Obviously there are industrialists who are very angry with us and attack us claiming we are holding up growth and development. On the other hand, we are saying that we need even stronger regulatory institutions.'

I wondered whether Sunita got threats against her life. She laughed, 'Only from the pesticide industry, which is really the crassest of the lot; the rest are too sophisticated to send us threats. We live and operate in Delhi; we live in a good democracy. We are protected here and I keep saying that we should not be made into heroes and heroines. We do nothing that gets us out of line. Now if you go and see the activists who work outside

Delhi you will see how they work against the odds. For example, in states like Gujarat, Chhatisgarh, and Jharkhand, it is not only tough but potentially dangerous.'

I asked Sunita to talk a little about herself and her upbringing. 'I don't really want to talk about it, because frankly it is very boring. I was born in Delhi in 1961 and have always lived here. My father was a businessman working in the handicraft sector, but he died of a heart attack when I was eight years old. I have three sisters, so following my father's death, it was an all-girl family of which I was the eldest daughter. My mother brought us all up herself, as she never remarried. Her father was a liberal thinker and I am sure he would have given permission for my mother to remarry, but it seems she decided to put all of her efforts into her four daughters. She was a wonderful woman and we only lost her two years ago.

'In his youth, my father was apparently involved in the freedom struggle. From what I have gathered, together with L.C. Jain [1925-2010], a famous supporter of Gandhi, and others at Allahabad University, my father became an activist fighting for independence. I remember one day, after my father had passed away, an old teacher of his came to our home. I will always remember how he told us that he had been a chemistry teacher at the university and taught my father and others how to make bombs. Whether that is true or not, who knows?

'My maternal grandfather was a leading journalist and wrote for leading British media organisations such as the *Financial Times* and *Reuters*. He was in every way the classical English Sahib of that era. He always wore a bow tie, seemed to have hundreds of pairs of immaculately-polished shoes and all his suits were tailored in London. Despite his British airs, he was very connected to the India of that time and his brother, my great uncle, Brij Krishen was known as Mahatma Gandhi's fifth son and was actively involved in the freedom struggle. My mother used to talk about how surreptitious meetings would be held in her house between Gandhi and Jinnah. She told me of how one morning, when they got up, they saw police everywhere. They could not figure out what was happening and then found out that Mahatma Gandhi had come the previous night to meet Jayprakash Narayan in her home. I often wish that I had been born in that time so that I could have been part of the struggle for independence – what a time it must have been. We used spend a lot of time at my grandfather's home at 1 Narinder Place, just off Connaught Place which has now become a hotel. My grandfather died only a few years after my father.

'Was your mother educated?' I asked Sunita. 'Oh yes. In fact I keep saying that I can have no excuse because I come from a third generation of educated women, because my mother's mother was also educated. All of these women were in arranged marriages but even so managed to be educated. After my father died, my mother took over his handicrafts business and she ran it to support the family. In India, it usually does not matter what you are educated in as you often end up doing what you have to do. So my mother did not need to have a business degree to successfully run the business. At CSE, we do not care about what degree a person has; we just want them to do what has to be done.

'I have no idea whether I was a good or a rebellious kid at school; I think I just went through school in a little bit of a daze. Towards the end of my time at school, I got involved with an environmental group. There were four or five of us and we used to meet up and go to environmental meetings. That is how I first met Dr MS Swaminathan [his life story was covered in *Added Value: Life stories of Indian Business Leaders*] in the late 70s as his youngest daughter, Nitya was a member of our group. He is now the Chairperson of the Executive Board Members of CSE but, at that time, he was Principal Secretary at the Ministry of Agriculture. We used to tell him how everybody was destroying the Earth and ask him what he was doing about it. We used to go to these meetings and observe how everybody was talking but doing nothing. We wanted action. When I think about those days, I think what brats we were.'

I asked Sunita why she became environmentally conscious, 'I am not sure. I think it may be partly from my mother – she was an amazing gardener – in fact both my mother and also my grandfather were incredible gardeners. So I think partly it was her passion and partly I just got interested in the environment. An important event in this evolution was a meeting I attended at the Gandhi Peace Foundation. I met two important people who awakened my activism; one was Ashish Kothari, who is now also an environmentalist and chairs Greenpeace India and has written many books; the other was Amit Baruah, a journalist who was appointed Head of BBC Hindi and was the BBC's lead editor for India. We became environmentally conscious together. For example, we travelled to the Himalayas to see the Chipko movement where the women worked to protect trees. *Chipko* means "to hug" in Hindi. These women were the original "tree huggers". The woodcutters in their district waited until all the men had left the village and then moved in to cut the trees. The women put themselves between the trees and the woodcutters, as they knew once the trees were gone they would no longer have enough firewood for their kitchens. So I guess my environmental consciousness just evolved over a period of time – it is very weird how it happened. The Chipko experience lead to us founding Kalpavriksh in Delhi – which I believe was the first student environment movement – we used to do all sorts of things like protecting trees from being cut in Delhi.

'We were really just kids, brats running around trying to protect the world. We did protect the trees in Delhi, but that was a very different fight from the one we had seen in the Himalayas, where the police came and often took the side of the woodcutters. When we did the same in Delhi, the scene was nice and cute. That was the difference – that was what I call the age of innocence.

'This is an interesting part of the Indian environmental movement. Initially everyone thought these poor women just loved trees. But what we learnt was that these women were protecting the trees because they needed them for their survival. In these early years of the 1980s, we realized that the movement to protect the environment was not just about pretty trees and tigers; it was not just that we needed to protect something because we needed to leave something for future generations but, much more importantly, you needed to protect something because you needed the resources for the current generation. Environmental protection was needed for the people living today to enable them to live tomorrow. This was a fundamental change of thinking and this is what has driven me since then.

'And so, by the time I finished school, I had decided to work in the field of environment. I must say it was amazing that my mother allowed me to do that because at that time nobody knew what "environment" meant. I tried to find university courses on the subject, but could only find things like "weather science". It was not the buzzword that it is now.

'L.C. Jain, who I mentioned earlier as one of my father's friends, suggested that I go to the Vikram Sarabhai Institute for Development

Research in Ahmedabad that was run by his son, Kartikeya Sarabhai. So off I went, but as it was the first time I had left home, my mother found someone to look after me. This was Ela Bhatt [see chapter in this book on Ela Bhatt]. Now she too is a member of the Executive Board of CSE. Whilst I was there, we worked on environmental issues and on a magazine she ran.'

I wondered whether Sunita got a university degree, 'No, I never did. I did a degree by correspondence but I am actually what can be termed "illiterate" by some who believe you need a degree to speak or write intelligently. I was actually called "illiterate" once on TV after we had done an investigation on colas and a fuss blew up. One of these TV interviewers actually said to me on air: "Oh but you are illiterate, how did you take up such a scientific issue when you are illiterate?" This was in 2003 just after we issued our report on pesticides in soft drinks, including Coca Cola and Pepsi. We had done an earlier report on pesticides in bottled water. We set up a Pollution Monitoring Laboratory because we needed our own research facility to do independent investigative analytical science. At that time, the public did not know what levels of toxins existed in our food and drinks. No sooner had we set up the lab, we started receiving emails from a doctor based somewhere in Kerala saying that he was noticing a surge in the number of cases of deformities in a village near where he worked. He had never seen anything like it, and he just could not understand why it was happening. We sent a journalist who worked with us to go to the village and collect blood, water, and soil samples. We found very high levels of a pesticide called endosulfan and published the results, which of course caused a huge fuss. The pesticide industry objected to our analysis, and the villagers then took the matter to the human rights commission, which ordered an independent scientific analysis. This analysis confirmed our results that such levels of endosulfan could cause birth defects and kill people. The dispute continues to this day, and frequently, I am sued for defamation. There is one mad industrialist in the sector who is very rich and who draws obscene cartoons of me and distributes them to all and sundry. From time to time, there are even paid protesters outside our office. We have done a lot of investigations into the pesticide industry and demonstrated the efforts they have made to persuade the public and government that all is well. After all, these are legitimate businesses and lobbying, of course, is legitimate. The trouble with pesticides is that it is difficult to prove cause and effect.

'But we have made great progress and the chemical has now been banned from use throughout India, and the Kerala State Government has agreed to pay compensation. Also there are now standards for the level of pesticides in bottled water and soft drinks.'

Returning to her life story, Sunita continued. 'I stayed about a year in Ahmedabad working with Vikram Sarabhai Institute for Development Research, and then I went off to Mumbai where I worked briefly with another environmental group called the Bombay Natural History Society before returning to Delhi as my grandmother was very ill. This is when I met up again with Anil Agarwal. I had met him for the first time some years before when we had set up Kalpavriksh to protect trees in Delhi. He had just come back from England and was setting up CSE and simultaneously working on a book called the *State of India's Environment Report*. Anil had been to Malaysia and seen a similar report produced by the Consumers Association of Penangon. Anil wanted this report to be one from the citizens to the government, and needed people to help him. I guess I was there at the right time and started work with Ravi Chopra and Anil in 1981 in a musty little two-roomed office in Nehru Place.'

I asked Sunita whether she had been paid enough to support herself during this immediate period after leaving school. 'I was very privileged as my mother looked after me financially. Once I joined CSE, I initially got paid 600 rupees a month, but it was not enough to live on. I have nothing to complain about. I have been very lucky as I have never had to struggle too hard financially. I was passionate about CSE and my mother gave me the space and the opportunity to do it. As for my sisters, my second sister got married and has two sons. The third sister is unmarried, works in financial research and the fourth one went to study in the US and then got married there and now works at the World Bank in Washington where she is an environmental economist. That may be partly my influence, as we are very close. She likes what I do and I like what she does. My mother was very happy to know before she passed away that we could all take care of ourselves.'

The Citizens' First Report on the State of India's Environment came out in 1982. 'The first thing I remember is Anil telling me to go to Mumbai and start selling the report as until we did so, we had no money to pay our bills. It is probably an appropriate point to say more about Anil. Not only did he found CSE, but he was the most amazing teacher for me. He had graduated as an engineer but moved into science journalism and after working with the *Indian Express*, he became the science correspondent for the *Hindustan Times* in 1973 before moving to Harvard in 1974 where he worked for and eventually ran the Harvard Institute for International Development. While he was there, he won one of the UN's prestigious Food and Agriculture Awards and it was with the prize monies from this that he founded CSE in much the same way Professor Swaminathan did with his foundation.

'When I joined Anil in 1981 at CSE, I was probably equivalent to a junior research assistant. I used to file material and, once the Citizens' book was published, I would keep the accounts for the book and mail them out to buyers. The book became a bestseller and even today people tell me how it changed their lives. There is little doubt that Anil was the person who made Indians understand why the environment is so important. Sadly, he was diagnosed with cancer in the mid-1990s before passing away in 2001. As the cancer progressed and he spent periods out of the office for treatment, he asked me to increase my management role. I think he formally asked me to take over directorship about a year before he died.

'We have deliberately never grown CSE too much. We have been very tough with ourselves on growth and we are still about 150 people, which we have been for the last decade. Anil never wanted us to get too big, and felt that we should focus on being a lean guerilla movement. We are now very firmly established, we hope, so in one sense we are hardly a guerilla movement but we still think like guerillas. The aim is to produce very high quality, high-impact work, because that is how you can bring about change. The bigger an institution becomes, the more you risk becoming compromised and then you also run the risk that the quality of the work will suffer. So we prefer a different model, where we remain a small institution which keeps screaming and shouting from outside the door; the other model is to get bigger and then power comes from being inside the door.'

When I suggested that Sunita was actually 'inside the door', she replied, 'I am "in" and I am "out". As far as funding is concerned we have a very tough set of internal rules. We are financed through multilateral grants but we have rules. For instance, we will never do a private consultancy, not even if the prime minister asks us to do it. All our research has to be made public. In fact, the prime minister did ask me to chair a committee looking at tiger conservation and come up with a report. My only condition to him was that the report had to be made public on the very same day that I gave it to him. We did the report and I think that it was one of the best reports that the government has ever had on tiger conservation and measures to protect tigers in a poor country like India. It gave some very tough messages and laid out a very bold agenda as to what the government needs to do. And indeed, the government did publish it on the day that I gave it to them. So they honoured our agreement and did not just put it in "cold storage" and say they would review it and come back to us. It was our condition that the report would be made public, but not that the government would accept it. The government must always have the right to accept or to reject. In this case, they have accepted the report and implemented many of the recommendations. As I said, we are "in" and we are "out". But we are very careful to preserve our space "outside the door".

'I think that is also why we have the respect of the government. I have been a member of the Prime Minister's Council on Climate Change since 2007 and think the reason I am there is because I am an articulate critic of the government on climate change policies. I see that it is important to preserve the respect in which democracy is held. As long as the criticism or the analysis is based on facts and even if it is strident, even if it is a sort of screaming at some point, the government will listen to the facts and that, I presume, is why I have been invited to be in it. So I do not see any reason for me to stop saying what I believe and my assumption is that I am "in" the room because they want me to be a pain in the neck; otherwise why would they want me there.'

Sunita then talked a little about the Climate Change Conference in Durban from which she had just returned. 'CSE attended as an NGO, and definitely not as part of the government. We do not ever want to fly under that flag. On the other hand, we are Indians and we strongly believed in the Indian government position in Durban. In fact, for the first time ever, we co-hosted with the government a side event in Durban because we knew they were in really bad trouble and under an unjustified attack. This was very unusual and uncomfortable for both of us; it was a strange temporary marriage. While in Durban a young person came up to me and said that he was a devoted fan of mine but could not understand how CSE was doing this side event "with the same government that you are always attacking in India". Sunita laughs in telling me that she told him: "That may be my job in India but it is not my role in Durban".

I mentioned to Sunita an article she had written in the *Guardian* post the Durban conference on the longstanding differentiation of the relative contributions to climate change between the developed West and the developing countries. 'We have taken the same view on climate change for a long time. Our argument has always been that we are very strong environmentalists and we want effective action on climate change but we also believe that climate change cannot be tackled without equity and justice; so that the Western world cannot tell the developing countries that we have to clean it up now when it is them who have created the problem in the first place. That is not acceptable.'

On this same topic many years earlier (1991 to be precise), Sunita co-authored with Anil Agarwal a report, *Global Warming in an Unequal World: a Case of Environmental Colonialism*. 'This created a huge stink at the time. We are talking about the pre-Internet era but, even then, it created a huge controversy because it was a fight between little CRE and the most powerful US institution in the sector, the World Resources Institute. They had come out with a report, which we critiqued and showed how fraudulent their data was. To prove our point we went back and recalculated everything that they had done and showed how they had never verified their assumptions and now simply wanted to redistribute the global ecological space in the favour of the developed West. We have been articulating the same position since 1991 and again in Durban in 2012. The UK press was rapidly anti-India on the position the government and CSE took in Durban. This so infuriated me that I wrote pieces, not only for the *Guardian* which you read, but also for the *Herald Tribune* and *Business Standard*.'

Given all the writing and speaking she does, I asked Sunita whether she was better at oral or written argument. 'There is no doubt that I am better at written. But I have had some very tough debates in my life. The last tough one was a CNN debate broadcast from Singapore where my opponent was Bjorn Lomborg. That was tough as he is such a contrarian, pro-West, and extremely right wing. He is the man who wrote *The Skeptical Environmentalist* in 2001 and became the favourite poster boy of economists and everyone who wanted to deny the importance of climate change. They even put him on the cover of *Business Week*.'

I asked Sunita what she thought was the big issue for her now in India. 'I think that the biggest issue is how to have growth in a way that does not destroy the livelihoods and resources of very poor people. All over the world, growth has come at the cost of the environment, but in the West they have had the money either to be able to mitigate those costs or to be able to repair the damage and constantly keep repairing them. But there have never before been such enormous human densities of people living and needing natural resources in order to survive. I guess Africa and China are probably comparable to India, but China has a very different strategy. They just move people away from the pollution. It may be an exaggeration but it is said in China when they take away a farmer's land, they give him two flats; one to live in and one to rent out so that there is the means for survival. I am not sure whether the farmers are happy, but at least they have something on which to survive. In India, we do not have the ability to compensate people for the loss of livelihoods. So the big issue for India is whether we can actually think through a different growth model. This is a very tough issue because all over the world, in spite of all the talk about the financial recession and the Eurozone crisis being the "big issue", I think many people know the environment is the real "big issue". I do not think that we have a workable model. I think that we have to be much more open to innovating ideas and to think "outside the box". It is true that after Durban nothing may happen again. In fact I think that the biggest tragedy of Durban was that they have basically agreed that they are going to fight for the next five years just to come up with something else.

'The fact is that the rich countries are now realizing that climate change is no longer the soft issue that it was when we began talking about it in 1990. Then you could talk about it and talk about the future of the planet and how everybody needed to be saved, but now there is a different context. Now China and India are growing and demanding their rightful share and we are telling Canada that they come from an extractive economy which is still highly inefficient and that they should learn to live more efficiently – their per capita emissions are one of the highest in the world, even higher than the US, but nobody wants to give up what they have. I was saying this yesterday when there was a panel discussion with some former diplomats. The trouble with tackling climate change is that we are talking about socialism in a highly capitalist world and it is very tough to even begin to see that change is possible.'

Sunita felt she should finish our discussion on a more cheerful note by talking about a CSE success story. 'I think that the biggest victory we have had is the one in Delhi on compressed natural gas (CNG). We pushed very hard from the 1990s saying that the pollution levels in Delhi had reached such high levels that we needed to do something about it to prevent it affecting our health. We had numerous lawsuits against CRE. For example, Tata filed a defamation suit against us because we were attacking diesel. The car industry also hated us and took us to court. We started a campaign for the conversion of all Delhi buses from diesel to CNG saying we needed greener technology. Those opposing our proposition told the courts that CNG was unsafe and it was explosive and people would just die, as it was an untested technology. We were indeed thinking about doing something that had not been done anywhere on the scale we were proposing. The largest fleet of CNG in the world at that time was some 30 or 40 buses in LA. We were talking about hundreds of buses. The government lacked the resources to analyse what it would all mean, so we had to do the research on all the major issues like safety, how certification would be carried out and how the transition would take place. Eventually after a long battle, it was agreed all the buses would indeed convert to CNG. Delhi today has the largest fleet of vehicles that run on CNG and we have definitely brought down the air pollution levels. It was an incredible victory.

'Of course, now we are losing clean air again because the number of cars keeps going up and so we are fighting a new battle which is to restrain the growth of cars in Delhi. That is where Singapore comes in and we keep using it as an example but keep being told that it is a fascist country, which we cannot hope to emulate. Well whatever; Singapore still has great things that we need to learn from. We are arguing that we need to change the whole mobility system so that we push commuters towards a comprehensive mass transit system to be built by government or the private sector. But this will not be easy. A few years ago we were involved in promoting the introduction of a bus rapid transit system. On the day it was launched I went onto the streets to see how it was working. It was fascinating as car owners were shaking their fists at me saying that I was the one responsible for the traffic jams. It was madness, but the best thing,' Sunita says mischievously, 'was the way people in the buses were waving to people in cars, because they were moving and the cars were stuck. So, as I keep saying, socialism on the roads is very, very tough.'

As I left Sunita to the next big fight, I wondered what my takeaway was from this passionate social entrepreneur. Certainly she exhibited many of the characteristics of her private sector counterparts but there was stand out difference. She needs to be fearless.

---

[1] Centre for Science and Environment (www.cseindia.org) is a public interest research and advocacy organisation based in New Delhi. CSE researches into, lobbies for and communicates the urgency of development that is both sustainable and equitable.

' I believe we have to think differently. It will be foolish for us to try to replicate the factory model of China. In India we have the capabilities to design even a complex product in electronics, but the rest of the supporting ecosystem is missing. We have to leverage our large domestic market to get economies of scale, and we need access to low-cost capital and finance. '

SANJAY NAYAK

CEO and Managing Director, Tejas Networks[1]

Listening to Sanjay Nayak talking made me think that it is a pity that readers cannot hear the subject of a biography sharing details about their lives. When Sanjay talks about anything there is an incredible and unmistakable passion in his voice interspersed with laughter. It makes him a very appealing subject. We met in one of the Royal Orchid Hotels in Bangalore. This one fronts a private golf course and is a pleasant and quiet place to stay. We chose to do the interview outside in one of its open-air pavilions in the garden. But unfortunately, as it was what is called 'the mango season', we were frequently interrupted by rain storms passing through and this led to us seeking refuge several times until we found somewhere both quiet and dry.

I started by asking Sanjay about the family he was born into and his childhood, 'My grandparents came from Damoh in Madhya Pradesh. It is not a very well developed place even now. We are

Hindus from the Vaishya community that is a caste traditionally involved in trading. My ancestors come from a wealthy family; my grandfather was involved in several businesses including gold jewellery, money lending and other related businesses. My father's two elder brothers went into the family business, whereas my father studied to become an engineer. He was the first in the family to get a professional degree. He was probably also the first engineer in the town in those days until my father's younger brother also became an engineer. And that is how it often is in India. Someone in the family breaks out a little and then other family members and friends follow. My parents had an arranged marriage; they both lived within one kilometre of each other in the same town and their families knew each other well. As you know from others who you have met in India there is nothing unusual about such arranged marriages, although it is changing fast now.

'My father was a government civil engineer at a time when various dams were being constructed around the country. Every three years, he was transferred to a different place to supervise the construction of a dam or some other infrastructure project. This meant much of my childhood was spent travelling to different places. When I was in fifth standard, my father realized that I was doing well academically and the moving around was disturbing my studies. So my parents sent me, when I was just ten, to a boarding school called Rajkumar College in Raipur, where I stayed for seven years – from standard fifth to twelfth. Fortunately for me it was one of the good boarding schools where princes studied during the British Raj. Whilst the initial days of staying away from my parents at such a young age were very tough once I got into the groove of the school I came to love it. We had lots of sports, study and other activities like drama, debating, etc. There was a strict discipline of how we spent our days – we got up at a certain time and then had a very rigorous routine, but of course, there was enough time for everything. I really think it did help me to become a very disciplined and independent character because we were pretty much on our own and were given the choice to decide what we wanted to do.' I have four elder sisters who stayed with my parents. I also have a younger brother who studied at the same boarding school for a few years. So we were a family of eight. I always felt that we always had enough in the sense that we were never deprived of anything, but we never had excess of anything either. I have to say it was a nice childhood and I grew up in a happy family.

'My father never placed high expectations on me. He believed that whatever I did or happened would be good for me, which I actually found very useful. There was no pressure to become something or do something; it was more that whatever I might like to do would be good for me. So for that matter, since I had been at boarding school, whether I should take maths or biology or commerce was my decision. This applied to what course I should take on leaving school; it was all left to me.'

I asked whether he was a 'topper' in school and college. 'That is quite interesting. I was indeed a topper at my school and, prepared to take the Joint Entrance Examination for the Indian Institutes of Technology (IIT). As fate would have it I reached the examination hall half an hour late and, as a result, eventually failed to get into an IIT. But I was not despondent and I followed the principle that it was important to take what you get and make the best of it. Of course, I was upset, but I moved on very quickly. I think that is one of my strengths. Move on without regrets. Indeed my father had an interesting "take" on me not getting in. He told me that he knew I would have got selected had I been able to complete the exam and that itself was enough satisfaction for him. He was always very supportive and encouraging.

'I finally joined the Birla Institute of Technology Mesra, which also is one of the top colleges in the country. I was also the gold medalist of my batch, which meant that I not only topped my branch of electronics engineering but was the topper of all of the engineering courses. From there I went on a scholarship in 1985 to North Carolina State at Raleigh in the US where I did my master's degree. Frankly, I did not have to put a lot of effort into getting good grades; it was more about discipline and studying smartly which I had learnt at boarding school. There is also one important lesson I learnt from my father and that was the importance of doing things well, no matter what; not to be a perfectionist but for the pleasure of doing well. I continue to follow that philosophy. If you are doing something, you might as well do it well, as there is no point just going through the motions.

'I really enjoyed myself in the US; it was a very good learning experience. It was not just about studies. I made many friends and had a lot of fun as well. For instance, in one of the winter breaks with three other friends we got a car and drove all the way from the East Coast to the West Coast via Mexico and then to LA and back in fifteen days. One of the highlights of this trip was that we neither rented a car nor did we drive our own car. We used 'drive-away' car agencies, which used to move people's cars across cities and in turn looked out for drivers who would do this for free. The first car we got was a Mercedes that we had to take from Winston-Salem, 50 miles from Raleigh – and it had to be driven to LA, which was great. So, we just drove all the way and then seven days before we reached LA we needed to find a car for the return, so we called up agencies and got one car for some of the distance and then another car for rest of the trip. For accommodation we used the huge diaspora of Indian students studying in the US and slept on their living room floors or beds if people were away. We did this for the entire 3000 miles to LA and return. It was amazing.

'I think the US experience was very good for me personally. It taught me a lot. Before I went, I would read someone's textbook and think the author must be a genius. Then I went to the US and some of the university professors who were teaching me were the authors of the books I had read. And for some reason I thought the US students must be much brighter than me. It did not take me long to realize that I was just as bright or capable as many of those students. This gave me confidence to recognize that it does not matter what nationality you are and that I could compete globally. I really think this exposure and experience is very valuable because you meet people from different societies and cultures in an energetic and competitive environment.

'After I finished my studies, I joined Gateway Design Automation, a startup in Boston as a R&D engineer. To get my first job was quite simple. Someone told me about Gateway, I sent my resume, was called for an interview, and then got the job. Gateway was a unique startup that developed design software for chip design; they invented a language called Verilog that is a hardware description language – you can basically describe hardware in software. This was revolutionary stuff then, but today the whole world designs hardware using that language. The founder was Prabhu Goel, an Indian. He was almost certainly one of the most successful Indian hi-tech entrepreneurs in the US in 1980s. He sold Gateway in 1989 to

Cadence Design Systems for about $80 million, which was a lot of money in those days. Since I was keen to get back to India, I was happy when they set up a R&D centre in India and I moved to Noida.

'Mine was an arranged marriage. Anju is also from Madhya Pradesh from the same community. Our parents knew each other. They by and large did the background check to make sure that we would be compatible; we only met once before we were married and we both liked each other. She knew that her dad was looking at a few prospective grooms and as I was at the top of the list; she was happy she got the person at the top of her father's list. I actually feel that in an arranged marriage as you spend time together you get to know the person better. We were married in Raipur which is where my parents were settled. After we married, Anju and I returned to Noida where I was establishing Cadence's presence in India.

'Anju has a master's in Economics but has never worked. She has been a homemaker, which has been very convenient for me. I am being very selfish here because life becomes very hard if both of you have business careers with significant travel obligations. We have two boys; the elder is Shravan – he was born in 1992, and then the younger Anmol was born in 1994. "Anmol" means "priceless" in Hindi whereas "Shravan" is a Hindu mythological character who is supposed to be the best son in the world.

'In the early 1990s, I travelled a lot to the US, to handle major software releases or during design development stage of a project, since the communication links in those days were not great. Typically, the way it worked out was I would spend three to four months of the summer in the US in Boston area which is very pleasant compared to the heat of Delhi summers. From 1995 to 1997 we were full-time based in the US where I was working for Viewlogic (which later merged with Synopsys) on the condition that they transfer me back to India at the end of the period to establish their Indian operations. In fact that is how I came to Bangalore.

'By 1999-2000 I had already realized that there was a lot of action happening in India and there were many opportunities in the hi-tech industry. My work in India at Cadence Design Systems as well as Synopsys was technologically cutting edge but all the profits from this were being generated for the US parent. But this experience gave me the confidence of how to hire raw talent, really bright people and how to train them and quickly get them up to speed, and get them into building world-class products from India, even if they did not have prior domain expertise.

'This is also the culture we have tried to inculcate in Tejas Networks – our motto is very simple, if someone in the world can do something, so can we. It is of course easier said than done, but we always try our best and make it happen. Over the years I have had to learn that everybody is not the same and some may find intellectual issues harder than others, some may lack passion and some the ability to work hard. But I believe that, despite the differences between people, what is needed is the combination of intellect, passion and hard work. If all three are together the difference is not too much. I am not saying everybody will or can become an Einstein – that never happens. But I think you need each of the three things to succeed at the maximum level.

'In 2000 I took the plunge and started Tejas Networks. It was one of the most freaky product startup stories that you ever come across. Usually when you do a product startup you have a brilliant idea of what you are going to build. In my case, I had no clue as to what product to do. In fact I had spent thirteen years in a completely different industry before starting Tejas. I had been in the semiconductor and chip design software industry, whereas I was going to do something, but I did not know what, in the telecommunications sector. We are really the first ICT product company in India but had started without any prior proven record in the sector. However, we had a great founding team with each of us being first generation, first-time entrepreneurs with complementary skill sets. There is Arnob Roy, who is my co-founder, and heads our R&D. We had worked together at Cadence and Synopsys. The third co-founder is Kumar Sivarajan. He was earlier a professor at the Indian Institute of Science in Bangalore. He was a silver medalist from IIT Madras before going on to do his PhD at the California Institute of Technology. Then he worked at IBM's Research Centre doing all the fundamental clever stuff in optical networking. He also wrote a book on optical networks that became the most important textbook on the topic. So Kumar is our man who knows telecom, whereas Arnob and I are the chaps who can build anything and say "no problem, we will crack it". This is how the three of us came together in Tejas.

'The person who brought us together was Gururaj 'Desh' Deshpande. At that time Desh was co-founder and chairman of Sycamore Networks, which was for many years the hottest startup ever in the history of NASDAQ. On its opening day its stock increased 3000 per cent and at the peak the market cap was 40 billion USD. Prior to that Desh had founded Cascade Communication, which he sold in 1997 to Ascend for 3.7 billion USD. Given his success, Desh was probably the most iconic Indian in the world in terms of technology business and I was introduced to him through a common acquaintance in Sycamore, since Sycamore was planning to set up an operation in India.

'I still remember it was early April 2000 that Desh called; it was my father who answered the phone and told me that a Mr Gururaj Deshpande wanted to talk to me. I could not believe it. Desh went on to say he was thinking of establishing Sycamore's Indian operations and asked if I was interested. Of course, I said I was interested, but not in setting up Sycamore India, but a separate company, since I had set up Indian subsidiaries before and wasn't excited about doing it again. I also told him that I was from a different industry and did not know much about telecom. He said he was open and suggested that I come to Boston to meet him. Within a couple of days, I was on my way to Boston. I have to admit I was very nervous meeting Desh for the first time but he was very down to earth and just came and met me at my hotel. We got down to talking about building a business in India. I kept telling him that my expertise and experience was not in that sector but this did not seem to worry him at all. We talked most of the day and at the end of it he told me he would invest in the business and asked me if I was interested in joining him. It was moving far too fast and I said I needed time to think. He told me that the flight back to India should provide plenty of time and to call him when I got home. I really wanted to talk the opportunity through with my wife in person but when I went off to the US she had taken the opportunity to visit her mother. So when I got home all I could do was chat to her on the phone. It was a big decision to leave the secure world of being MD of a multi-national company in India, but we decided it was worth the risk since someone like Desh was behind the company. Desh invested 2.5 million USD of his own money and Sycamore Networks put in the same amount because we were also going to do some stuff for Sycamore in India. So Arnob, Kumar and I started Tejas on day one with a funding of 5 million USD. We said to each other that now we have got the money we have to figure out what product to do with it. It was as bizarre as that.

'"Tejas" in Sanskrit means brilliance or radiance of light. We had decided that we would be making a product in optical networking where all the communication signals are carried on a beam of light and different signals are carried in different colours of light. Basically, you take a beam of light and split it into the different colours. Now you use every colour – which is every wavelength – as a communication channel. One can modulate, demodulate and carry gigabytes of data on each wavelength. We wanted to do something out of India, we were based in Bangalore, and we wanted to have an Indian name. So Tejas seemed like a good name because it was connected to the business. Later on we realized that in Mexico, Texas is actually called Tejas in Spanish.' Sanjay laughs adding, 'We actually have an office in Mexico and as some Indians and Mexicans look alike, our people are often mistaken for Mexicans and particularly with the name of our company.

'Kumar and I decided to find out what product we would develop we should talk to potential customers. Along with Desh, using his contacts, we met Mukesh Ambani of Reliance on day two and Sunil Mittal on day three of our company. Bharti Airtel and Reliance Communication were just starting in 2000, when the tele density in India was only 1.5 per cent. We predicted that telecom boom was going to happen in India, even though at that time nobody imagined the magnitude and pace of growth. At that time India had close to 20 million phones but now a dozen years later there are almost 1 billion mobile phones.

'By talking to these different potential customers we were able to identify our first product – a multiplexor/switch which could carry voice as well as data. Similar products existed in the rest of the world but they were designed for much higher capacities and cost, which were not suitable for India, as the needs were much more modest in terms of capacities. What we did at Tejas was adapt that new technology and come up with a product that suited the Indian market. It was like taking the latest jet fighter technology and putting it in a simple four-seater plane, because that is all you can afford.

'The fact that we got associated with Desh made sense for Tejas to focus as a product company in telecom area, since telecom is a global industry and we had a large local market whose needs we could connect with. Part of the reason why a lot of product startups in hi-tech do not happen in India is because it is very hard for someone sitting in India to imagine, what product a Japanese or a US user would want. You have to be in that market to know about the habits and what kind of services they would like to use. That is why a lot of the innovation in technology products happens in the US, Europe or Japan and once they invent then the rest of the world catches on. Sitting in India it is very hard to do that kind of stuff. But we felt that telecom is an industry where every country in the world needs a network. So after you outgrow your home country, your advantage or disadvantage in any foreign market is the same as anyone else.

'The electronic design automation (EDA) industry in which I had been earlier involved, was a total industry of USD 5 billion. So even if we did well as a start up the logical thing was you would get acquired by one of these big guys and be done. Telecom is a USD 300 billion industry. Clearly, it is a much more competitive industry but if you can somehow get going in a global industry of a seriously large size, you can do something much bigger. Another part that attracted us was that India would have a huge and growing telecom market because telecom density was very low in 2000 and the Internet had yet to make its full impact in India. The impact would be even greater in India because we at least felt, even in 2000, that the Internet would be the way you would get leveled out in terms of the city guys and the village guys – much of their access to internet would be the same thing; it would not matter where and who you were, but you would be as effective in getting access to information. All of this analysis led us back to focusing on telecom products.

'We had a very simple deal with Desh and Sycamore. We formed Tejas Networks and divided it 50/50. We sold them 50 per cent of the shares of Tejas for USD 5 million and Desh became the chairman. The other 50 per cent was divided between our employees, Arnob, Kumar and me. From day one our company has issued stock options to employees. Once we started, we contacted bright people who had worked with us in the past and picked the twenty-five brightest people who had the combination of intellect and passion and who were prepared to work hard. Many of these employees had worked with the top companies in India and the world and had joined us based on Desh's reputation and ours. We had a talented team, we had money, and we had the brand name of Desh behind us as an investor. All we had to do now was go and figure out what product to build and we were on.

'I have not said much about Desh to this point. Desh is still the chairman of the company and the largest investor. We have done five subsequent rounds of funding and raised about USD 75 million. Desh is first of all an extremely down to earth person, very accessible to the point if you send him an e-mail you will get a response promptly. He is also very approachable, very helpful, and he has a very good management style, where you get space but he gives you the right inputs at the right time. He is as true a mentor as one could wish for. Given his phenomenal success, Desh spends a lot of his time these days doing not-for-profit work. Although he still lives in Boston he has started a major not-for-profit centre in Hubli, in his hometown in Karnataka. He has come up with a new concept of social entrepreneurship "Sandbox" and that model is now being replicated globally. Desh also serves as co-chair on President Obama's National Advisory Council on Innovation and Entrepreneurship.

'One of the interesting things was that most of the people who started Tejas had never done any telecom products before. So the way we approached how to build telecom products was completely different, without the baggage of prior knowledge. We did not know that it was supposed to be so complicated. We just said "okay this is what has to be built, yeah, sounds easy, it will take six months". We did not know that new products in the telecoms' sector usually took eighteen months to develop. We used to tell Desh we were thinking about a particular product and he would ask how long it would take, and we would say that it would take six to nine months. He would say "yeah, sounds fine". He knew that everybody else took much longer and that we did not know that it was going to be much more complex than we first thought.

'I was CEO and acting as head of sales. But I had never done sales before I started Tejas. Before Tejas, I used to be a "techy" but I had grown to become a General Manager as the MD of Synopsys. However, I was not a heavy hitting sales guy and I had no idea of how to sell. Despite all the doubts we produced our first product in six months and we got Tata as our first customer in less than a year. Tata Power Company had optic fiber cable spread across Mumbai for the last twenty years, which was laid alongside the power lines. Tata Power wanted to build a high capacity network on their existing optic fiber cable, which would be the first such optic fiber metro network in India. They asked us to do a presentation about the equipment and also our capabilities to build and operate the network because they did not have much experience about telecoms. We said "no problem, we will design and then operate the network". We told them we will use existing products from Sycamore and complement it with an appropriate product that we will build, by the time the network rollout happens. They trusted us and that is one of the good things about Tata; it is a relationship built on trust.

'We won the contract because they thought – and they got it so right – that if they bought the equipment from someone else, they would just get the equipment, they would not get the support and services they needed. They would just be a small USD 2 million dollar customer for the big giants like Cisco and may not get the attention they wanted. They trusted us and we built and ran the network for them. Then, as Tata got in a bigger way into telecom, we of course grew with them, with Tata Communications and Tata Teleservices. Tata now has bought telecom businesses outside of India such as in South Africa. This of course, creates new opportunities and work for Tejas too.

'But going back to the problem of getting the first customer, it is not easy, especially in hi-tech businesses, with no track record, because nobody gets fired buying from Cisco. The customer sees a brand new company and knows that he will be the first customer. By the way the standard reliability requirement in telecom is 99.999 per cent – that is called "five 9s". What that basically means is you run your equipment seven days a week 24 hours a day for 365 days a year and in that whole year, you get fifteen minutes of time to shut down, do any maintenance, or cover any unexpected fault or a failure – fifteen minutes and that is it. You are supposed to build equipment to that degree of reliability. It was very hard but somehow I think we did deliver. I think that finally at the end of the day it was just a comfort factor because we told them what we would do and then we did everything which we had told them – and we did a lot more than anybody else was offering to do,' Sanjay says proudly with that passion in his voice I mentioned at the beginning of this chapter.

'The second contract we won was a Pan-India network for Indian Railways. It has optical fiber across the whole rail network. The Railways wanted to connect at that stage 500 major stations across 45,000 kilometres. To manage this business they formed RailTel. We met their team and told them that there is a new technology, Ethernet-over-SDH, which we could adapt for their use. As you know some of the brightest engineering techies join the Indian Engineering Services from which some of these engineers were assigned to work with RailTel. It was a "meeting of minds" as our techies appealed to them. But of course there was an open tender as no Indian government procurement ever happens without an open tender. So the specifications were framed. All the global players tendered and Tejas not only came in as the lowest bid but we offered the latest technological products rather than the standard products offered by the majors. Like Tata, RailTel remains an important customer to this day.

'One of the issues we are addressing is that we can only service about 10 per cent of the various telecom products that an operator like Reliance, Bharti, or Tata needs to buy. But over recent years we have invested a lot in R&D and hope in the not too distant future, we will be able to address 50 per cent of their product requirements.'

I asked Sanjay Nayak for his vision of the future. 'The global telecom industry is going through a rejig of the business model. There will be a new set of leaders and a new set of competitive advantages that have to come into play, especially after the Chinese have come up with the low-cost products. We are gunning for it. I see no reason why, unless we mis-execute or get hit by a misfortune, we should not be able to take advantage of our cost-effective innovation from India. There is a problem with the business model in hi-tech ICT product industry. The traditional model has been that a lot of innovation in hi-tech comes out of US, Europe, and Japan, where customers can afford to pay premium prices for such products which in turn supported the high cost of such innovations, and once enough profits were made, the same products came to emerging markets later. The problem is that today a lot of the growth and demand for ICT products is coming from the emerging markets like India, China, Africa, where the affordability of people is very low. So, today the challenge is to do cost-effective innovation and develop products while using more technology, but offer it at price points that are very low. So, I think that for most ICT products, over a period of time, the design and manufacturing will shift to the East. It can only be done affordably in India and China. You need a lot of technology, a lot of innovation and a lot of R&D as well as low-cost manufacturing. The Vietnams and Thailands do not have the critical mass of high-end talent so they will excel in low-cost manufacturing. But the product design and R&D can happen in China and India.

'China has already played its cards and the country has bet on ICT products. They started with a big base of low-cost manufacturing and then they joint ventured or entered into technology transfers to go higher up the value chain. So, now they are no longer interested in low-cost manufacturing alone but are interested in the whole value chain of telecom products, mobile phones, laptops, PCs, and defense electronics. They want to build the equivalent of a Motorola walky-talky, they want to build the equivalent of a Cisco router. Their expectations have gone up significantly.

'India has so far focused on ICT services but missed the product opportunity. We neither did the low-cost manufacturing which is happening in China, Vietnam, Thailand, nor the high-end stuff that happens in Cisco and Apple. For efficient manufacturing, it will be difficult for India to fix its infrastructure problems, ports, utilities and so on – all of which are required if you want to set up all manufacturing factories with super efficiency. But what India has is the brainpower. So, we should focus on the front-end of the process, which is design, development, hardware and software, and for the physical manufacturing we could outsource, whether it is within India or outside of India. Then we would have captured 90 per cent of the value. The beauty is for ICT products, the last 10 per cent involving manufacturing actually requires ten times more investment then the first 90 per cent that involves design. Because to build up a factory, you need land, you need power, you need capital, you need machines, you need several things, but the first 90 per cent is all here – we have the brainpower, entrepreneurs, we have the ideas, we have the skills, we have the connection, and we have the networking. I really feel that the plot is going to change if India can get this act together.

'I believe we have to think differently. It will be foolish for us to try to replicate the factory model of China. In India we have the capabilities to design even a complex product in electronics, but the rest of the supporting ecosystem is missing. We have to leverage our large domestic market to get economies of scale, and we need access to low-cost capital and finance. Tejas has a little bit of advantage and role to play because we are probably the first and biggest guys in this game. But if we do not change the game, it will be very hard for us to become ten times larger than we are today; not because it is a competitive issue but because globally it is countries that are involved in the game. China is putting its finance and banks behind its companies and so is US, Europe, and Japan. As for India, the government needs to create a favourable policy environment to remove the handicaps faced by the Indian industry. If this is done, I feel comfortable in predicting a USD 400 billion dollar industry in India for ICT products in the next ten years. It is probably by far the single largest industry that India can create in the next ten years.'

I asked Sanjay where he saw himself in five years. 'We have a long way to go; Tejas is still a very small company. In the global scheme of things, or even in the Indian context, I still think of Tejas as a "start up" in my mind. We have proven a lot on many things to date and I hope and believe in the next five years we can fully realize our potential. I would get a lot of satisfaction if we can be globally recognized as the pioneering product company from India in the ICT sector, like Infosys is recognized as a pioneer company in the IT services sector.'

My last question was for Sanjay's advice for young Indians today: 'First of all, I think they should have confidence in their capabilities and not be worried about where they will end up in future. Everybody has enough knowledge to get to the next stage and you should not worry about what is after that. Just take a few "steps" since the "view" often changes once you have taken those steps. Another thing I would say is that the most important ingredient in the success of people is how strongly you believe in your passion and are willing to pursue it. Don't spend too much time worrying about what could go wrong. It is easy to get de-motivated and throw in the towel too soon. I see a tendency for young people these days to change tracks too quickly when something goes wrong. Things go wrong for all of us – and they are supposed to, as that is life – but if you are sure about what you are capable of and if you truly believe in your passion and you have an optimistic outlook, you will be successful. There are so many things in India that can be blamed on others. It is better to be positive and make things happen rather than waiting for bad things to be rectified.'

With these words of guidance to the young I left Sanjay and made the trek to the airport and, as I endured the inevitable traffic jams, I reflected on our meeting. Certainly most of us are not going to be outstanding entrepreneurs like Desh Deshpande or gold medalists like Sanjay and Kumar, but many of us do have at least one or more of the ingredients Sanjay identified for success; namely intellect, passion and the preparedness for hard work.

---

[1] Tejas Networks (www.tejasnetworks.com) is a leading provider of end-to-end optical transport solutions to telecom service providers. Tejas customers include telecom carriers (telcos) offering fixed telephony, mobile services, enterprise connectivity and ISP services. These carriers are spread across verticals like telecom, utilities, media, and defence.

> My family has been successful in recent times. ... And thus there is indeed an obligation or expectation for me to succeed too, but it is not something that bothers me too much. All I can do is my best and if that is not good enough, so be it.

HARSHAVARDHAN NEOTIA

Chairman, Ambuja Neotia Group[1]

I met Harshavardhan Neotia or Harsh, as he is universally known, in his office at Ecospace, the sparkling new business park in New Town, Kolkata, built by the Ambuja Realty Group (now Ambuja Neotia Group) of which he is the chairman. The Group consists of an inter-related network of private companies, which are partly the result of Harsh's own business efforts in real estate and associated ventures, and partly the inheritance of Neotia joint family business.

It was about the Neotia family origins that I asked Harsh to speak first. 'I come from a Marwari family originally from Rajasthan. But for the last 120 years or so our branch of the family has been in Calcutta (now Kolkata). Some time in the 1890s the family came to Calcutta in the search of commercial success and this dream continued to be here for the successive generations until today. It is interesting that, for most of the generations, there was only one male offspring.' This was certainly the case for Harsh in his own generation. But Vinod Neotia, Harsh's father, was youngest of three brothers. The middle brother was Suresh Neotia and the eldest brother, Bimal Kumar Poddar, was adopted out to their maternal grandfather, Janki Prasad Poddar, who was a partner in Tarachand Ghanshyamdas, arguably the oldest and, at that time, the most celebrated Marwari business firm in India. It was also one of the first wholly owned Indian firms in British India and which eventually had trading interests from Karachi in Pakistan to Shanghai in China. It also had interests in banking and insurance, and later diversified into the distribution of petroleum products as a franchisee of Burma Shell. The three Neotia brothers started work in this Poddar family business.

In the 1950s the businesses of Tarachand Ghanshyamdas was divided amongst the members of the then joint family. This led to the three Neotia brothers then setting up Radhakrishna Bimalkumar (RKBK) as the vehicle for their joint family business. Harsh continued, 'The business was initially involved in trading and one of the most important products traded, was petroleum products where they continued the Tarachand Ghanshyamdas business of acting as a franchisee of Burma Shell. They eventually expanded this business across Uttar Pradesh, Bihar, and West Bengal.'

The eldest brother Bimal Kumar Poddar died in 1968 and Harsh's father and uncle continued the business expanding the trading into products like cement, fertilizer, and cotton. In due course they established a textile mill in West Bengal and various collieries, which were later nationalized. They also set up Macmet India Limited, an engineering firm (which also provided software solutions).

Bimal Kumar Poddar died childless and Harsh's uncle Suresh also had no children. This meant that Harsh, who was born in 1961, together with his two younger sisters were the only children of the three brothers. 'I was extremely close to my extended family and, although we lived in one joint family compound, we had different homes within it so we had enough space. Although there were only three of us children in my generation, before my uncle died, it was like having three sets of parents. And also living there until they passed away were my grandparents and my great-grandparents. We also had a fairly large garden so, if I had my friends over, I did not really have to be treading on my parents' or my uncles' and aunts' physical space. But, like many joint families, we had most of our meals together.

'Unlike many Marwari families there was no rigidity or strict rules and everyone had the freedom to do their own thing. For instance, my father was a religious man and spent a lot of his spare time on charitable trusts. My uncle, Suresh has always been an avid art collector and student of Indian art and antiquity, whereas my widowed aunt, Bimla Poddar, has been deeply involved with Indian classical music and now runs the Jnana Pravaha cultural institute in Varanasi where she moved to some fifteen years ago. It was a very liberal, yet rooted, atmosphere and we were allowed and encouraged to do the things that we wanted to.'

During his childhood the joint family business fortunes varied. When I asked Harsh whether he thought his childhood was akin to living in a 'golden cage', he responded, 'No, it was not. Although the family has 120 years of business history behind it, there have of course been "peaks and troughs". When I was born the family was not doing particularly well, so I guess you could say we were in a "trough". That does not mean to say that we could not live in part off the family legacy and that therefore we had some security in the form of our own home and some of those things, but from a business perspective it was not in the "pink of health". Soon after I was born and for about ten years after that, there was a good upswing in the business fortunes of the family, but then again from the mid-1970s on there was a decline. I am not sure exactly what went wrong but I think some business decisions did not work out. We had purchased the engineering firm, Macmet from a family that was moving to the UK. Not long after we took over the company there was a major power shortage in Calcutta leading to the cost of power going up exponentially. This crippled the business. But that was not the only problem. Labour problems sprung up everywhere, including at our unit, Macmet. The family lost a lot of money; it was a very big blow. I remember there were even small austerity measures like not going on our annual holiday. I was in my teens at the time and I remember that there was a sense of everyone holding back a little bit because things did not seem to be going well.'

Fluctuations in the joint family prosperity did not prevent Harsh Neotia from going to La Martiniere[2] and then on to do his bachelor's degree in commerce at St. Xavier's College [which many of the people covered in this book attended if they were brought up in Calcutta]. Nor did it affect his happiness, 'My childhood was very pleasant. I do not think it mattered at that time how rich we might have been in the past or we would be in the future, I mean it just was not relevant to me as a child. I was pampered by love "yes", but not pampered in materialistic terms. I think most of my friends had more toys than I had and that kind of thing. But as there were only three children in my generation and I was the only boy, I have to admit I got a lot of loving attention from our parents and extended family.'

Nor did the fluctuations affect his inclination to join the family business after graduation, as he made clear when I asked if he had thought of doing anything else after graduation, 'Frankly, no. I think I always had an interest to join the family business. It was not as if it was something that was imposed on me, it was something in which I was interested. From the time I was a young boy I had seen my father and uncle carrying on business when there were no mobile phones and not even easy telephone connectivity. In those days, I did not have my own bedroom but shared one with one of my sisters. She used to sleep in the room whereas I used to sleep on its verandah, as it was cooler as we did not have air conditioners at that time. The verandah interconnected with many rooms, including my father's and uncle's bedrooms, and in one corner of the verandah was the home's only telephone; one of those big black telephones with a rotary dial. Every morning, between 6 and 7 a.m., my uncle and my father would make trunk calls – you know you had to book calls in those days – so I was woken up by them and used to hear them conducting business with their agents in Bihar or UP. I was, of course, not involved with what they were talking about and frankly did not understand most of what they said. This was an everyday affair so I think I grew up with all this going on around me and, despite a bit of bewilderment as to what all this business was about, I wanted to be a part of it. I remember all of this very clearly.'

My next question was about what his sisters had done. He said, 'My sister, Smriti who is two years younger than me got married, just when I passed out of college. She lives in Mumbai with her husband and two children. She runs a boutique selling saris in which she has had a hand in designing. Her husband owns a sugar mill. My other sister, Shraddha is ten years younger than me and she was the first amongst us to have gone overseas for education. She did her first degree in England and then went to do her post-graduate degree in the US where she met her husband who is an American, born and brought up there, but with Indian parents who had emigrated years ago. Her husband is a plastic surgeon and they live in Toledo, Ohio.'

When I asked for the family's reaction to this first instance of a non-arranged marriage in the family, in the sense that she found a husband by herself, Harsh responded: 'Well, in the first place, he was not a Marwari; he was from UP, from Himachal Pradesh actually. But that was not the main thing – I do not think there was very serious concern that he was not a Marwari; at most it was a fleeting issue – I think the worry was much more that she would settle overseas. Being the youngest, she was the "apple of everyone's eye" and we were devastated at the thought that she would actually live so far away in the US. Amongst all three of us she is certainly the most cerebral and also probably the most determined; in many ways she is quite a firebrand. She was very clear about what she wanted and she used me very effectively to lobby her case, because my mother was naturally very close to her and very protective of her youngest child. But she was very effective in convincing me to use whatever influence I had in the family to convince them that she was serious. I met her husband-to-be much before my family because she introduced me to him when I was travelling in the US. She told me that he was a close friend and that she would like me to meet him. So I sensed that, if she wanted to bring someone very specifically to meet me, even though she had said nothing, she might be serious. But, when I asked her, she said "no", they were just very close friends and she just thought I should meet him. And I thought the boy was wonderful, he was intelligent, and he was nice – so those were not issues for me, but yes we would all have been happy if she had stayed in India. And we still worry for her because, you know, she is alone and far away and we are all a little helpless and, those still alive in my parents' generation like my mother, are now quite old, so for them to travel to the US too often is also an issue. But we do meet her and her family once or twice a year and meet my Mumbai based sister nearly every month.'

When I suggested to Harsh Neotia that I would have expected him, as a dutiful Marwari boy, to have had an arranged marriage himself, I was surprised to get a qualified affirmative response, 'Yes, in the sense that my wife was introduced to me by my uncle. But it was not arranged in the way that traditionally Indian marriages are where the two sets of parents speak together; it was not like that. My father-in-law was an eye specialist in Sunderland in England. My wife, Madhu, is the third of four sisters. Her eldest sister was married and living in Calcutta and her second sister was married and living in Lucknow. The Lucknow sister was married to a boy who was in some way a family friend's nephew. When my uncle, Suresh was in Lucknow he met her at a party and she mentioned in casual conversation about her sister who had been in England but had just returned to Calcutta and was staying there for a few months with their elder sister and they were looking for a suitable boy for her. She had no clue that my uncle had a nephew; anyway what is interesting is that my uncle was so impressed by this sister that he thought that her unmarried sister must be a very nice girl as well! So he came back from Lucknow and said that he had met the sister and here was the name of this girl whose other sister was in Calcutta and why did I not meet her. I thought this was very crazy: just because she was nice, that was no reason why her sister should be. I asked, "Have you met her?" to which he replied he had not. I then asked him, "Have you seen a photograph of her?" to which he again replied he had not. Anyway I was told to meet her. So I met her and then we met a few more times and it went from there. At about the third or the fourth meeting, when I went to pick her up from their home, her sister invited me to have a cup of tea. I said sure. So I went upstairs. She brought tea and suddenly asked me what I had decided. I asked, "Decided what?" She said, "Are you planning to marry her or not?" I thought to myself "Oh God" this was really "in your face" question. I told her no one had suggested I had to make a decision and that we were still getting to know each other. She didn't give up and told me that her father would be upset to know that his daughter has been seeing me and going out with me without him having met me so I had to decide or otherwise stop seeing Madhu. It was like an ultimatum of a sort – anyway by that time I think we had already almost decided to go ahead. The more interesting part of the story – the twist in the tale – is that we fixed a date for our engagement, which was to be in July. But my father-in-law suffered from indifferent health and was a little hesitant to travel so he could not come for the engagement. So I got engaged to Madhu and her sisters represented their parents. The plan was that they would come a few months later for our wedding. But a few weeks before the wedding, my father-in-law had a massive heart attack and he underwent a bypass surgery. Fortunately, he was okay but he could not travel for the proposed wedding date. So, there were two options: postpone the wedding or go ahead. By that time it was only fifteen days to the wedding, so everyone felt that it would not be a good idea to postpone and that we should go ahead with the wedding. So we got married and because we wanted a very small wedding where there were only about 70 to 80 close friends and family present. As you no doubt know that is very small for an Indian wedding,' but Harsh adds with a smile, 'the following day we did have a reception at the home for a thousand people. We went to Udaipur for our honeymoon because after that, there were some family rituals – I had to go to a temple and a few other things – and I was finally to go to England in January to meet my parents-in-law. But, believe it or not, I had a severe attack of jaundice and was laid up in bed for several weeks. Finally, a couple of months later I managed to get to England to meet my in-laws for the first time and we all had a great laugh about it.'

By the time he married, in December 1985, Harsh had been working for a couple of years in the Neotia family business, RKBK. Just before that, and coinciding with the end of his college years, the family had started working on what became their major business success. Before describing this, it is necessary to fill in the rest of the family background.

The eldest Neotia brother, who had been adopted to become Bimal Kumar Poddar, had married Bimla, the daughter of Satyanarayan Sekhsaria, one of the leading Mumbai cotton merchants. She had a brother Narottam Sekhsaria, who joined hands with Suresh and Vinod Neotia to establish Gujarat Ambuja Cements Ltd. in 1983 – these were the two founder promoters in what was a first-generation family industrial enterprise. Narottam Sekhsaria was the driver towards the growth and success of what soon became known as Ambuja Cements Ltd – what Harsh Neotia calls 'certainly the most notable industrial success of our family'.

'The cement business was just starting at this point so there was an option to be a part of the cement plant that was being built in Gujarat rather than join my father. In fact my father was closely involved in the construction of the plant that even I visited with him a few times. But I found myself a bit overwhelmed by the scale of that operation and could not muster any excitement to be just a small "cog" in this very large "wheel". So I persuaded my family to allow me to do something in Calcutta. In fact we had no business in Calcutta at that point of time, though we lived here. Most of our businesses, the traditional family trading businesses were in Uttar Pradesh and Bihar, which are neighbouring states. However, another opportunity came around the same time when a small property was available to be developed into apartments. The property belonged to a family friend who was moving to Mumbai. He visited our home one evening and said that he would allow us to develop the land. I don't know why but property development seemed interesting to me and, with my family's approval, I did a deal with the owner and built twenty odd apartments – two bedrooms in each with about 1000 sq. feet for each apartment – so 21000 sq. feet in all for the total development. This was my first project and I spent about two years doing it and, with God's grace, it turned out a little better than we had anticipated and that was my beginning as a property developer. I continued as a small property developer with a hospitality division from 1985 until 1996 and had no involvement in the cement business during those eleven years.'

That was about to change dramatically. 'In 1997, Ambuja Cement was interested to take over an ailing cement company in eastern India, Modi Cement, which belonged to another group. The company had been transferred to the Indian Government's Board of Finance Reconstruction (BIFR) that was the "hospital" for "sick" companies. Narottam Sekhsaria never allows me to forget the family discussion in January that year when our entire family was at Ambujanagar in Gujarat for a family annual temple ceremony. Over breakfast Narottam mentioned to everyone that Suresh and he were interested for Ambuja to bid for the company and turn it around. However, he added turning to me, "We should buy it. But we will only buy it if you take charge and run it." I looked around at everyone and responded: "I have no experience in cement so how can I make a commitment? I would not like to let you down or the family." Narottam chipped in that he was sure I would not let anyone down and I would just "learn on the job".

'I was actually doing quite well on my own, but at my peak I was doing two or three projects in the city each year with each project involving 20,000 to 30,000 sq. feet, and thus it was not really anything to "write home about". And it was miniscule compared to the scale of the family involvement in Ambuja Cements. So essentially, Narottam and Suresh were saying, "Enough is enough, you have spent time doing what you like, but this is the family's main investment and we need you to get involved." I was in a little bit of a dilemma but then finally felt that if I did not do this, I might not be able to do anything of any large scale, because all the family's fortunes were locked into the cement business and there were little resources available to do anything else. I was sure I could do another couple of buildings but that would be neither here nor there. So I agreed to take the plunge after a number of discussions.

'With my agreement to be involved, Ambuja indicated it would be interested in tendering for the business. The upshot was that Ambuja Cement won the bid and I joined the business. Looking back I can see my joining the family business was inevitable. Always at the back of my mind was the fact that our joint family businesses had existed for more than 120 years and I had an obligation to assist the family. Sure there had been ups and downs but I felt I could not really be an "outlier".

'From the day I joined it was a "baptism of fire". Modi's plant was shut. The electricity was cut off because they had not paid the bills. There were several hundred court cases that various people had filed against the company for various kinds of default. Yes, you heard me right, several hundred court cases. There was a demoralized workforce and a large number of senior executives had quit the organisation. Workers who were still there were in a state of daze and shock. They were not sure whether they would be paid their next month's salary. Just to put it in a perspective: in Indian rupees it had a paid up share capital of 40 crore and it had book losses of about 300 crore. So over seven times the net worth of the company was eroded. It was a disaster.

'Fortunately for me Ambuja Cements had a great reputation for being a very efficient player. But unfortunately, there was a feeling that as I was a member of the family which owned Ambuja I must have a "magic wand" to fix all of the problems. How wrong they were.

'I was getting increasingly worried because I could see that the challenges were absolutely enormous. It was as if I was peeling an onion – there seemed to be no end to it. I found more and more issues that needed to be resolved. I felt helpless. What made it worse was that I was very aware many people were depending on me to produce solutions to all these issues. Eventually it became all too much. One day after maybe six weeks in the job, I returned to my guesthouse – you know typically in Indian factories management has lunch and takes a short rest before returning for the second half of the day – and sat down in my restroom. And although I had no idea it was going to happen, I suddenly just burst into tears and cried uncontrollably. At some point my assistant came to bring me my cup of tea and to tell me it was time to return to the office. He knew me very well, as he had been my assistant in my real estate business; he thought I must be very ill and called for the doctor without telling me. The doctor was there within minutes. I feigned that I had a severe migraine but, looking back, I had of course just suffered some sort of emotional breakdown. I reacted irrationally and fired my assistant on the spot for calling the doctor and not asking me what was wrong. Of course, I regret having done this, but I was not thinking straight, and to have fired someone who was only trying to help me was unforgiveable.

'Anyway I told the office manager to cancel my meetings for the second half of the day as I needed to rest. I sat in my room and thought about everything that whole afternoon and evening. The next morning I requested the company's president to call the twenty or thirty seniormost people to meet me; we used to have separate meetings with different parts of the business but not usually with everyone. He asked me was there any specific agenda to which I responded that there was not and I just wanted to meet. When everyone was assembled I said to them words to the effect "Over the last six weeks or so, each of you has been raising a lot of questions and I have heard you out. But I have to tell you that I do not have any answers. By now you must know the truth of what I have said before on one or two occasions, that I really have no experience in the cement business." Now these people knew that, but their thinking was that it did not matter that I had no experience, because I was a part of a very successful business family and it was as if I would know genetically what to do. But you do not know these things genetically; you may have some business sense genetically, but you do not have knowledge of the particular business where the technical complexity was very great as it was in the cement business. As I continued my address to them I told them, "Perhaps my family made a mistake in appointing me to this job and I made a mistake in accepting it. It is clear to me that the problems of the business are complex and that I do not have the answers. But there is one thing that I can offer, and that is to be available to work shoulder to shoulder with you if you can come up with possible solutions. With this input from you I can use my common business sense to guide us and hopefully overcome the various problems." Of course I am just summarizing what happened over a couple of hours. I was not trying to be clever but was just telling the key management my honest feelings. The effect of this meeting was transformational as from that day on management started coming to me with their problems but also with their recommended solutions. If they offered me two or three possible solutions, I could say "okay let's try this one out" and if they offered only one solution, I would ask a few questions, and if that it seemed to be the only possible solution I would agree we should go ahead with that one. I think that my admission of helplessness made the management feel somehow a little more emotionally connected with me as in the normal ownership situation in India which existed at that time it would be rare for the ownership to ask for their assistance; they would be more used to implementing decisions rather being a part of the decision making process.'

When I asked whether he had sought advice from his uncle and his father or experts, Harsh replied, 'Of course their advice was always available, but when experts – like technical people and others – came in to help, they were most often not deeply involved with my people. They would come in for a few days, look at the issues on which their advice was sought, make recommendations and then go away again. I would be left to discuss these recommendations with the local management and make the final decision. Quite often the recommendations were isolated from an understanding of the whole business. Sometimes you can get a doctor who can fix your eyes, but he cannot fix your knees or your back, which are also aching. One doctor may not have all the answers when often one thing affects another. Besides, if outside experts were supposed to be deciding everything, then what the hell was I myself meant to be doing? It took three years to turn the company around. The first thing that happened was that we were able to establish a greater amount of rapport and relationship within all the levels of the organisation. What seemed to be a huge burden for me gradually started to melt and eventually became something that was a pleasure to deal with – the problems were still daunting – but at least the relationships improved. By 2006, the financial position had completely flipped over from a 300-crore loss to a 300-crore profit. I am proud to say that when I left as Managing Director on 31 March that same year, Ambuja Cements Eastern Limited was one of the more efficient and well-run units of the entire Ambuja Cements Group.'

Harsh Neotia was obliged to leave his executive position (and his directorship of Ambuja Cements itself) in 2006, because Narottam Sekhsaria and Suresh Neotia, divested a substantial portion of the family stakes in favour of the Swiss company Holcim, the world's largest cement company and, at the same time, also handed over the family management control. The previous year, the two companies had jointly taken control of ACC, India's oldest and most prestigious cement company, in which Ambuja Cements had already made a strategic investment in 1999 by acquiring a 14.5 per cent stake. By 2006, Ambuja Cements and its associated companies was probably India's largest cement producer.

The divestment was very heavily debated in the family. Harsh explained: 'It was not something I think everyone understood. Looking back it is pretty clear we grew the business too quickly which meant more and more investment was required from the shareholders. This involved increasingly large amounts of capital that we did not have and thus our shareholding in the company continued to be diluted. But there were other issues too, such as my uncle Narottam, who was Managing Director, found he had a major health setback [from which he recovered] which meant he could not devote his full time and attention to running the business.

'To be frank I was certainly very unhappy and disappointed at that time but, having said that, I completely went along with the decision because that was certainly expected of me and I was brought up in that way. Why should I oppose a decision that my senior family members are taking which in their opinion is in the long term best interests of the family?

'And again, with the benefit of hindsight, the sale provided the two families with money and freedom to invest in other enterprises. In my case I have been able to build or rebuild an enterprise much more to my likes and to my capabilities. Maybe it has given me the opportunity to "soar" a little more, maybe see the world from a little more independent perspective, and sometimes I feel – to be a little philosophical – that I was like a "bird", which lived in a "golden cage" in a "beautiful garden", safe from "predators" and where "food" was plentiful. And then suddenly the "food" stopped and the "cage door" was opened. For me it was a little scary to leave the "cage" for the unknown but, having done so, I realize how lucky I have been. To be given the opportunity to soar, of course with the attendant risks.'

The decision effectively not to pass the business on to the next generation clearly deeply affected Harsh but 'I picked up the threads where I had left them when I joined Ambuja Cements. Incidentally, during these ten years while I was deeply involved in the cement business, the real estate companies which were subsidiaries of the cement business continued. It was not that they were closed down, but they were then a side business and they were operating in a small way – we had a small team of about thirty people and my colleague Mr. Jain, who is the president of our company, was effectively the person running the show. What was excellent was that the three or four projects that we did during that period all turned out to be very good projects which confirmed to the market that we knew how to do developments. When Holcim bought the cement business they made it a condition of the sale that they did not want any of the non-cement businesses. This meant I had the opportunity to buy out the Ambuja companies involved in real estate and hospitality and others, such as one involved in housing finance, was sold to HDFC. Also, we were able to keep the Ambuja name and thus in 2006 Ambuja Realty was born.'

I mentioned that I understood Ambuja Realty now operates in four verticals. 'Yes, we have real estate, health care, hospitality, and education. In education, in 2008 we acquired an engineering institute, which we rebranded as the Neotia Institute of Technology, Management & Science (NITMAS). It is a fully residential institute with around 1500 students and which we hope to grow by around 300 students per year. Of course this is not a "for profit" venture but

I see it as important to our future and thus it sits under the group umbrella.

'In terms of healthcare, in 2002 we set up a specialty 83-bed hospital in Calcutta which is dedicated to woman and child healthcare, called the Bhagirathi Neotia Woman & Child Care Centre (BNWCCC). That was our first hospital. Our second hospital, Neotia Getwell Healthcare Centre, is a super specialty hospital in North Bengal that opened in 2012, and we have plans for another in Calcutta.

'In hospitality we built the Swissotel Kolkata Neotia Vista, which is the first time in India a hotel has been incorporated onto a mall – at City Centre in New Town and we also have the Fort Raichak, which was our first real initiative in the field of hospitality in 1997. But our new focus is to build and operate a chain of small ecologically friendly "up market" resorts located in the mountains or by the sea. They will each be called Kutir, which denotes a peaceful abode in Hindi. The first one, Ganga Kutir, was opened in 2008 and is located on the Ganges in Raichak. We have also opened a number of others, including one in a tea plantation, one in a forest, one by the sea, and another in the mountains of Sikkim.

'In our core real estate division, we have been doing townships, malls and corporate offices like this one.' This brief summary does not do justice to Harsh's achievements in this sector and, in particular, his success in doing public-private sector partnerships in West Bengal. The first partnership, Bengal Ambuja Housing Development Limited, was with the West Bengal Housing Board for the development of mass housing projects in the state. The initial project, Udayan, established a new landmark in providing social housing. Another successful public-private partnership was with the Calcutta Metropolitan Development Authority for the development of City Centre, a residential-cum-commercial complex comprising half a million square feet of built-up area on about seven acres in Salt Lake, Calcutta. This was followed by a number of other City Centre projects.' However, with the appointment of Mamata Banerjee as chief minister of West Bengal I wondered to myself whether it has now become much more difficult to do such projects with the West Bengal government; one hopes not, although I suspect for Harsh to succeed in the current environment he may need to use every bit of the negotiating skills he developed during the early days of his time with Ambuja Cements.

When I met Harsh he indicated that he was thinking about changing the name of the group from Ambuja Realty to Ambuja Neotia and by the time I came to write this chapter he had done it.

When I then asked Harsh whether, being from such a successful family, he felt an obligation or pressure to succeed, he replied: 'I think there is a certain amount of that. I am hesitant to be too analytical about this because I am too close to it, but I have a sense that yes, my family has been successful in recent times. And thus there is indeed an obligation or expectation for me to succeed too, but it is not something that bothers me too much. All I can do is my best and if that is not good enough, so be it.' With this time honoured truth I thought there was no better time to bring my time with Harsh to a close. But, if the developments he is doing are similar to his Ecospace where we met, I have little doubt that he will continue to 'soar' as the 'bird' which escaped from the 'cage', subject of course, to the vagaries of working in Calcutta.

---

[1] Ambuja Neotia Group (www.ambujaneotia.com) is one of the most respected corporate houses headquartered in Kolkata. It has developed residency housing, townships, malls and business parks in a city that has seen little development over recent decades. It has also expanded into hospitality, healthcare, and education.

[2] La Martiniere School in Calcutta was established from funds from the Will of Claude Martin. Martin was born on 4 January 1735 in Lyon, France. He came to India when he was seventeen and served in the French East India Company. After French influence declined in India and, following a spell in British custody after a military defeat, he accepted a commission in the British East India Company's army and rose to the rank of Major-General. After taking up residence in Lucknow he again switched allegiances and occupied an important position in the court of Nawab Shuja-ud-Daula and later his son, Asaf-ud-Daula. During this period he is estimated to have accumulated a fortune of about 400,000 rupees. He built the palace of 'Constantia' and his house named Farhat Baksh, both of which he equipped with luxuries that included a library of some 4,000 volumes written in many languages and a picture gallery. He died in Lucknow on 13 September 1800. According to his will, he was buried in the vault prepared for his remains in the basement of the college in Lucknow. The major portion of his monies and estate were left for founding three institutions, one each in Lucknow and Calcutta and his birthplace Lyon. It took 30 years to dispose of the litigation arising out of his Will. Finally, La Martinière Schools opened in Calcutta, on 1 March 1836. (Source Wikipedia)

"Our use of the Nicholas name is an interesting illustration of our values. When we acquired Nicholas in 1988 we agreed that in 1990 we would cease using the name. But they saw that in those two years our new investment in the business and the growing of the business had enhanced the reputation and value of the Nicholas name; not only in India but internationally. As a result in 1991 they told us we could keep using the name in perpetuity as long as the Piramal family owned the business."

AJAY PIRAMAL

Chairman, Piramal Group[1]

I met Ajay Piramal in the group's headquarters in Mumbai which was once the site of one of the family's textile mills. As anticipated with someone 'at the top of his game', he was relaxed and comfortable talking about his life and the various 'ups and downs' along the way.

'Like many business people covered in your first book on India[2] and, I suspect this one, our family are Marwaris from Rajasthan.' This seemed an appropriate point to ask Ajay why he thought the Marwaris have been so disproportionately successful in Indian business. 'I really don't have an answer for this, other than to point out that many of the Marwari businessmen who founded what, generations later have become large businesses, left Rajasthan with nothing. I think there was an element of survival in the beginning and the drive to ensure financial security for the extended joint family. My own grandfather, Seth Chaturbhuj Piramal [1892-1958] is a case in point. He left his village of Bagar in Rajasthan in the early

1900s and it is said that when he arrived in Mumbai he only had Rs. 50 in his pocket. With no capital he became a trader of numerous agricultural products such as cotton and opium, the latter of which was, at that time, legal. He also started to speculate on cotton futures; successfully it appears as it allowed him to acquire a very small percentage in a textile business called, Morarjee Goculdas Spinning & Weaving Company Limited. He was however not a builder of businesses. That was done more by my father, Gopikrishna Piramal [1923-1979] who consolidated the family presence in the textile business and entered other businesses.

'By the time I was born one would say we were a well-to-do family. Still we lived a pretty simple life. We were never short of anything but, at the same time, we were not extravagant on anything either. I was the youngest of three boys; my eldest brother was seven years older than me, and my middle brother was five and a half years older. My mother did not work but concentrated on raising her three sons and taking care of my father. I was much closer to my father than to my mother and I think it is fair to say I was my dad's favourite; perhaps because I was the youngest but, for whatever reason, he did not conceal his fondness for me.

'I went to the Catholic St Xavier's Boys' Academy in Mumbai where the students came from a range of religious backgrounds. It was certainly not the most elite school in Mumbai and there were children from different socio-economic backgrounds. All three of us went to this school. Each of us was quite good academically; my brothers were smarter and were usually top of their class, whereas I would be in the top half dozen, but never the top.

'I took a different line from my brothers in sports. My eldest brother was good in many sports but I started horse riding when I was around ten and stuck to that. My father in fact owned horses many years ago in his hometown in Rajasthan but it was not through him I inherited a love of horses. In fact, I never saw him ride. It was much more happenstance. One day my mother, without asking me, took me to a riding club and signed me up. I guess I took to it like "a duck to water" as I not only loved it but also started to do well. I was the junior champion in the western zone for three years in a row. The competition was a mixture of show jumping and some games that you play on horses when you are young. From this I moved into playing polo.

'I can remember often trying to persuade my father to let me have my own horse because I used to just ride the horses which were owned by the club. I would try to justify this to him by explaining how much we were spending on hiring horses. One day when I was much older he allowed me to buy a few and explained why he had refused for so long. Apparently he had a deep-seated fear that my love of horses would inevitably lead to a love of racing and gambling.'

I remarked that horses can be pretty fickle animals and wondered if he had ever seriously hurt himself. 'You are right,' he laughed, 'they can indeed be erratic. I vividly remember not long after I started riding that I fell off my horse and landed on my head and became delirious. Although my dad was very worried for me, he was a deeply spiritual person and consulted his guru to whom he used to go regularly. The guru apparently said, "Don't do anything; just let him be and tomorrow he will be okay." He was, fortunately for me, correct.

'After school, both my brothers followed the same path and studied commerce at university. My eldest brother then wanted to go on to do an MBA at Stanford. But this did not sit well with my parents who figured he would never come back to India. This was a pretty reasonable prediction as many did just that – went and never came back. So the family was very concerned about that and they persuaded him not to go.

'By the time it was my turn, my father was keen that I study something different and so I pursued my studies in science. Maybe I could have done engineering but I did a bachelor's specialising in Chemistry at the University of Mumbai from which I graduated in 1975. The first couple of years in college actually did not go well because I could not adjust to academic life but, more importantly,' Ajay grins, 'I also met Swati, the woman who is now my wife so maybe that was somewhat of a distraction as well.

'So I scraped along for the first couple of years and then started to focus on my studies and eventually, graduated with a distinction. Actually, how I did at university, provided I received a degree, was largely all that mattered as it was assumed I would join the family business. Following this, like my brother who was not allowed to go the US, I did an MBA at Jamnalal Bajaj Institute of Management Studies.

'While I was studying for my MBA at the age of twenty-one in 1976, I married Swati. Although Marwari families are generally more conservative than others, my family is quite liberal in matters like this. They did not try and push me into an arranged marriage. Actually my father was delighted as he wanted to see his youngest child settled; especially as he was certain that he was going to die early. Swati was in the middle of her medical degree at the time but pressed on after we got married and became a doctor.

'Her family was more worried about the marriage than mine. There were two prime reasons. Firstly, they felt that she should have completed her studies before marriage. Secondly, she was from a conservative Gujarati family who felt that Marwaris were much more flamboyant and were worried what sort of difficulties I would get her into. But these were largely just pre-marriage jitters and once we were married her family relaxed. One of my characteristics is that I do not worry too much about anything, including getting married.

'My father's prognostication that he would die young proved accurate as he died in 1979 at the young age of fifty-five. It was very sad and, looking back today, so unnecessary how the end came. Swati, my mother and I travelled to the US with my father to keep him company while he had a comprehensive check-up. My father suffered from labile hypertension and the doctors knew from his CT scan he had at some stage suffered a mild heart attack. But none of the doctors in India at the time knew why and what needed to be done. They recommended him to be taken to the US where there were doctors with this sub specialty. Believe it or not, within 24 hours of him meeting for the first time with the doctor in New York he suffered a massive heart attack and died.

'Needless to say, it was a huge shock for the family. Whether he died because of a reaction to the dies used in the tests he undertook or for some other reason, we will never know. But of one thing my father was certain and that was that he was going to die young. His own father, my grandfather also died young of a heart attack and, as my father was a heavy smoker, he knew he was taking a big risk. Another sign he knew he did not have long to live was the fact over the previous few years he had began to devolve management responsibility to my brothers and me for the family businesses.

'The family businesses at that time consisted of the textile business, a luggage business which operated under the brand name of VIP, a very small pharmaceutical business called Kemp & Co (and after which was named the famous landmark Kemps Corner in Mumbai) and a small cutting tool business called Miranda Tools. It was this last business that he asked me to run not long after I joined him in 1978 when I was twenty-three. This experience taught me many lessons; it taught me to take independent decisions, it also taught me to succeed on my own and to cope with failure. I certainly did not repeat this with my own children when they were of the same age but that is what happened back then.

'The fact that both my father and grandfather died in their fifties is certainly something I am very aware of and particularly as I have now passed the age my father was when he died. In fact my oldest brother reminded me on my birthday when I became the same age as my father when he died.

'As mentioned earlier, my grandfather was Chaturbhuj Piramal, after whom we have taken our family name, and he had three sons and three daughters. Two of his three sons were in the textiles business together; one was my father, Gopikrishna and one was my uncle, Mohanlal but they separated out their business in 1971. This was done amicably. From what I know from my father and Mohanlal, the reason they separated out was because my father had three sons and my uncle had three daughters. So their views of life were different. At that time, girls did not work in family businesses. On the other hand my father wanted his sons to be in the business and the way my uncle saw it, there was a partnership between the two brothers, and not necessarily with the next generation. The separation was done without any lawyers, with just an understanding between the two brothers. This is certainly unusual but this is how separations of the family businesses have happened in my family. Mohanlal kept some of the textile businesses as his share. Sadly, his businesses did not prosper and he died in 2001.

'In 1982, three years after my father passed away, my two brothers and I separated the businesses we had been left by my father. Ashok, my eldest brother and I decided to stay in the textile business together and Dilip, my other brother received his one-third share, which was the VIP branded luggage business and a ferrite manufacturing company. Our textile business was known as Morarjee Textiles and we also owned Miranda Tools and a small auto component business.

'It was an amicable separation but I have always thought Dilip negotiated the best deal as he knew that Ashok was passionate about keeping the textile businesses in any separation. As the youngest brother I just "went along for the ride" but if it had been my call I would certainly have suggested a different way of dividing up the businesses and particularly if I had been able to predict what happened next.

'We separated the businesses on 1 January 1982 and on 16 January the whole of the Bombay textile industry went on strike – all 250,000 workers went on strike. And not just for a couple of days but for 18 months. I believe it is the longest strike in Indian history. By the time the strike ended the value of our textile businesses were negative.

'But a year later we were to receive another shock when it was detected that Ashok had kidney cancer. It was particularly a shock because not only was he only thirty-five years old but also as he was the fittest of the three brothers. As he won a tennis tournament in Bombay just before the diagnosis it made it even harder to understand. We all flew off to the US to ensure he had the best treatment but it was all to no avail as the cancer had spread beyond his kidneys. It was terminal and he returned to Bombay and died early in 1984 within 12 months of the diagnosis. Apart from my father, I was closest to Ashok and he trusted me with everything. In fact, my wife, who was a doctor by that time, and myself, managed all aspects of his illness.

'I do not know what effect the stress of the strike had on his health but one has to think it played a part. Not only did Ashok feel the full effect of the financial aspects of the strike on the business but there were also fears for one's safety. The strike was led by Dutta Samant who had a reputation for violence and I know that unnerved Ashok. But, more important than all of this, I think my brother felt that he had let down the family as he struggled to keep the business going. Ashok left behind his wife Urvi, who was only thirty-one at the time, and their three sons between the ages of three and eleven.

'So, within a space of four years, I was catapulted from being the youngest son to being effectively in charge of two thirds of the family business. It was also an extremely difficult time for my mother as, not only had she become a widow at a young age, but had also lost her eldest son.

'I think it is fair to say there was a lot of skepticism as to whether I would be able to resurrect the family businesses owned by Ashok and me. I was largely unknown in the business community as I was the youngest brother and Ashok was very much identified with the textile business. And of course the strike had seriously damaged the viability of the textile business. There are two things, however, that work well for me: firstly, I do not feel stress so much and, secondly, I believe that whatever has to happen will happen. This was also very much my father's philosophy. I very strongly believed it then and I believe it now.

'You might be surprised to know that two months before Ashok passed away he agreed we should acquire a glass business I had identified. Despite the fact the strike was continuing and the family was in difficult financial circumstances I felt this was a good opportunity and should not be passed up. I was certain that our textile business did not have a great future and we needed to diversify, just as my father had started doing with the VIP baggage acquisition.

'So we continued with the diversity strategy and in 1987 something happened that changed my life completely. I had gone to lunch at a friend's place, where I met R.A. Shah who was a lawyer I had not met before, although, we knew of each other. He was also the chairman of an Indian company called Nicholas Laboratories, which was owned by Aspro-Nicholas of the UK and which in turn was owned by the Australian Nicholas Kiwi and had been acquired by Sara Lee of the US. Sara Lee was essentially a consumer goods company and wanted out of the pharmaceutical business. So he told me that they wanted to exit out of India, and asked me why we should not put in a bid. His job was just to get more and more people to bid; it was not that he was giving any insider information. So I gave the okay. It was literally at the Sunday lunch where I first heard of a possible transaction and on Monday we put in a bid. I do not know how. I do not even know why I did that.

'It took about eight or nine months of trying to persuade them to sell to us because there were many other bidders, many larger, much larger companies, who were interested in Nicholas Laboratories. I was a nobody then; I was not only young but was unknown in this sector. But I had one thing: I had the enthusiasm of youth. When you are young, you have much more passion and you can pursue things harder – the hunger is greater. So I persuaded the British who were running the business that they should sell to us. I think others probably offered a higher price. In those days the government determined how much an Indian group could pay for a foreign company. These were done by a department called the Controller of Capital Issues that would regulate the price according to some formula. Foreign bidders of course were not caught by this and could "top up" the payment outside India. My task was to persuade the government to allow me to pay an amount higher than the formula produced being "x + y" instead of "x".

'It was a very torturous process taking several months because not only did I have to get the approval of the majority owner and the government but also from a number of minority shareholders such as the Unit Trust of India. I do not know how but I got there and all the relevant parties agreed. As a young man confronting all these issues for the first time I found the whole process exciting and got immense satisfaction in solving all the problems that came up. Of course at that point I did not then have a passion about the pharmaceutical sector; I just felt that it was a good deal and then I wanted to win it. My passion for pharma came only once I got into the business.

'There was also a twist in the deal which is worth mentioning. Right at the end while we were waiting for final approval from the government, an interesting problem came up. The top five senior employees of Nicholas India who had wanted to do a management buyout, but had failed to get the approval of Nicholas, lodged a complaint with the government that some payment had been made "under the table" by us and therefore approval should not be given by the government. They also approached the parliament to conduct an investigation and placed the story in the newspapers.

'Luckily for us, I had established a good relationship with the executive who was the chief negotiator for Nicholas. He did not want the deal to fall over and so appointed me to the Board with the mandate to run the company until the approval was given or rejected. My first action was to sack the five employees and my second was to approach the senior parliamentarian who was to raise the matter on the floor of the parliament. He was a former finance minister and, given his seniority, if he had pursued the transaction there is no doubt it would have created significant problems for the approval. But as luck would have it, he had known my father and did not realize I was his son. I went and explained everything to him and, once he understood it was just part of a political strategy by the executives to try and buy the company, he decided not to raise the matter in parliament.

'In the end two of the senior managers came to me and said that they wanted to come back to the company and I agreed to do so. But I did not take back the ringleader. So that is how we got into pharmaceuticals. We grew the business, both organically and inorganically.

'I always say that it has been our values that have held us in good stead such as whatever we agreed upon, whether it was in writing or verbal, we would stick to it. And that is very important. For instance, we did not export any of our branded generics, although they were much cheaper, because we had said that we would not. Part of the deal was that we would stick to India. We also said that we would do business of a high quality and that we would look after our employees. We did that too.

'The Nicholas deal was finalized in 1988, and I think it was in 1989 that they sold the rest of their business, which was mainly over-the-counter, to Roche. We had invested in a new world-class plant in 1991 at a time when few were investing in India due to price controls and so by the time Roche decided to exit India in 1993 they saw us as a logical buyer as they knew we behaved in terms of quality, in terms of not exporting and in terms also of looking after our people well. Once again there were many foreign and local companies interested in acquiring Roche's business but we prevailed for the reasons I have mentioned and, of course, the price we were prepared to pay.

'Roche was particularly concerned about the quality of our production as some years before there had been a famous court case involving the question of liability surrounding a gas leak at a Shriram Food & Fertilizers Ltd chemicals plant in Delhi. The case, M.C. Mehta vs. Union of India went all the way to the Supreme Court, which laid down the principle of absolute liability on the manufacturer for damage to the environment. Part of what Roche was selling was a chemical plant outside Mumbai and they were scared that should there be some issue even once they had sold there could be reputational damage for Roche. Fortunately for us they saw us as a manufacturer they could trust to manage the plant professionally. It demonstrated, again, the effectiveness of all our business values. I always emphasize to our people that, if you maintain those values, ultimately you will reap the economic benefit. In the short term you may feel that your cost is higher or that you have not been able to take advantage of things, but ultimately it helps.

'Our use of the Nicholas name is an interesting illustration of our values. When we acquired Nicholas in 1988 we agreed that in 1990 we would cease using the name. But they saw that in those two years our new investment in the business and the growing of the business had enhanced the reputation and value of the Nicholas name; not only in India but internationally. As a result, in 1991 they told us we could keep using the name in perpetuity as long as the Piramal family owned the business. So that is why we changed the name to Nicholas Piramal.

'Following the Nicholas and Roche acquisitions we purchased Boehringer, which is another interesting story. Boehringer Mannheim had a quality issue and two of their customers died in 1996 because there was some mix-up in the bulk manufacturing process. The authorities came down strongly on them and Boehringer were very worried. So when they decided they wanted to quit India, naturally they came to us. It was a unique deal as rather than us paying them for their business they paid us to take on their contingent liabilities. And because of the credibility we had with the authorities that we did things cleanly and that we would do everything properly with a high quality, we managed to sort out the liabilities. It is a perfect example of where our reputation for integrity and manufacturing had a tangible financial value.

'When we began with Nicholas, our rank in the pharma sector in India was number 48 and by 2010 once we had absorbed Boehringer and other purchases such as Rhone Poulenc we were number three. The Rhone Poulenc acquisition in 2000 was actually another interesting experience. We were not the highest bidder but they still wanted to sell to us for the same reasons as others I mentioned earlier. But in this case one of the higher bidders threatened to take Rhone Poulenc to court for trying to sell the business at a lower price. Fortunately for us Rhone Poulenc was able to demonstrate that it was their business and it was up to them to decide on what basis they wanted to sell the business. For these global groups price was only a part of the story; they were concerned about their global reputations and wanted to feel confident the Indian business would be in reliable hands.

'In 2010 we were approached by Abbott of the US to sell the Nicholas Piramal business to them. We eventually agreed on a price of $3.7 billion making Abbott the largest pharma company in India. The price Abbott paid provided us with the highest valuation that has ever been obtained globally for any branded generics company. The price was about 9.5 times sales and 30 times our annual operating profit.

'The reason that I agreed to sell was because I did not think that we could ourselves create the value which had been proposed. It seemed to us that if we grew at 20 per cent year on year for the following fifteen years and in which our profit margin was consistently in excess of 35 per cent, then we would have probably attained the same value. So it did not make sense for us to stay on as the owners. And, as for me, I am not attached to any specific business we own. I see my primary job as a trustee for all my stakeholders and I would not have done justice to them by clinging on to the pharma business. Many people have asked me how we could sell out of our main business, but I see my job is really to create value for my shareholders and I need to be objective about this.

'Whilst at the time we purchased Roche back in 2000 the textile business was still bigger than the pharma, I had come to the conclusion that it just was not viable to run a textile business in Bombay. But there was a strong undercurrent from socialists and non-business types that textiles formed an integral part of the true old city of Bombay and should not be allowed to move out of the city. But this was just not practical. Everyone in the sector knew it was suffering whether it was a worker whose employer was unable to pay him or was being paid a pittance for his work, shareholders who no longer received dividends, unpaid suppliers or the banks who were not being paid for their massive outstanding loans to the sector. The state government was very hesitant to take any action and that is when I can say with some immodesty that I managed to convince the government that the right thing to do was to allow the planned re-development of the textiles industry and the land it occupied.

'We became the first company to re-develop land on which a textile mill sat and the result is the development where we are meeting today. You can see outside the window behind me some of the chimneys of the old mill that we preserved in the redevelopment. We moved the cotton mill to a site outside Mumbai where we joint ventured with an Italian company to produce world-class fabric and at a cost of operating significantly lower than at the old site.

'Our workers were given the choice if they wished to move to the new site but most of them preferred to just get paid off. I am happy to say that every one of our workers was paid in full and we have never had an issue in this regard and which sadly was not the case with some of our competitors, where even today some workers have still not been paid or paid in full. I think the fact we paid all our workers and repaid our loans in full has given us a certain credibility that has stood us in good stead over the years. Even though perhaps we could have settled for less with the workers and persuaded the banks to take a "haircut" on their loans, our business approach in the long run definitely pays off.

'Around the time of redevelopment and movement of the textile business, I decided in 2004 that we should separate the business between my late brother Ashok's wife, Urvi and their children and my family. When my brother died in 1984, 95 per cent of our turnover was in textiles but by 2004 it was only 5 per cent because the pharma and other businesses had grown significantly. In the separation we agreed they should get the textile business, the Crossroads shopping mall and other real estate where we are meeting today plus the Miranda Tools' engineering business where I started my business career. My family kept the Nicholas Piramal business and the glass business Ashok agreed we should buy shortly before he died. The separation was done amicably without lawyers just as my father and uncle had done and my two brothers and I had done years ago.'

Both Ajay and Swati's children, Nandini and Anand work in different parts of the family business. Nandini went to Oxford before taking her MBA at Stanford whereas Anand did his MBA at Harvard.

'Our business success has allowed Swati and me to establish Piramal Foundation[3] and also associate with Pratham India.[4] Piramal Foundation pursues projects that fit into one of the four broad areas – healthcare, education, leadership development, livelihood creation, and youth empowerment. The idea is to develop innovative solutions to address issues that we see as critical roadblocks towards unlocking India's economic potential. On the other hand, Pratham India, is the largest non-governmental organization in the education sector and reaches out to 33 million children through its "Read India" campaign.

'On the personal front I try to spend time to better understand the spiritual side of mankind through reading the Bhagavad Gita and other religious books. In fact I believe the Gita is one of the greatest management books as it prescribes optimism and freedom from stress.' I remarked to Ajay that in this regard that I heard one of his favourite spiritual stories was "footprints in the sand". 'Yes, I heard this story back around the time my father passed away and it has always comforted me. The story goes like this – one night the author of "footprints" dreamt that he was walking along the beach with the Lord. Across the dark sky as he walked flashed the scenes from his life. For most scenes, he noticed two sets of footprints in the sand, one belonging to him and the other to the Lord. But when he looked more closely, he noticed only one set of footprints at the lowest and saddest times of his life. Disappointed, he asked the Lord as to why He had left him when he needed Him the most. The Lord whispered to him, "My child, when you saw only one set of footprints, it was then that I carried you".

This story silenced me and I felt if ever there was a time to end an interview, this was it and I politely took my leave, impressed that this extremely successful businessman, who seems so practical and unemotional in discussing the 'ups and downs' of his life, underneath it all has a much deeper softer spiritual side.

---

[1] Piramal Group (www.piramal.com) is a diversified conglomerate with operations in over 30 countries and brand-presence across 100 markets around the world. Since the late 1980s, the Piramal Group evolved from a textile-centric business to a diversified pharmaceutical-based global organisation. The Piramal Group operates across sectors such as healthcare, life sciences, drug discovery, healthcare information management, specialty glass packaging and real estate.
[2] Peter Church, *Added Value –The life stories of Indian business leaders*, Roli Books, 2010.
[3] http://www.piramal.com/content/piramal-foundation
[4] http://www.pratham.org/

❝ The investment by Disney was a necessary part of UTV's growth because the media business has always been a very undercapitalized business and we needed more financial muscle to expand on an international scale. Also, the media business is risky and, whilst we were confident we would succeed seven out of ten times, realistically we would fail three times. Not because we had made bad decisions or had not delivered, but because that is the nature of the industry. ❞

RONNIE SCREWVALA

Founder UTV and CEO Disney India[1] /Unilazer

Before I meet the people covered in my books I make a point of not reading too much about them in the media as I do not want to be too influenced by what others have written. But I would have to say my impression of Ronnie was consistent with what I read later. Smooth, professional and confident come to mind. And yet fully cognizant that, despite his success, he may still not be seen as an insider by some in India's notoriously fickle film industry.

I met Ronnie in his UTV offices on Lower Parel late one afternoon. They were professional but certainly not opulent or flash. We started with him telling me about his childhood. 'I was born, bred, and grew up in a small Parsi family in Mumbai. There were my parents and an elder brother who is six years older than me. My mother was a homemaker since my parents married. My father was an executive for his entire career. His last assignment, which was the longest one, was as Managing Director for a British company called

JL Morison (India) Ltd which sold Nivea cream and other personal care products.'

It is a small family even by Parsi standards as there is only one cousin on his father's side and none on his mother's. Other than this his parents' siblings either did not marry or have children. 'My brother was far more academic than me as not only did he complete a management degree but went on to do a PhD in human relations.

'I went to Cathedral and John Connon School in Mumbai. This is a co-educational private school established back in the middle of the nineteenth century.' I told him I was aware of the school as Rahul Bajaj and Yusuf Hamied, covered in my last book, too had attended the school. Ronnie went on to say that he thought the education was first class and I said I had heard it was recently ranked as the top private school in India.

'Yes, I think private primary and secondary schooling can be better in India than in the West but it is at college level where things drop off. The three years or four years I spent at the Sydenham College of Commerce after school disillusioned me. I just could not see it was relevant to my life after study. College in India is a completely different discipline and a different teaching style; it is not like any university abroad. I think that, if I had studied overseas, my appetite to continue to want to study might have been higher – and I think my daughter has been fortunate to do that. But I did not and I have no deep regrets for that because I think I always wanted to take the steep dive into entrepreneurship in some form or the other. I was always in the top 5 per cent academically at school, but then at college I just lost interest and everything nosedived.

'I used to do theatre at school and college and after that continued the hobby at weekend theatre repertories. It was hard work as one rehearsed in the evenings after work and, given the travel issues in Mumbai we finished very late indeed. I enjoyed acting and I think that the acting experience gave me a strong bedrock to be articulate as well as the confidence to do a lot of other things in life. I also think that the experience of being on the stage teaches you to be able to think and act extempore. It helps you to think on your feet for the rest of your life so that you are able to speak to an audience of one or one thousand scripted or unscripted. In my case certainly it helped me create a level of confidence that you exude day in and day out.

'I think theatre must have been in my destiny and I stumbled into it. I choose to get involved in it like any undergraduate might anywhere in the world. Then suddenly you find you have a liking for that subject and decide you want to remain involved in it in some way.'

I asked Ronnie how he remained involved in theatre as part of his professional life. 'I finished Sydenham in 1978 and then started working as a small entrepreneur, although I know my father wanted me to become a chartered accountant. At that stage, I think it was more or less by default and for the first two or three years I worked in what I would call the audio-visual field. I started doing a lot of television anchoring. These were the days when Doordarshan (the Government monopoly broadcaster) was the only television channel. It used to have a lot of game and quiz shows that I sometimes anchored. It was actually in my last year of college that I went for an audition at Doordarshan and was selected to be a host of game and quiz shows that went out at prime time on Wednesday nights.' Ronnie smiles as he adds, 'A large proportion of the country watched these shows as there was nothing else to watch.

'These shows were in English. I think we created a game show called "The Mathemagic Show" which was really about making maths fun; it was a game show. And then we had a show that was along the lines of a very old British format called "Contact" that was about words and simply connecting them together. It was called "Let Us Make Contacts". There was also "Young World" which was a talent show along the lines of "Saturday-night Live". It was a one-hour show where I would bring in a celebrity, do a little bit of standup comedy that was followed by music or dance. I was always clear that this was not going to be a permanent occupation but it was a fun thing to do in one's early twenties.'

I asked Ronnie how he moved from this to his first business of cable TV. 'At that time there was no cable TV in India; there was, as I mentioned earlier, just Doordarshan with only one channel. Funnily enough most TVs in India at that time did not even have remote controls as there was nothing to switch to! Many of us realized India would not move for some time to satellite television but we thought there would be a market for cable as we saw how this operated in a number of developing and developed countries. It took about a year of doing door-to-door, building-to-building concept selling in key cities and with hotels where we indicated we wished to provide the second channel in the house or hotel through cable TV.

'The start was to sell the concept. If the committee or society running a building thought that they wanted to have the channel, then there was an initial subscription charge and one year's rent in advance. That way it was a kind of self-funding. But before that it was all guerilla and garage operations of a core team who went out to sell the concept. We got the first contract and then the second contract and so on. I think that this was an important basic lesson and which I talk about to young people today. Young people will come to me and say that India is not a great environment for entrepreneurs. I am saying quite the opposite and that, if you are looking at how our growth here can be sustained, it is going to happen through self-employment. And the cynicism among the young is high that they do not have the bankers or investors who want to cut them cheques and that they will move Silicon Valley where the grass always seems to be greener. My basic answer to them is the lesson that I have learnt starting businesses – you have got "cut your coat" according to your "cloth". So if you have got an idea which nobody is buying because you want half a million dollars, then you had better start it at fifteen thousand dollars and build it up through hard work from thought process to realization and then go on to the next level. I think that was the crux of some of the lessons I learnt in starting up businesses. This will also stand you in good stead because sooner or later a business cycle will change for the worse and where you may "run aground". There is never going to be a cycle where you face a tougher problem that starting a business with no funding. So that is the best example I can give to first stage entrepreneurs.

'Initially we were just selling the concept or idea as to how we could do the cable channel. The presentation was high impact but it was curiosity that attracted all the building residents down on a Sunday morning when we did the presentation for them. We used to say something like "Here is the possibility that you can have a multichannel TV set in your home." We succeeded first with the building societies of the buildings in which we were living in as at least we had the credibility of being someone they knew who went up and down the elevators each day and that we would not run away. Again theatre helped a lot because I was a known entity and for some people they probably felt ok, he understands what he is doing and yes we know who he is as we have seen him on TV and in plays. It was similar to the way Prannoy (Roy), Raghav (Bahl[2]), Aroon Purie and all other people involved in news at that time built their credibility.

'As far as pricing was concerned there was a fair amount of working backwards from the calculation of the number of residents that we would reach in one complex. With our cable TV concept without a dish it meant that you had to stop every time you crossed a road, so we had to sell only to colonies or complexes that were private and where you could interconnect but did not have to cross a road. We would look at the density – take 25 per cent for instance – and if we could secure it, that was the reason we would "green light" a project. We worked backwards from that calculation to find the price and allow it to be self funding.

'The funding was for content and technology; once those were covered, the running cost were not high. As what we were doing was a private enterprise we did not need any regulatory approvals. If we had been starting a broadcasting channel it would have been a different story. Our cable TV was in separate clusters of buildings and multiples and within three years of commencing in 1981 with our first building we had cable all over Mumbai with about 40 control rooms. But we still could not cross a road. Then we started to cable up all the hotels – the Oberoi, Taj and ITC chains – and that is how the business grew.

'It was certainly not without struggle to launch the cable business because it took a couple years of development and marketing before we got our first sale. I remember that the one car that we used to borrow between three or four friends would never have a full tank of gas. There were many times that we had to push the car to the gas station. And when we started to make money, all the money went back into the business. But I think that has been in my DNA. Some people put their money into gold, some people put it into silver, some people diversify their investment portfolios, fair enough, but my DNA has been to reinvest. I believe one's standard of living should change incrementally and not exponentially and the rest should go back into the business.

'The cable TV business was owned by my former father-in-law Suresh Nanavanti, who owned the special-effects powerhouse Western Outdoor Advertising and me. He largely funded the business. By the time we sold the business after five years we had cabled up a lot of Mumbai and Delhi and a lot of hotels all over India. We sold the business for a good price but primarily because we could see the business was changing rapidly. Newer entrants to the cable TV market had started crossing municipal roads and in many cases were doing so without approvals and for which we knew approvals would either take long to come by or were very expensive.'

The mention of his former father-in-law led me to ask him about his family life. 'I got married in 1985 when I was thirty to Suresh's daughter, Manjula. It was a love, not an arranged marriage. We were school friends for many years and then dated before Manjula went to the US to study for four years. When she returned we continued dating and then got married. Sadly, we separated after six years but have a daughter, Trishya who is now twenty-six and did her IB (International Baccalaureate) at Sevenoaks School in Kent. From there she went to UCLA and on to USC. I don't think either of us see her wanting to join me in the business world as she is quite independent.'

I asked Ronnie what he did then after exiting the cable business. 'Believe it or not I started making toothbrushes in India.' 'Toothbrushes in India,' I said startled at the difference to his just existed media business. 'How on earth did that come about?' I asked. 'It was actually completely by chance as I was in a factory in London which made Addis Hair Brushes. Addis was one of the partners in JL Morison where my father worked. I was in England for something completely different but my father said the factory was interesting and asked me if I wanted to join him. There were four tooth brush manufacturing machines in the factory that were being scrapped even though they were only two-years old. We were being shown around by Robert Addis, who had in 1980 just celebrated the bicentennial of Addis where he was the tenth generation descendant of the founder William Addis, the inventor of the modern toothbrush. They only wanted one thousand pounds for each machine.

'I asked him to hold the machines for four weeks because I wanted to find out whether there might be a business in India. I met with Colgate and others involved in selling branded toothbrushes. One of the groups agreed to give us a contract if I imported the machines.

'It took me three months to get the approval to import the machines as we were still in the time of the "licence raj" but we persevered and by around 1995 were the largest contract manufacturer of toothbrushes in India. As it was contract manufacturing it was essentially a low-risk business of cost plus a margin. We called the business Lazer. I think the reason we succeeded was again largely due to our credibility in delivering on time what our clients wanted for the agreed price. In due course we sold the business around 2004 when I needed funds to buy back News Corporation's shares in UTV. But I will come to that in due course.

'While the toothbrush business was growing, and where I was more of key shareholder and non-executive chairman, it was starting to become clear to me what I wanted to do in the media and entertainment sectors. I decided to produce television games and other shows and was joined by two people as minority shareholders who I had met many years before in the theatre – Zarina Mehta and Deven Khote. A number of years later Zarina and I married. UTV Software Communications formally opened its doors in 1990.

'But the idea of UTV becoming a diversified media and entertainment business started not long after we started producing shows. Every time we had finished a TV show there was a gap before we got next contract. The main reason was because at the time we started there was only Doordarshan as a buyer and Zee only started in 1992. We expanded into making ads and doing in flight programmes for airlines. Nobody was carrying Indian content on airlines back then.

'At the same time, Cartoon Network, Turner, and all these people were coming into the country with their kids' channels so we established a dubbing division to dub all foreign animation. There was also an increased demand for more local content from players like Discovery. But at this point all of these were small businesses and at least half of the business continued to be the production business. I think after about three years we had about 60 people employed in UTV.

'The funding for growth in the early days was self generating. We only took on a little bit of debt and then repaid that. We were a

B to B[Business to Business] company. And again it was a cost plus margin business. So it was not like we were just making something and if it did not work then we were out in the cold. Although we presold, that did not mean that every time we got an advance cheque – there would be days on which we would all live on a little bit of credit and stretched objectives, including all our 60 people but, by and large, that is how it worked.

'Looking back there was one particular show which caused us huge trouble. We had invested a lot of money into the game show we were producing for Doordarshan as it did not pay us upfront. The first show ran into trouble because there was a question on Mohammed Ali Jinnah who was the first president of Pakistan. Someone brought this up in parliament and there was an uproar about the show and Doordarshan took the show off air. Now the question was: "Who was the show boy of Pakistan at the time of independence?" to which the answer was Jinnah. Now for some reason the Member of Parliament heard the question as "Who was the playboy of Pakistan at the time of independence?" It took us seven days to prove that it was "show boy" that was asked and that is how he was referred to in the history books. But Doordarshan was an extremely conservative government entity and they still cut the show off the air for six months.

'We had already produced 39 episodes and we could not do a thing about that until we got the show back on air as the sponsors had not yet been signed up. Nobody was paying us for this show and at the same time we had many creditors seeking to be paid. Doordarshan did eventually put the show back on the air and ran all 39 episodes. But those six months off the air were a crossroads for the company. My point is that running a media company always has plenty of ups and downs and when you are an entrepreneur without the business being properly funded there are significant risks.

'So those are the risks and the learning experiences, especially in a country like India where everything is evolving and in the media business where anyway you never know necessarily that the next thing you are going to do is the right thing. I think that at UTV we are known for being pioneers but that can be costly if you get it wrong. For instance, we got into home shopping TV programmes around 1996 because I really believed that we understood the content part of and could sell products to TV viewers. But actually we did not anticipate the "touch and feel" Indian consumers need and although we had one successful product it was not enough to make the business a success. Overall, I think we were before our time.'

I asked Ronnie how News Corp came into the picture. 'I think it must have been in 1995 or 1996 that Rupert Murdoch came to India and wanted to explore the opportunities here as he had just bought Star TV from Li Ka-shing. He came across to our office and we had a good chat. Three weeks later we had a follow-up chat in his BSkyB office in London. The upshot was that they bought 49 per cent of UTV for USD 4.5 million. A couple of years later we needed more funds to diversify and Warburg Pincus invested. By that time the valuation had grown to USD 30 million as we were growing in leaps and bounds.

'By 2000 we started thinking about doing an IPO but it took us until 2005 to do so. But before we did the IPO we bought back the News Corp shares in UTV. The primary reason was that we were no longer relevant to News as it had developed its own infrastructure in India and there was no longer much in common between us.

'By that time I would say UTV was decently successful but we were still a production house – by that I mean that 100 per cent of our business was B to B; we were either producing or an intermediary. Post the IPO, our core team sat down to explore how we could become B to C [Business to Consumer] in two years. To do this we needed to build the UTV name and brand with consumers. Globally we also started to take some strategic steps, sometimes in gaming, sometimes in high-profile Hollywood movies. If, for instance, we were creating content, we wanted to make movies because that are as good as it gets in terms of B to C. So we phased out a lot of our other B to B activities. We still do dubbing but it is not a significant part of the business. Ad films were also largely phased out.'

As part of the B to C strategy following the IPO, UTV started broadcasting. UTV acquired a channel, Vijay TV, in South India from Vijay Mallya. It was a leading Tamil-language channel and, according to Ronnie has done pretty well. UTV also reactivated its relationship with News Corp and involved them, not only in Vijay TV but also in other South Indian channels.

'In 2004, shortly before the IPO, we started Hungama TV. This was a kids' channel and many in the industry advised against us doing so and said we were mad. They pointed out India already had Disney, Cartoon Network and Nickelodeon; each of which had free libraries with massive content. But within eighteen months, Hungama TV became the number one kids channel because we had the flexibility of not using their libraries where in many cases the content was quite alien for Indian audiences. Based on our television production experience we knew what our audiences wanted. Indian children had not grown up with American animation. We researched the market and ended up selecting really mischievous but nice animation characters from Japan – Doraemon and Shin-Chan. The cartoons just went gangbusters. Combined with this we did one local kid superhero live action programme. That was it; with these three programmes we went straight to number one.

'This led to Disney ringing me. It was actually the first time I had contact with Disney and the person said something along the lines of "I believe that you might be looking at outside investment into the kids' channel, so do you want to talk." I flew to LA and within a month we reached an agreement to sell Hungama TV to them and, at the same time, they agreed to take a 15 per cent stake in UTV. This all added up because they had a good vision of what they wanted to do here and they had lost a lot of time in India. And, on the other hand, for us with Disney as a shareholder we were in a much stronger broadcast position.

'The investment by Disney was a necessary part of UTV's growth because the media business has always been a very undercapitalized business and we needed more financial muscle to expand on an international scale. Also, the media business is risky and, whilst we were confident we would succeed seven out of ten times, realistically we would fail three times. Not because we had made bad decisions or had not delivered, but because that is the nature of the industry.

'Within two years we built a much larger business where lot of investment had gone into broadcasting, gaming and making movies. The Board of UTV started thinking about hiving off some of the subsidiaries and bringing in outside investors. However, Andy Bird, Chairman of Walt Disney International who was on our board counseled us against doing this. He said, "I can only tell you that in three years from now you are going to regret hiving off some of the parts because the whole is always bigger than the sum of the parts."

This definitely rang a bell for me even though I knew this was in Disney's own interest to suggest this. Indeed one can see some of our competitors having demerged their companies, are now putting them back together again."

The upshot was that Disney increased its shareholding to 32 per cent. Disney's first investment in UTV when they bought Hungama was at about Rs.190. Eighteen months later Disney made an investment at Rs 860 totaling around USD 200 million and which took them not to 32 per cent but to 52 per cent due to the global financial crisis of 2008. The reason their percentage escalated so much is that the public and Ronnie also had a right to take up their pro rata entitlement to shares at the Rs 860 price. Meanwhile, the UTV share price dropped to Rs 460 so virtually no one other than Disney took up the share entitlement.

'The business continued to run well and towards the end of 2010 Disney got in touch with me again. They said that they needed to figure out a broader strategy for Disney in India. They indicated that they had their Indian subsidiary, which was small, and they had their 52 per cent investment in UTV. However, in UTV I had the right to purchase 20 per cent of their shareholding bringing them back to 32 per cent as it was the stated intent that each of Disney, the public and me would own one third each of the company. Their options seemed to be to sell their investment in UTV and build up their 100 per cent subsidiary or increase the investment in UTV to 100 per cent and put everything together. I think a substantial part of that decision depended on whether I was willing to take the plunge to be part of it, because owning 100 per cent of UTV without the core management team would not have made much sense from their perspective.

'It took the better part of three to six months for us to understand what that would imply for my position and for me to take the major leap from being an entrepreneur all my life to being a professional CEO working for someone else. As you have heard from my earlier comments, the Indian media business is by and large undercapitalized and funds obtained by listing are both a positive and negative. Listing dampens growth because the shareholding public and their advisors assess the company's performance on a quarter-to-quarter basis rather than a longer-term basis. The five to six years I had running UTV as a listed business taught me that, if you want to go on up to the next level, you need to be free to scale up; otherwise you will end up doing pretty much the same as you did in the past with only incremental values.

'The upshot was I agreed to the deal and the company was delisted in February 2012. As part of the deal I agreed to run the Walt Disney Company India for five years and will give it my full care and attention because, even though I am no longer a shareholder, a large part of my soul is in the business and wants the company to succeed in the long haul. And I am sure I will learn a lot from Disney. It would be great for me if this were to be the culmination of my media career but I am still relatively young and there are other things I wish to do once I have fulfilled my obligations.'

With that we drew our meeting to a close. As I waited for my car to take me back to the hotel I speculated in my mind as to how the Ronnie Screwala story would unfold. Will he enjoy being full time with Disney India and complete his career as a CEO just like his father? Or will his entrepreneurial juices bubble to the surface leading to him strike out in a new direction once his contract expires? At this point I suspect even Ronnie does not know the answer but it will certainly be interesting to watch.[3]

---

[1] UTV Software Communications Limited (www.utvgroup.com) was acquired by Disney in 2012. UTV has developed into a global integrated entertainment content production and distribution company with five business verticals: Television (content production and airtime sales), Movies, Broadcasting, Games, and Interactive.

[2] Raghav Bahl was covered in my first Added Value book on India.

[3] My interview with Ronnie was some considerable time ago and it was indeed interesting to learn that Ronnie exited UTV/Disney in January 2014 and followed his entrepreneurial spirit and has now founded Unilazer, a private equity and venture capital firm.

" It is quite amazing to note how my grandfather planted the seed and his elder sons acted as his lieutenants and built a solid foundation. Then every brother who came along after them added something to it. What is amazing is that each of my grandfather's five sons did exactly what your book is about – they "added value". As you would know from your studies of Indian joint families this is quite extraordinary, as usually there are one or two members who are not interested, who "coast" or cause the joint family to lose value. "

VENU SRINIVASAN

Chairman, TVS Motor Company[1]

Finding a time and place to meet many of the people covered in this book is not an easy task; not because they are being difficult but because they are constantly on the move responding to the demands of their businesses which are usually spread throughout India and for some internationally as well. And so it was in arranging my meeting with Venu where, having decided on Chennai, we needed to arrange a location that tied in with his day. It ended up being a breakfast meeting in a hotel close to where he had agreed to give a speech on the occasion of the opening of a business colleague's factory.

Venu launched straight into the history of his family. 'We grew up in a family which was simultaneously very traditional and also non-traditional. I think that India is always a country of contradictions where a bullock cart may be delivering a nose cone for a rocket. So on the traditional level we behave like a joint Hindu family; I grew up in a large joint family. Although all of us did not live in the same house, we really behaved like a joint family. On the other hand, it is a very non-traditional family, because my grandfather Thirukkurungudi Vengaramaswamy Sundram Iyengar broke off from being in the priestly class – from being a Brahmin – by starting an ironmongery business. This was considered really something beneath the dignity of a Brahmin.

'He started making auto parts and the business in due course went on to have dealerships for GM, a large bus service and distribution of auto parts. Then in the 1950s we expanded into finance and insurance businesses and in the '60s into manufacturing auto parts, and then into motorcycles in the 80s. So I grew up in a family that was completely self-made.

'My grandfather had five sons and three daughters. All of his sons joined him in the business. My father was the youngest and actually much younger than his four elder brothers, so that it was really originally a partnership between my grandfather and his five sons. It was a partnership in a very real sense because my grandfather retired very young; he retired in 1933. He said, "I am fifty-five and I have done my duty to my sons; now it is your business." He gave away all the shares, every penny to his sons and did not have anything to his name when he died. He lived for twenty-five more years. He was a remarkable man because he said that it was the sons' responsibility to look after their mother and father. The shares were split equally among the five sons and when one son died early, his shares were given to the other four because my grandfather had the traditional view that only males could have shares in his company. The company was T.V. Sundaram Iyengar and Sons Ltd and it is still the holding company of the TVS Group.

'As I mentioned, my father was the youngest in the family. There was a twenty-year difference between my eldest uncle and my father. My eldest aunt was born in 1899 whereas my father was born in 1922 and therefore he really grew up more of the same age as his nephews and nieces. This huge difference in age has continued through the generations and so when I was growing up I was one of the youngest cousins and my brother was actually the youngest. As one of the youngest cousins, my bonding was always with people who were ten to fifteen years older than myself. And, therefore, I grew up thinking and acting older than my age.

'I think I have been greatly influenced by all the stories about my grandfather and my uncles – as, for instance, the stories of his concern for punctuality. This meant my grandfather was fanatical that every TVS bus ran on time. Even now my children make fun of me about my concern for punctuality but to me it is very important that you should be early at least by one minute for an appointment and certainly not more than two minutes late for the appointment. I was taught that being late showed a lack of respect for the person you were meeting. Apart from stories of punctuality, I was brought up with stories of cleanliness – of how my grandfather used to keep an absolutely spotlessly clean workshop. The third thing he lived by was to retain complete trust with employees, customers and society. So these were the broad values with which we were brought up: the importance of punctuality, exactness, cleanliness and trust.

'My eldest uncle was the chairman and I think he was the glue that kept the family together. He was really the patriarch after my grandfather. He and his immediate younger brother really built the GM dealership and the bus transport business. Then the third uncle expanded the dealership and parts distribution into the neighbouring states. My fourth uncle built the entire finance and insurance businesses. He also looked after trading and a significant mark that he left was Sundaram Finance, one of India's most respected automobile finance companies founded in 1954. Finally, my father created the industrial base of TVS. He was a visionary far ahead of his time.

'It is quite amazing to note how my grandfather planted the seed and his elder sons acted as his lieutenants and built a solid foundation. Then every brother who came along after them added something to it. What is amazing is that each of my grandfather's five sons did exactly what your book is about – they "added value". As you would know from your studies of Indian joint families this is quite extraordinary, as usually there are one or two members who are not interested, who "coast" or cause the joint family to lose value.

'From the day that he retired in 1933, my grandfather insisted that no one should talk business to him. There is an anecdote where one of my uncles came and started talking to him about business. My grandfather apparently turned his back on him and picked up the newspaper and started to read it.

'Given his concern for punctuality I suspect you will not be surprised to hear that he was a man who had very fixed habits. For example, he would go for a walk every morning and evening. On returning home he would decide what food he wanted to eat. He would personally weigh the food and say that he wanted so many ounces of this and so many ounces of that. He was a strict vegetarian and ate very few carbohydrates. There was also a routine to his walks. During the rainy season he would go to the foothills of the mountains, whereas in the summer he would walk at the top of the mountains. Clearly he was very exact and exacting. Sadly, I never really knew him as I was only two and a half years old when he died.

'He was also very laconic; he did not like to speak very much and, when he did, it was very exact. I am sure you can understand how very unusual it was in India that he had every bus running to time every day, for every stop, all 400 of them. He ran the business so that every customer (even passengers on his buses) was served personally just as Lexus did when they started their business. When he retired, GM considered his as the greatest dealership network they had anywhere in the world.

'So this was the influence on us in childhood and we grew up with all these much larger-than-life stories. Let me give you an example. I remember that one day I got up early in the morning – I must have been only about five years old – and I walked out of the house and I asked the guard standing outside the house what time it was. In those days, they did not have watches. But he told me that the first bus had not yet gone past so it was not yet 05.15 am.

'My father told me how he would go and sit in the cheapest seat in the cinema and could often see the company's workers were sitting in higher category seats as my grandfather would allow him only so much allowance to see a film.

'My grandfather started working as a clerk for a British manager of Indian railways. The story goes that he was upbraided for being one day late from leave because his father was seriously ill. He told the manager that he had been obliged to stay with his father and thus had come back a day late. The manager did not believe his explanation. My grandfather said that he was a man of his word and resigned on the spot and from that day he decided he would not work for anybody else. He started with a lumber business and then moved on to metal auto parts. In the early days, it must have been quite a struggle.

'By the time I was ready for school, the family was already established as a well-respected family. In that sense we were wealthy by the standards of those days. All the family houses were on the same street so that we could walk to each other's houses. Both my grandparents lived with my father because he was the youngest. By the time I came along, I think I grew up with much more luxury than my older cousins. We were driven to school in a car and there were always two cars at home. I do not think our wealth affected our treatment at school. That was one of the good things about school and particularly the Christian schools we attended. In those days the schools were very big and based on merit and I do not think anybody got treated any better. You might have had some jealousies and sometimes teachers might have resented you because you came from a well-to-do family. But, allowing for normal human behaviour, you were treated with equality and equality was enforced. You had to buy the same brand of shoes and clothes, whoever you were. You were told that you had to buy Bata in this style and you had to buy the same coloured Binny clothing – "Khaki shade" and white shirt were specified. So everybody was in identical clothes; there was not someone in homespun and another in fine yarn. Everybody wore exactly the same uniform which I think was great and I really enjoyed that.

'I was not a good student because I could never apply myself to anything that I did not like. I was strong-willed and the very antithesis of my grandfather who would do everything with great diligence. I would only do things that gave me a "buzz" and in those I would do extraordinarily well. Not only was I a middling student through my high school years, but also I was not very athletic. My sisters were much more diligent in their studies as girls tend to be.

'Given what I have said you will not be surprised that I was a mischievous child. I was also very accident prone because I would do anything that had some risk to it.' Venu suddenly laughs as he remembers how his mother used to be always terrified about how and in what condition he would come back from play or school. 'On the first day I went to school, for instance, somebody threw a stone at a mango tree and I was the person on whose head the stone landed – I still have the scar on my head to remind me of my first day at school. Perhaps you will be surprised to know that from the time I was a small boy I used to like to set fire to things – and I am embarrassed to say that I still do; fire has always fascinated me and fortunately,' he says with a laugh, 'I have been able to control these pyromaniac tendencies and apply them to controlled combustion in motorcycle engines. In general I was always mischievous, dropping things, throwing things and seeing what would happen if you threw a toy: whether it would break or not.

'Whilst we are still a joint family in a business sense we no longer live as a joint family. I think this must have ended around 1970. But when I was young, we lived as a joint family to the extent that the holidays were always spent together. I used to go to the mountains in the summer for two months with all my cousins; there was a flock of us with myself being the youngest. And being the youngest you did not get bullied; actually you got protected and nurtured which was great fun – the elder cousins looked after you. Some of my cousins' children are of my age because of the difference in the ages of the uncles. So some of my aunts' and uncles' grandsons were even of my age.

'In India we treated each other as first cousins despite being second or third cousins. To us we were just cousins. We went on all our holidays together right through the first twenty years of our lives. Whilst the six or seven families shared two homes in mountains we were all together from breakfast through to dinner.

'When I finished high school, I would only go to the mountains for about a week because my father made me work as a garage mechanic for six of the eight weeks of vacation along with two of my cousins.

'It was an incredible childhood and, believe it or not, we did not have friends outside the family; we grew up only with family. We were truly sheltered and I was completely raw and "wet behind the ears" when I went to university because I only knew my extended family.

'At the time I went to school, India had adopted socialism and it was really on a "slow boat to China" where there was no great pressure to gain admission to college or to study once you got there. Discipline was at the lowest point in educational history. But ten years after my school years, discipline was back and the pressure to study became intense and continues to be the case today. As a result, school for us was not serious and we had a "ball".

'But the thing that really defined who I am today is that my father made me work during my holidays right from the time I finished high school. From that year on I spent five straight summers in the garage as a mechanic trainee, learning things such as repairing cars and trucks. One of my uncles had bought all the surplus equipment of an American air force base left after Second World War which meant we had the best machine shop in Asia and I learnt a huge amount and saw firsthand the desire for excellence which my grandfather had instilled in the workers which was actually then later built on by my uncles and father. This experience laid the foundation for my practice of TQM [Total Quality Management] later in life.

'My father was a self-taught industrial engineer. He did go to GM Tech in the US but he told me that the instructor there did not give him any work because he said that my father already knew everything he was teaching. After all, more than me, all his spare time was spent working in the garage and it was probably true there was nothing he could be taught about automobile repair and service. However, on his return from the US my father did introduce a lot of automation and systems that were strongly based on US industrial engineering practices.

'My father was a real book worm. By the age of sixteen, he had read every book in both Tamil and English in the local library. He was omnivorous and would read romance novels, books on the arts, books on the brain, anything on industrial engineering or human resources development – essentially anything that came his way. I don't think it is an exaggeration to say he would spend four hours reading every day and maybe more.

'But what really defined my father was his vision of the future and his golden heart. He really cared about people; both those who worked for him and those who worked for the poor and disadvantaged in society. He was the first to set up clinics for his employees. He also provided nutritious meals to them at next to nothing because he believed healthy and satisfied employees would be loyal and productive. No employee was denied access to him. His door was always open and he always had enough time to listen to their problems. This was true for poor people from society as well. And they always went away happy that they could share their burden with him, and, more often than not, go away with money or a job for their son or daughter.

'It was his vision that TVS should become a manufacturing giant. In his lifetime he built one of the largest auto component manufacturing groups in India. He laid the foundation for the motorcycle business but, alas, he didn't live to see the start of that business. However, as his son I feel fulfilled that I could make his dream come true.

'Our upbringing was dominated by the concept of the family business. You were told right from the day you entered kindergarten that when you finished school, you would do engineering and when you finished engineering you would join the family business. So I think that we were well and truly brainwashed and had no other thought in life. This was the great vision with which I grew up, the dream that I would work in the family business and contribute; and that I would want to make a mark that would make my father and grandfather proud.

'When I finished school I studied engineering at the University of Madras and then went to Purdue University in the US to do a master's in Industrial Management. My father chose it because it had a good industrial engineering school and he said that half my courses should be from industrial engineering. I may not have done all the courses, but broadly I took the majority of my courses in manufacturing and industrial engineering.

'We did not have much of a choice and in the days when I grew up I would say that most Indians were doing courses and pursuing education that was largely led by what the parents wanted them to do. Even today I think in India it is much more common than in other countries. Everybody in the family went to university in the Midwest of the US because we were all GM trained. My uncles who went there long before me went to GM Tech as did many of my cousins. The younger cousins and I went to a wider selection including Wisconsin, Michigan, and Purdue. It was only later that the next generation that our family started going to the East and West coasts.

'I am sure you will be surprised when you learn that during my summers, to earn money I sold Bibles and other books door-to-door. How I got into this strange job was because of a university friend. He asked me what job I would do during the vacation and I indicated that my father would probably line up a summer internship at automotive company. He said I would only be a "gofer" and why didn't I join him selling door-to-door which would allow me to meet "real" Americans and be my own boss. He said we would meet 'real'

Americans because we would be absolutely out in the "boonies" and see the people who we would never meet in the cities.

'I will say this, it was an unusual experience for a young Indian. I can remember one day I knocked on a door and a woman answered. I said with my best Southern accent: "May I come in?" She said, "Son, how come you got no accent?" I said "Ma'am, I am from the south, the south of India, and we all speak like this all the time." I had quickly learnt that if I wanted to sell I needed to speak with a good southern accent. And I could switch accents; it is something that comes to me very naturally. When I went back to school, I went back to a Midwestern American accent.

'I was in the top ten student salesmen in my day. I would get doors slammed on me, the sheriff called on me, dogs ordered to attack me, and guns pulled on me. Yes, you heard correctly "guns pulled on me" just because I knocked on their door. I was never physically assaulted but I had everything just short of that. But it was great fun and taught me a lot.

'I think what book selling does to you is put a mirror to your face every minute of the day. Every time a customer is nasty to you, you ask yourself what it is in you and the way you presented yourself that made her respond like that. And the answer is that she is responding to what she is seeing and that was quite a tough thing to learn. But I think that selling Bibles was a very major exposure to the real world for me, especially coming from my very sheltered family upbringing. Further, the hours were long and hard – six days and eighty hours a week! I really would never exchange that experience for anything else and I would say,' Venu says with a smile, 'the best thing I did at Purdue was selling books.

'Before 1974, the whole TVS family business was run by one group of people in the family. Then there were some differences which came to the fore and the family had some very bitter divisions. And so in 1975 the family decided that each family member would run only one business. So my father then had only one business to run being the design and bringing to market of a moped.

'I came back from Purdue in 1978 when I was twenty-six. I resisted the pressure to get married immediately on my return, as was the normal custom. I decided I was not going to get married until I was quite clear as to what I was going to be doing in the family business.

'I had come back to India with all my American ideas and I was very unmindful and insensitive to India and Indian traditions. I kept saying things like we are "going to shoot from the hip" and things like that – the typical American management style. I made a lot of mistakes. Fortunately, I had inherited an extremely good core group of people who worked as managers who were patient and able to guide me. Indeed, one of them Mr. Lakshmanan is still with me today. He joined my father the year after I was born and so he has been with the company for sixty years. Also Professor Lord Bhattacharyya,[2] who was my mentor when I was an industrial trainee at Lucas in England for six months before I went to the US, played a key advisory role.

'Professor Lord Bhattacharyya helped me hugely in management and technology and how to run businesses as well as in my personal transformation and growth. As a result, despite the mistakes I made, the moped business took off and within seven years grew from an annual turnover of some Rs 160 million to Rs 1 billion. The other family businesses grew too but it was the moped business that truly flourished and morphed into a full motorcycle business.

'I decided to get married in 1981 to Mallika Sivasailam[3] after running the business for three years. I thought I had enough freedom and independence that I could now take on another responsibility of a marriage. Since we married Mallika has continued in her family's Amalgamations Group[4] founded by her grandfather Sivasailam Anantharamakrishnan and then run by her father A. Sivasailam until his death in 2011. Mallika is currently the chairman and chief executive of Tractors and Farm Equipment Limited [commonly known as 'TAFE'], one of the Amalgamations Group's most important companies. She has successfully grown its tractor business into the third largest tractor manufacturer in the world and the second largest in India with presence in over 82 countries, including developed countries in Europe and the Americas.'

We then turned our discussion back to what happened to TVS post his marriage to Mallika. 'I arranged for us to enter into a joint venture with Suzuki but after that I made a number of mistakes. For example, one of the biggest strengths of TVS has been its industrial relations and in this area I made a number of critical mistakes including the choice of the right people to lead it in the joint venture. A combination of these mistakes came home to roost in 1987 when the Suzuki motorcycle business collapsed. This led to a huge strike and the company became financially very vulnerable. With Lord Bhattacharyya's help we started turning it around, and by 1993 it was healthy again and since then we have had very good success.

'There is one other thing which I have missed out and which reflects all the values from the stories of my grandfather: the exactness, the discipline, the timeliness, the cleanliness, and taking care of employees and stake holders. These are all the values that I have stood by after all the lockouts, strikes and industrial actions of the late '80s early '90s. From then until now I have followed the lessons of Japanese manufacturing sector.

'Once we went into the Suzuki joint venture, we saw that the Japanese were the only country which seemed to follow my grandfather's values. At that time in England the shop floors were terrible. In the US, the shop floors were also terrible. There was constant fighting between the unions and management. In TVS, we had never had a strike. There was no separation between the union and management. There is one company; the union worked for the company and the management worked for the company. If the company prospered then everybody prospered. That was my grandfather's philosophy. It was this philosophy with which I was imbued from my childhood and when I went to Japan and saw how they operated I said that this was manufacturing paradise.

'When I first went to Japan their Total Quality Management professors were unwilling to talk to an Indian company, let alone come to India. But we were persistent and eventually they relented; and we became the first Indian auto manufacturer to adopt Japanese quality practice. When I say "quality practice", I do not mean just on the shop floor; it also includes all aspects of management from design to marketing. As a result we have built over twenty years a world-class outstanding quality company in India. My grandfather's and Japanese philosophies are very similar. It is the adoption of our quality practices that has made our company quite unique and now we are respected for trust, ethics, and good governance. You would never hear of problems with any of those issues when you talk about TVS because we grew up with these values. Although we might not have grown as fast as some others, we will never leave the relatively straight and narrow path of adhering to our values. Life is tough and you do not go as fast but whatever you do is very stable and is hard earned. For a number of years the Japanese were also shareholders in the venture but we ended up buying them out in 2001.

'I owe my gratitude and thanks to my Japanese sensei – Professor Washio and Professor Tsuda. They have selflessly and tirelessly worked with our company for over twenty years. It would be no exaggeration to say that TVS Motor would not be such a high quality competitor in the motorcycle field but for their sincere contribution. My colleagues and I owe them a great deal for improving the design, manufacturing and marketing to such high standards. The Japanese sensei helped us to recapture the essence of everything my grandfather TVS stood for and practised during his lifetime.'

I asked Venu to look back over his career. 'As far as I am concerned, it has been a very fulfilling life. If you ask me whether I have any regrets, I would say that I have very few. I know what mistakes I have made and if I went back in time I should not make them again – but knowing me I would probably make those mistakes in those circumstances again. I think it has been very satisfying working within the family, and within the culture and the values that have been passed down the generations. In the last fifteen years, we have started a huge social initiative. We have been working in a thousand villages and in these villages we have really been eradicating poverty. We are seeking to introduce a harmony that crosses castes, that crosses religions and that largely involves making sure everyone has a chance to be educated. We have found, for example, that if we support the infrastructure already in place, such as the local government schools and primary health centers, we get a much greater output than we would get trying to put in place a new infrastructure. Doing this we have found no children drop out of school. I have not yet personally spent much of my time on these activities, but I intend to spend much more time on them over the next five years.

'I do not regret having gone into the family business. I wanted to be what I am and with what I have achieved, but of course life is not a bed of roses. Many in our family of around my age – give or take ten years – will say that they have all been forced to go into business because there was no other choice and it is very clear that some of them today will say "I regret my life because I should never have accepted this – I should have said 'no' I want to be something else". Only one cousin had the real courage to tell his father after finishing his chartered accountancy and MBA in America that he was not going to join the family business. He set up a foundation and started a hospital and his father supported it. I think that more people will do that in the future.

'But, on the whole with God's grace – I think that one thing that is provided to our family is a deep faith in God and God's grace. Here I am talking specifically about my nuclear family, my wife and children, Lakshmi[5] and Sudarshan, and we have had the blessing of Sri Sathya Sai Baba of Puttaparthi[6] who is a messiah for us and his followers. I think that this religious faith has really moulded our values and therefore we are very happy doing what we are doing.

'The next chapter in my life will be putting into practice Sai Baba's teachings and the care for people that my father cherished. Over the last twenty years the foundation in my father's name "Srinivasan Services Trust" is working in fifteen hundred villages uplifting the lives of over a million people. We adopted the Millennium Goals of the United Nations. Today we are so fulfilled by the developments we see. We have the best levels of health, education, income, and social harmony in the country. Through a large micro enterprise movement run by over sixty thousand women we have been able to transform these villages into, by Indian standards, societies that are empowered and have sustainable local leadership to create prosperous, harmonious, and self-reliant communities.'

Venu and I agreed that on such an uplifting note it was time to bring our meeting to a close and allow Venu to return to more earthly duties of opening a factory.

¹ The TVS Group (http://www.tvsgroup.com) is India's leading supplier of automotive components and one of the country's most respected business groups. With a combined turnover of more than over $ 6.5 billion, the TVS Group employs a total workforce of close to over 39,000 employees. Charting a steady growth path of expansion and diversification, it currently comprises around over 50 companies. These operate in diverse fields that range from two-wheeler and automotive component manufacturing to automotive dealerships, finance and electronics.
² Sushanta Kumar Bhattacharyya, Baron Bhattacharyya, CBE, born 6 June 1940 is an Indian British engineer, educator and government advisor. He was born in Dhaka (then part of British-India, now capital of Bangladesh). His father was a Professor of Chemistry at the Indian Institute of Technology, Kharagpur. Bhattacharyya studied at the same institute and the University of Birmingham where he attained an MSc in Engineering Production and Management and a PhD in Engineering Production. In 1980, he became Professor of Manufacturing Systems at the University of Warwick and founded the Warwick Manufacturing Group (now WMG of which he has been Director and then Chairman of since its inception. WMG is focused on research, education and innovation in collaboration with private and public sector organisations in the UK and internationally. He was made a life peer in 2004 and sits on the Labour benches in the House of Lords.
³ Mallika is a university gold-medalist in Econometrics from the University of Madras, she graduated as a member of the Dean's Honor List from the Wharton School of Business at the University of Pennsylvania, USA, and was ranked as one of its top 125 most successful alumni.
⁴ http://amalgamationsgroup.co.in/ The Amalgamations group was founded in 1938 with one man's vision. Shri Sivasailam Anantharamakrishnan, or 'J' as he was fondly known as, was a visionary who dared challenge the impediments to India's Industrial future. He pioneered many ventures and spearheaded the quest for sourcing the finest technologies in the world. The Amalgamations saga was born when it took over the 100 year old Simpsons in 1941. Amalgamations soon brought under its shade some of the oldest companies in Southern India like Higginbothams, Associated Printers, Associated Publishers, Addison & Co., SRVS, George Oakes, T. Stanes, The United Nilgiri Tea Estates and Stanes Amalgamated Estates. From the mid-1950s, the auto component manufacturing companies of the Group have worked with practically every major OEM in the country, to bolster their import substitution requirements. Strong collaborations with international market leaders have influenced the technology advancements. These, combined with technological innovations and strong initiatives on new product development, have contributed substantially to a strong equity in the After-markets as well, ably supported by vibrant national distribution networks. The Group's overseas presence and distribution have over time, moved from strength to strength. Today, the Group is one of India's largest light engineering conglomerates. It has 47 companies and 50 manufacturing plants including TAFE which Mallika Srinivasan runs.
⁵ I was interested to learn that in June 2011 Lakshmi Venu married Rohan Murthy who is the son of NR Narayana Murthy, one of the founders of Infosys and whose life story is covered in my first *Added Value: The Life Stories of Indian Business Leaders* (Roli Books), 2010.
⁶ Śri Sathya Sai Baba (born as Sathyanarayana Raju; 1926–2011) was an Indian guru who claimed to be the reincarnation of Sai Baba of Shirdi and is considered by his followers to have been an avatar, spiritual saint and miracle worker.

" I have until 2018 when I turn 65. So I look forward to the next few years as I still enjoy doing business. I believe that the group is hugely privileged because we are in a position today where the entry barriers are very strong because of our size. We have chosen to focus on seven areas of business where we seek to be dominant: fertilizers, sugar, tube, cycles, abrasives, financial services and insurance. "

ARUNACHALAM VELLAYAN

Executive Chairman, Murugappa Group[1]

My colleague Matt Gorman and I met Arunachalam Vellayan in the Boardroom of Murugappa in Chennai. The office had a very British 'feel' with leather furniture, an impressive board table to seat up to 25 people and photos and paintings of previous chairmen hanging on the walls. That my feeling was correct came out in the meeting.

Before we got into the details of the life story of his family I asked him how names were given in his family as it seemed quite complex to me. 'I can well understand that. My name is Arunachalam Vellayan but I could have been named Murugappa Arunachalam Vellayan. I am named after my grandfather who was named Vellayan and my father's name was Arunachalam. In my Chettiar[2] community the first son is named after the father's father and the second son is named after the mother's father. So my grandfather Vellayan was the second son. It works the same way for girls. But,' he says with a grin, 'you have a choice of names after the fifth child.'

He continued: 'Actually, I am from the fourth generation to run the company and my great-grandfather whose photograph is there,' he said pointing to the wall, 'started the business in Burma which is Myanmar today. We had a small business here in Chennai or Madras it was previously known but the main fortune was made in Burma. Basically, there was no banking or moneylending business there in the 1860s and my community introduced this business to Burma.

'My great-grandfather, Dewan Bahadur AM Murugappa Chettiar went to Burma in the early 1900s to work as a clerk. The way that the Chettiars worked in Burma was that they went for three years, came back for six months and then went back again. Over time they built Chettinad in our state of Tamil Nadu which consists of about 60 villages and is quite like the villages of the Marwaris in Rajasthan. The Chettiars could be called the Marwaris of the South of India because of the similarities – we are a Hindu sub-caste of traders and bankers.

'Anyway, the money lending business in Burma developed well and expanded into landholding. The family became more or less permanently based in Rangoon [now Yangon] and then my grandfather A.M.M. Vellayan Chettiar took over. He was an extremely successful businessman; he spoke fluent Burmese and became a member of the Burmese Parliament. He was very much part of the establishment and one of the few Indian members of the Rangoon Club that was primarily reserved to the British and Burmese aristocracy. Like most Indians in Burma he fled back to India during the Second World War[3] but when he went back at the end of the war in 1945 to see if he could rebuild the family business, he was shot dead. So, in 1949 the family started off from scratch back in India. Everything in Burma was lost – and it had been substantial in those days. So the whole banking thing, all the land, everything was gone.

'So for my great-grandfather and my two grand uncles it was a tough experience – of course we had some capital which had been transferred from Burma over the years but the main business was there. My great grandfather took a back seat after the murder of his son, my grandfather. It was my grand uncle A.M.M. Murugappa Chettiar [1902-1965] who took over as the first chairman of the group in India. He was a visionary and he saw that there were needs in India which were very basic and that is how our first business of bicycles started.

'Sir Ivan Stedeford was the Chairman of Tube Investments which owned Hercules bicycles. A very good friend of the family, Arcot Ramasamy Mudaliar, who incidentally was a member of Winston Churchill's War Cabinet, introduced him to my grand uncles in Chennai. This led in 1949 to the establishment of a joint venture between Tube Investments and our family to make Hercules bicycles and Mudaliar became the first chairman of our Tube Investments of India joint venture. The first factory was built in 1951 and sold so many bicycles in its first year that it caused Hercules' major competitor, Raleigh to also set up in India. We eventually bought out Raleigh in 1960.

'My granduncle was quite astute because he signed the joint venture with the clause that we could claw back as we earned. We did not have much money at that time but Sir Ivan trusted us so he put in 85 per cent and we put 15 per cent. He let us manage the business; we sent many of our people to the UK for training. We went through the graduate training course in Tube Investments and all that. So that had a big impact in terms of how the group took shape. This joint venture was really the beginning of the Murugappa Group.

'So my granduncles, as the second generation ran the business with Murugappa Chettiar, the older brother, in charge; he was a visionary and very "hands on". That was the time when India was importing everything. So they said, look let's start indigenizing. So, they started first with cycles, then with tubes, then with chains, then with braces and that is how we grew. We had collaborations with the help of our other friends to link us with the people who had a large presence in those countries. So TI Cycles of India Ltd was with Tube Investments in 1949, Tube Products of India Ltd was with another UK company in 1955, and TI Diamond Chains Ltd was with the American Diamond Chain Company in 1960. 'As Murugappa Group grew we had a slightly different feel from other Indian family businesses, because of the Tube Investments influence. We also got in professional management, so that we did not adopt an exclusively family-style management. Right from the beginning we started employing people, some of them brought from TI, some of them from other companies, professionals who came to manage the company. There were a few family members in the business, but not that many who were actually running the show which, as you know, is very different from a traditional Indian family business.

'Then the business passed to the next generation, the third generation, which was headed by my father M.V. Arunachalam [1929-1996]. During this period we actually grew by acquisition because we found that it was not possible to grow just organically due to the licence raj; one needed existing licences as in most cases new licences were not available. We wanted a particular rate of growth, which would not have happened otherwise. So we also had the opportunity to purchase companies like the one whose boardroom you are sitting in now. This company is called E.I.D. Parry; it is a 225-year-old British company that we took over in 1981. It had set up the first sugar plant in India in 1842.' [And thus explaining the distinctly British 'feel' to the room in which we were meeting and mentioned above.]

'Another opportunity came towards the end of British ownership of the tea plantations. We joined the management of the company owned by the CWS – the Cooperative Wholesale Society – of the UK in 1981. What happened was that some of the British executives who came to India to run their businesses were frankly not, as it were, 'the best of the crop' as management back in the UK saw that they would have to sell out of India. We bought many of these companies from the market at a fraction of their real value. It was unbelievable. Because we did not have that much money at the time, we bought about 35 per cent to 40 per cent of the company from the Commonwealth Development Fund and the market for around three million dollars and we bought the entire tea gardens from CWS for something like six million dollars. They were hemorrhaging losing money. We brought in quality professional management and turned them around.

'I am pretty fortunate because by the time I came into the reckoning there was a business that was running profitably. I was born in 1953, so one of the first things that I was asked to do was to propose the vote of thanks any time that we signed a joint venture, because we were doing deals all the time; there were new ventures coming on stream; one venture would be the introduction to lead to another. This was even while I was at Don Bosco school in Chennai run by the Catholics. Vijay Amritraj was with me at the same time so we occasionally played tennis together, although,' he says with a smile, 'not at the same level. We are still in touch and get together whenever he is in town.

'Early in my childhood my granduncle and my dad decided that if I was one day to run the family business I could not live and study only in the south of India. So they sent me at the age of around ten to Doon School in Dehradun, which is right up in the north in the foothills of the Himalayas. Doon was a great learning experience for me because it was the best public school in India; it still is. More importantly, I now realize that the cosmopolitan nature of the student population there gives its students a huge advantage.

'The first year was difficult because when I went past Hyderabad station, I was further north than I had ever gone and I could not speak the language and even English was spoken differently there. So it was tough as it was very cold in winter whereas here in Chennai it is warm all year long. But it did not take more than one term to get used to everything and by the second term you built the camaraderie that lasts even until today. Doon has got a very different approach to study; it is more about the development of the person. We had an English headmaster called Jack Martin and before him, A.E. Foot who was the first headmaster who really took up this approach. So they used to send us rock climbing, whitewater rafting, and try to use these things for confidence building, with public speaking as well, which were all unheard of in India at that time.

'Foot created the Fat Boy Society which was followed on by Martin. The idea was to make the fat boys realize that it was not good for their health being fat. They thought if you just keep teasing them then nothing would happen. However, if you got them together in a group where they could relate to each other you had more chance. They would have experts come and talk to them and I must say it seemed to work. They also created other societies to help in other ways; often indirectly. In my case it was suggested I join the Indian music society; not so much for the music but to help me meet others and build up my confidence.

'At dinner time they used to ask us to come and sing songs to the other students. It was quite hilarious because I had to sing Tamil songs that 95 per cent of the guys could not understand what I was singing. Some of these boys from the north became my best friends. Vikram

Seth, the famous author was in my class; and our class of 1968 was one hell of a batch and even now almost all 40 of us meet once a year.

'It was a mixed batch; there were people from all over India. The Nizam of Hyderabad was there, as was the Maharaja of Dholpur and the Maharaja of Kaswanda's son. There were a lot of the Rajputs,[4] sons of army officers and other leading families. Certainly Uttar Pradesh and Delhi were more heavily represented but we did have about 15 or 20 guys like me from the South. There were no foreign students. Then we had a lot of old boys' children as there was that tradition. Last year my son got married and fifteen of my Doon friends came to Chettinad from all over India with their wives and they had a hell of a ball because we dressed them up in our traditional things; we had all just decided that we would each go to the weddings of our children. So I went to Bihar where one of the guys, the Maharaja of Dumraon's son, was having his son married; so we went there and it was great fun.

'I spent five years from 1964 to 1969 in Doon and came out totally different with a network of friends who have ended up in many different walks of life including politicians, army officers and even writers like Vikram Seth. Before I went to Doon, I was very naïve and I had not been exposed to the rest of India; I could not speak Hindi or curse in Punjabi or whatever. This was still so much so that I stayed on in the north and went to college in Delhi at Shri Ram College of Commerce from 1969 to 1972.'

I asked A. Vellayan if he was the oldest in the family. 'In my fourth generation, I am the eldest. I have a brother and a sister. My father also was the oldest of his generation. The joint family still exists to the extent that our money is invested together even if we do not live together. And we are into the fifth generation; my sons are in the business as well. What we do now is we follow a system of meritocracy and we also follow a fairly equal lifestyle. So what happens, for instance, in our fourth generation is that there are seven of us and, despite the size of the group now, only four of us are in the mainstream business. The other three are reconciled to not being in the mainstream business because we have an independent Corporate Board that makes the decisions as to who should be involved and who not. But all of us drive the same car and are more or less paid the same amount, except as I have more responsibility I have an incentive because of that.

'The third generation took the enlightened view that we would go for value creation and look at enhancing value. We now have seven listed companies and we have followed the principle that a family member does not have to run those companies unless the Corporate Board decides they should; certainly we do not just put a family member there for the name's sake.

'As for the girls in our community, we encourage them to become very much part of the husband's family when they are married. So more or less they do not get involved in our family's business. That is because there is a deep-rooted belief that, if a daughter gets involved in the business that is the best way to create problems in her husband's family. In this cultural environment it works like this: for instance, suppose I have a sister and that her husband has a rubber parts' company. If my sister becomes involved in our business and this business is larger than his rubber parts' business, it may be quite demeaning for him and that could mess up his family life. But at the time the daughter gets married she has to be given her share of the family's business in cash or shares at the time of the wedding and on special occasions like when she has children, etc., but basically they do not come into the business. She can hold stock but not get into management. This has worked well for us because otherwise, as my grandfather believed and as we continue to believe, if in-laws start coming in or if girls start becoming dominant, it does not help the familial harmony.

'Immediately after my studies in Delhi I went to work in the UK with both Raleigh and its parent, Tube Investments. I lived in several places including Nottingham, Birmingham, and I lived in a place near Scotland where they had plants. At that time Tube Investments was at its peak and its graduate training programme was top notch. Again, I found myself in a totally different environment – like going to Doon School – and I was the only Indian there. The first few weeks I was a little out of place but after that I became good friends with a lot of locals and in particular my fellow management trainees such as Ian Simpson. Tube Investments then sent me to do a master's in Business at Warwick Business School in the very early days of that business school. I lived on campus and learnt a lot. In particular I remember being taught by Professor Derek Waterworth who was one of the world's leading academics in marketing.

'I was on a reasonably comfortable stipend from Tube Investments and I used to spend time with Ian Simpson and a couple of other friends from Doon who had come to the UK and were living in London. I kept gravitating to London but also frequently visited Scotland. We were regulars at the Edinburgh Festival and one of the crazy things I did was to get a street trader's license to operate on the Royal Mile for one particular summer when we sold clothes, skirts, ties and such things; it was quite an experience. That year we stayed on through the Fringe Festival. Ian's sister and his girlfriend were modeling what we were selling and we picked up a couple of thousand pounds. I bought my first car out of my share – an old Simca for one hundred and fifty pounds or something like that in those days. I also had other Scottish friends from a small village outside Edinburgh whose homes I used to visit for their New Year celebrations called Hogmanay. They used to kid me by telling me that normally it was tradition that you had to enter their homes carrying a sack of coal.

'I enjoyed my time in Scotland. After that I came back to India and was assigned my first job in the group's Tubes business. My role was in marketing because by that time I had more or less decided that this area was my forte, although I had done my MBA in Finance. When I joined, my father was the managing director of Tube Investments and my surviving granduncle was its chairman. There were about four to five members of the family in the business but I was the first one from my generation. In our setup the family starts in the ranks – I did not come in and become MD – so I was actually a marketing services manager for the Tubes division of Tube Investments.

'The two-wheeler boom was just about to start in India and I was moved into the chain business. I had got married to Lalita just before that. It was an arranged marriage – you meet and you get to know each other but you are both from the same community. My dad thought that it would be a good idea for us to spend some time abroad together, so it was decided we should move to Indianapolis in Indiana where Diamond Chain, the company with which we collaborated on chains, had its headquarters.

'We moved to Indianapolis in 1975-76 and we both really enjoyed our time there because it is a small friendly mid-western town. A number of the Diamond Chain executives had already been to Chennai and knew our family. They made us feel extremely welcome which was particularly important for Lalita who had never been abroad. The first winter was still quite a shock for her. But I am certain that being in Indianapolis was much better than being in San Francisco or New York because irrespective of the weather it would be more difficult to find warm and friendly people in those big cities.

'Diamond Chain manufactured roller chains for power transmission on oil rigs and escalators and things like that. We were their only joint venture abroad so it was important for both of us. It was my first time in the US and after five to six months I took eight weeks off. My brother-in-law – my wife's brother – and his wife came over and we rented a car and we drove around the United States. I knew that it was highly likely when we returned to India it was unlikely I would ever get a chance to take this much time off so we took the opportunity. We started off from Indianapolis and went to New York, then to Winston-Salem, North Carolina, and from there to Miami, cut through to Houston, then on to El Paso, the Grand Canyon, and finally came to LA.

'Once we were headed for the Grand Canyon where the temperature can change suddenly. One moment it was sunny and then it was snowing. We saw cars veering off the road and hanging over the Canyon cliffs. We had the heater fully on with the wipers working furiously but for about six or seven minutes we could not see a thing as we crept along. We really thought we were going to die and particularly as there was a pastor on the car radio preaching 'fire and brimstone' for non-Christians. Finally, somehow we skidded into a bay at the side of the road, which, as luck would have it, was a truck resting station, and one of the truck drivers kindly towed us into Flagstaff.

'Another time outside Houston in Texas, my brother-in-law drove onto an expressway on the wrong side of the road. Luckily, the highway cops stopped us almost immediately. They looked at our passports and said "so what do we do with you now?" We showed him our maps and we showed him everything that we had done. We had already been on the road for some four weeks and so there was plenty to show the cops. And despite the image one has of US cops they were extremely understanding and let us go without any charge and even escorted us back into Houston. So that was real luck.

'After a year we returned to Chennai. This was the time that Honda and Suzuki were entering or interested in entering the Indian market. It was the turning point both for the chain and the tube business and that is probably when I earned my colours as the managing director of Tube Investments. Tube Investments needed a technology, which neither Diamond nor Tube Investments had. The Japanese had the technology, both for the chain and the tube – the tube is used for the front fork of the motorcycle and the shock absorber. Their idea was to import the technology from Japan. I believed that if they had done that our business in a short time would have been dead or we would have been limited to selling it to a few Indian bikes like Royal Enfield and Java; most of which were going out of business. I proposed as an alternative that a team of us should go to Japan and discuss a wider collaboration arrangement with Honda.

'So first dealing with the chain, the offer we got for the technology transfer was equal to our turnover, so clearly we could not afford it. We got a group of seven to eight IIT engineers together with our people and told them: "Here is the challenge; Diamond can help us only so much; beyond that we need to indigenise this and have it approved by Honda or we go out of business". Fortunately in ten months flat this team actually designed and made a product that was approved by Honda. Of course, Hero Honda, the Indian partner of Honda also wanted indigenization. And fortunately our two companies not only knew each other as we were both from the cycle business but also,' Vellayan laughs, 'Sunil and I both had gone to Doon.

'We had a tougher time on the tube front because that was critical also with safety considerations. But it was the same team that worked with me on both the chain and tube. That was the turning point for the group because until then we were doing okay but we were small. At that time in 1994 we ramped up and did our first Euro GDR issue for USD50 million which we launched in the UK market through Cazenove. This was a lot of money at that time, so we expanded. We built chain plants, one in Hyderabad and one in north, and then tube plants, one in Pune and one in the north. As a result we built up the point we were supplying 50 per cent of the Indian market. So wherever Bajaj or Hero was, we were there too and we became national.

'In 1999, we formed a Corporate Board for the group. My father had died in 1996 when the chairmanship passed to my granduncle

AMM Arunachalam [1918-1999], and my uncle MV Subbiah became the group CEO. At this point we had an advisor, Dr. Ganguly, who was chairman of Hindustan Lever who gave the group some shape when my uncle decided to resign in 1999 and my granduncle died. We established a formal advisory board, we had different verticals with different people looking after them and then we had the listed companies with professional MDs and for the first time we appointed a professional as overall chairman of the group. With all these changes it was felt that I should move out of Tube Investments, as I had been there long enough.

'I moved to EID Parry which, at that time, had a small fertilizer business and a reasonable-sized sugar business. I saw an opportunity in the fertilizer sector because there were a lot of plants in the government sector, which were ailing. We had for a long time held some equity in a company called Coromandel Fertilizers in Hyderabad. This was founded by Chevron and IMC and one of the last deals that my father did was that he bought Chevron out in 1995. This was the same time as Coca Cola and a number of US multinationals were withdrawing from India. Then in 1999 we bought out IMC so that EID Parry had a majority shareholding in Coromandel. Dr Arun Bharat Ram was our chairman at the time and encouraged me to pursue a growth strategy. This led us to get more into fertilizers with Hyderabad as the base and to merge EID Parry and Coromandel. Then, in 2003, we aggressively bid and bought into a government company called Godavari and became a large player.

'When we bid for Godavari, there were two other companies bidding for it too and which were both producers of phosphoric acid. One was South African, Foskor (controlled by Industrial Development Corporation) and the other was Tunisian, Groupe Chimique Tunisien. Although they both lost out to us within three months I brought them back in as suppliers and gave them equity in Godavari. We more than made up for the high price we paid but also got a long-term supply contract of phosphoric acid. It has worked very well and took me to the next big phase in my life. South Africa is a country I have spent lot of time in.

'The background to this strategy is that Kaya Locula, who was chairman of Industrial Development Corporation is quite a wild guy and we knew he really wanted Godavari for Foskor and would bid very aggressively. But we also knew that if we lost in our bid for Godavari then we would not grow, so we bid even higher than what we thought IDC would bid and in the knowledge we were paying way over the value. When I offered Locula equity for Foskor and to renew its supply contract, we became friends. We signed our deal in front of their president when he visited India, so it was a big deal for him. This was the time when the blacks were kicking out the whites in South Africa. Unfortunately, Foskor's phosphoric business had been totally run by whites. Locula had brought in black management to Foskor and then the company tanked. He rang me up and said, "We are going down the tubes and we are losing money, can you come and help?" So, I sent my team there and then I went myself. We did due diligence, they had a Rolls Royce plant, but they did not know how to run it because they had kicked out all the white guys. We did a very interesting deal, similar to what Mittal had done in South Africa with Iscor, the steel plant. In 2005 we took a small stake in Foskor and then we said we would run the plant for them and then convert to set equity. We invested 2.5 per cent initially and finally now, as of today we own 14 per cent. We helped turn Foskor around from a loss making company; they were running a Rand 300 million loss and we converted that to a profit in the third year.

'I am on the board of Foskor now and we have got such good relationship that when they wanted to sell down their interest in Foskor Zirconia in 2008 they sold a majority to us. We have also had recent invitations to invest with the black empowerment people in sugar where we will do the management. Our relationship with black empowerment partners has been very good and we actually brought 50 to 60 blacks and trained them in our factories in Vizag and Kakinada. Importantly this was noticed by President Mbeki that we are not just trying to grab everything there but we are also giving something back.

'And of course we were developing Tunisia simultaneously because we know that we could not depend solely on one country. But of course Tunisia has had problems of its own which only goes to demonstrate the dangers of a single supplier. Our partner there, Groupe Chimique Tunisien, is the country's largest producer and exporter. We are currently building a new plant there. Once that is completed we will be No. 2 in India with a 4 million tonne production compared to the largest in India, IFFCO (Indian Farmers Fertilizer

Cooperative Limited) that has a 5 million tonne capacity. This is a large increase from our original capacity of some 300,000 tonnes, a little more than a decade ago.

'I realize I have not mentioned our abrasives business, Carborundum Universal Limited, whose chairman is my cousin, MM Murugappan. In 2008 we came to hear of Volzhsky Abrasive Works in Volgograd, Russia, which was doing poorly. The business was owned by two Russians who had lost interest and, as a result, they sold it to us for around USD 50 million. As with Foskor and Zirconia we went and turned it around. It is now the second largest silicon carbide producer in the world after Saint Gobain. Again the whole strategy is forward and backward integration, as it is for all our products whether it is fertilizer, sugar or abrasives. That is China's strategy today. As for forward integration in India, we have gone into retail. In our fertilizer business, for instance, we have 650 retail outlets that we own. We do the soil testing, we sell all the micronutrients, we provide loans, crop and weather insurance and we sell the seed and the pesticide – as you can see – everything.

'We have not always had family members as chairman of the Murugappa group. From 2001 to 2006 we had P.S. Pai; he had previously been vice-chairman of Wipro. When Mr. Pai came in, our group had size but did not have profitability and I learnt a lot from him in terms of how to review, how to push, how to grow, how to manage profitability well as he was a tough hardcore manager. I was the lead director for the agri businesses while he was in overall control. My uncle MA Alagappan took over from him and became chairman for a period of three years and then I took over from him in 2009 because we have got a rule that at 65 you retire.

'So I have until 2018 when I turn 65. So I look forward to the next few years as I still enjoy doing business. I believe that the group is hugely privileged because we are in a position today where the entry barriers are very strong because of our size. We have chosen to focus on seven areas of business where we seek to be dominant: fertilizers, sugar, tube, cycles, abrasives, financial services and insurance.

'I am also on the board of Indian Overseas Bank. The government said that they would like me to be an independent director and it helps with the networking. In between, I was on the Board of Governors of Doon school for six years, because they wanted somebody from the south. It was fun, as on the board with me was a Scindia from the Maharaja of Gwalior family, R.C. Bhargava who was the chairman of Maruti Suzuki and Sunil Munjal of Hero Honda.

I asked if A. Vellayan had sent his sons to Doon. 'No, unfortunately not. Our younger son is a lawyer. He did his law in Bristol and then he worked with KPMG in London, did his CA and now he is heading our organic fertilizer business. What we do with younger children is that for three years they have to work outside the group; after that they can come back and are offered an opportunity in the group. Our elder son is in our finance business. He is running the home equity side of the business. He did his master's in Finance at Lancaster University Management School. And then worked with DBS in Singapore.

'Most of my time is spent in environment management with the government in India and with the industry and associations. A large proportion of the rest of my time is taken in reviews and visiting customers and factories. I travel about ten to twelve days a month. My beat is Hyderabad, Delhi, London, Johannesberg, and Tunisia. I just take commercial flights because it is not part of our culture to have a private jet. We are very conservative. I drive a Toyota Camry – that is it; I would hate to drive into one of my plants or sugar mills in a fancy car.'

And then Vellayan took us back to where we started our meeting by commenting on the room in which we were sitting. 'Indeed this boardroom is a lot more formal than we would create for ourselves but, as you can see, it has history all around it and I still find it amazing that on its walls are photos or paintings of the Chairmen of EID Parry over the last 225 years and that now includes me. It is humbling.' And with that comment Matt and I decided it was an appropriate time to bring our meeting to a close.

[1] Murugappa (www.murugappa.com) is one of India's leading conglomerates and is headquartered in Chennai in the South of India. It is a market leader in a number of sectors, including abrasives, auto components, cycles, sugar, farm inputs, fertilizers, plantations, bio-products and nutraceuticals. The Group currently turns over annually around USD4 billion. The Group has a wide geographical presence spanning 13 states in India and 5 continents.

[2] The Chettiars or, to give them their traditional name, the Nagarathars came from a sun-baked homeland in basins of the Sittang and the Salween. The original Chettiars in Burma set sail from some Coromandel port and, hugging the coast, reached Rangoon after many weeks of sailing. It seems the Chettiar used to spend three years in Rangoon and then three years back in India before repeating the cycle again. Strangely, it was the opening of the Suez Canal in 1869 that was the genesis of the finance business for the Chettiar in Burma. Europe was clamouring for rice and the Chettiar identified that lower Burma with its plentiful rainfall was an ideal place to grow rice, albeit to that point the Burmese only grew enough for domestic consumption. For whatever reason the British Government was unwilling to finance the development of the area. And it was into that void stepped the Chettiar. Rice production increased one hundred fold as seven million tonnes of rice were produced. The Chettiar earned enormous profits from this intermediary role. Whilst without the Chettiar taking the financing risk the Burmese economy would never have developed like this, there is little doubt that some Burmese resented the influence of the Chettiar. See http://www.archive.org/stream/rajahsirannamala030779mbp/rajahsirannamala030779mbp_djvu.txt for a description of the situation by the Rajah Sir Annamal Commemoration Volume.

[3] Almost half of the population of Rangoon (now Yangon) at the start of the Second World War was Indian and perhaps 20 per cent of the total population. Most of them fled back to India before the Japanese took the country. Most had to walk by foot and many thousands perished. At the end of the War few Indians returned to Rangoon as it was clear that Burma was heading for independence and that the rights of Indians would not be protected. After independence, Burmese law treated a large percentage of the Indian community as "resident aliens". Though many had long ties to Burma or were born there, they were not considered citizens under the 1982 Burma citizenship law that restricted citizenship for groups immigrating before 1823.

[4] Rajputs (from Sanskrit raja-putra – son of a king) were members of one of the patrilineal clans of western, central, northern India and some parts of Pakistan.

www.ingramcontent.com/pod-product-compliance
Lightning Source LLC
Chambersburg PA
CBHW020323170426
43200CB00006B/247